THE BATTLE FOR NORMANDY

Eversley Belfield was born in 1918 and is married with three sons and two daughters. He was educated at Ampleforth and Pembroke College, Oxford. During the Second World War he served as an Air Observation pilot with the Royal Artillery in the North West Europe campaign and was mentioned in dispatches. His other works include *Unarmed into Battle* with General Parham, *Oudenarde, A Concise History of the Boer War*, and *Corps Commander* with General Horrocks. He was a senior lecturer in the adult education department of Southampton University, specialising in military history. He now lives in Sark.

Major General Hubert Essame (1896–1976) served in both world wars. He first saw action in the Somme in 1916 and was awarded the MC in 1918. He spent much of the inter-war years with the Indian Army. In the Second World War he commanded a brigade throughout the North West Europe campaign and was awarded the DSO in 1944. His books on military history included *43rd Wessex Division at War*, *The Battle for Germany*, *The Battle For Europe 1918*, and *Patton*.

Grand Strategy

THE BATTLE
FOR NORMANDY

EVERSLEY BELFIELD
and
H. ESSAME

PAN BOOKS
LONDON AND SYDNEY

First published 1965 by B. T. Batsford Ltd
First Pan Books edition published 1967
This edition published 1983 by Pan Books Ltd,
Cavaye Place, London SW10 9PG

© Eversley Belfield and H. Essame, 1965, 1983

ISBN 0 330 28034 1

Printed in Great Britain by Collins, Glasgow

PREFACE

THIS ACCOUNT OF the Battle for Normandy runs from 7 June, D + 1, to 22 August, when the Falaise Gap was finally closed. Only where relevant to D + 1 are the events of D-day summarized. Those wishing to study the Normandy landings will find many excellent books easily available.

We have discussed the fighting described here with many survivors of this battle as well as with others who have studied it; we wish to thank them for having given us the benefit of their experience and knowledge, they have helped illuminate many points.

We are particularly grateful to Mrs Diana Belfield and Mr Leslie Jaques who have kindly read most of the typescript and made many helpful comments and suggestions, and to our wives who have read the proofs and helped with the index. We owe a debt of gratitude to the Librarians and Staff of the Prince Consort's Library, Aldershot, the Library of Southampton University, the Devon County Library, the RUSI Library and the War Office and Air Ministry Libraries; the patient and cheerful assistance so readily provided by these libraries made the writing of this book a far easier task than it would otherwise have been.

CONTENTS

Appendices

ACKNOWLEDGEMENT

The Authors and Publishers wish to thank the following for permission to quote from the books mentioned: Jonathan Cape Limited, *From the City, from the Plough* by Alexander Baron, and *The Young Lions* by Irwin Shaw; Holt, Rinehart & Winston Inc, *A Soldier's Story* by General Omar Bradley; Oxford University Press, *BBC War Report*; William Collins Sons & Co. Ltd, *Triumph in the West* by Sir Arthur Bryant, *The Memoirs of Field Marshal Montgomery*, *The Rommel Papers*, edited by Captain B. H. Liddell Hart, and *The Struggle for Europe* by Chester Wilmot; George G. Harrap & Company Limited, *Invasion – They're Coming!* by Paul Carell; the Comptroller of Her Majesty's Stationery Office, *General Eisenhower's Report to the Combined Chiefs of Staff on the Operations in Europe of the Allied Expeditionary Force*, and *The Royal Air Force 1939–1945* by H. St G. Saunders; the Lieutenant-Colonel Commanding, the Welsh Guards, and Gale & Polden Ltd, *The Welsh Guards at War* by L. F. Ellis; Hodder and Stoughton Limited and the author, *The Enemy Within* by John Watney, and *Operation Victory* by Major-General Sir Francis de Guingand; Chatto & Windus Ltd, *Wing Leader* by Johnnie Johnson; the author, *Blue Flash* by Lieutenant-General Sir Allan Jolly; Hamish Hamilton Ltd, *Montgomery* and *Eclipse* by Alan Moorehead; the Air OP Officers' Association, *Unarmed into Battle* by H. J. Parham and Eversley Belfield; the Lieutenant-Colonel Commanding, the Scots Guards, *The Scots Guards, 1919–1945;* Martin Secker & Warburg Limited, *Defeat in the West* by Milton Shulman; The Queen's Printer, *Victory Campaign* by C. P. Stacey; and W. H. Allen & Company, *The Falaise Road* by A. Wood.

They also wish to thank the following for permission to reproduce the illustrations which appear in this book:

The Imperial War Museum

Verlag Ullstein GMBH Bilderdienst, Berlin

Thanks are also due to the Comptroller of Her Majesty's Stationery Office for permission to base the maps on pages 20–21, 58–59, 68, 92, 124, 150, 200, 216, and 222 on those in *History of the Second World War: Victory in the West*, Vol. I, *The Battle of Normandy*, and to Hodder and Stoughton Limited, for permission to base the map on page 168 on that in Major-General Sir Francis de Guingand's *Operation Victory*.

ILLUSTRATIONS IN PHOTOGRAVURE
between pages 128 and 129

MAPS IN THE TEXT

CHRONOLOGY

June

July

August

1

Normandy

'Si tu veux être heureux
Vas entre Caen et Bayeux.'
                    – *French Song*

THE BATTLE FOR NORMANDY marked the end of an epoch. During the summer of 1944, there took place inside a corner of the old Duchy of Normandy what will probably be the last great set-piece battle of the Western World. Never again is it likely that, without recourse to nuclear weapons, over 2,000,000 men will find themselves fighting, for several weeks, a battle which both sides knew beforehand must be a decisive one.

During an earlier and equally crucial period of European history, the Normans had dominated military affairs and it was, therefore, perhaps sadly fitting that this climax in the history of conventional warfare should have taken place on their soil. It was appropriate for the English-speaking peoples to have played such a leading part in these great events. Their history, to a great extent, derives from the Norman Conquest, and 1066 is perhaps the only date every Briton knows. Moreover, to many who fought there, Normandy was full of historical reminders. At Falaise the Conqueror had been born. The undamaged town of Bayeux, of tapestry fame, had nominally been the see of fierce Bishop Odo who had ravaged Northumbria for the Conqueror, his half-brother (by a most remarkable coincidence Bayeux was captured by the men of the 50th Northumbrian Division). In Caen, the body of William himself lies buried in the church of St Etienne. Crammed with refugees, this church was miraculously unharmed by the 1,000-bomber raid.

The local Resistance leader was not surprised at this near miracle, saying, 'Don't you know that there is an old Normandy legend that so long as the Kings of England are on the throne, no harm will befall the church of St Etienne, and, in this case, only one stone was dislodged by a shell.'

Even to the less historically minded, a deep sense of affinity with the Normandy countryside insisted on making itself felt, and, because it so closely resembles Britain, the devastation frequently had a disturbingly personal impact. Surrounded by small fields with high, thick hedges, the solid stone farm houses might have belonged to the West Country. Equally as typical of this region of England are the innumerable cider-apple orchards. Yet this sensation of being still at home was only spasmodic. The carefully tethered cows cropping rich fields of lucerne betokened a different approach to farming; on the wall, shell-scarred advertisements such as *Dubo, Dubon, Dubonnet*, did not fit in with the picture of being in Britain; nor did the straight poplar-lined roads with their low-set un-English signposts support this illusion. Venetian shutters on a turreted château set in its little stilted park gave the scene an alien look. Such scenes were sufficient to dispel any nostalgic daydream that this was only another one of those endless military exercises held in Britain.

Yet this fantasy, which many soldiers shared, of being back in an unfamiliar part of their own country would not be so easily dismissed. It constantly recurred, since as one observer remarked of Normandy:

The male inhabitants, on the whole, might have been imported *en masse* from Cornwall; they were bluff, red-faced looking specimens, who gave you the impression that they had spent many years in small fishing smacks off the coast. Admittedly some of the shopkeepers in their narrow pin-striped suits, would have seemed ridiculously old-fashioned in England; but there were few shopkeepers about the streets on D + 2. Children made up for the scarcity of men and many of the younger children had startlingly fair hair; so that once again the feeling of being away from home was lost. But when we looked at the women we knew we were in France; there was no mistaking their white faces and black clothes.

Normandy shared yet another quality with Britain. For centuries it had escaped being a battlefield. The last serious fighting had taken place here, just five centuries earlier, during the Hundred Years War. The Normandy countryside diffused an air of modest prosperity founded on centuries of undisturbed labour. This sense of solid well-being made the devastation of its hamlets, villages and towns almost as poignant as if this had happened at home.

Finally, the weather seemed to have taken a hand in this attempt at make-believe. Contrary to the usual British idea of foreign weather, June and nearly all July consisted of a succession of cool, cloudy days with much rain. To the damp and often dispirited troops, it seemed as if, by an impish freak of nature, Normandy had laid on a typical English summer for the invaders. Not until the very end of July did the weather change and then, for the next three weeks, there was a heat wave.

On the choice of Normandy for the invasion area, Montgomery has written: 'The first need was to decide how the operations on land were to be developed, and then to work backwards from that to ensure that we landed on the beaches in the way best suited to the needs of the master plan.' At its simplest, the 'master plan' meant that not only had the Allies to land successfully in France, but, above all, they must be able to build up their forces more rapidly than the Germans in order to be able to break out from the bridgehead. To fulfil these requirements the area chosen for the invasion had to possess several physical characteristics. In the first place, the maximum effective range of fighter aircraft had to be taken into consideration, and this limited the landing areas to those parts of the French coast which lay within 200 miles of southern England where these machines were based. Being about 150 miles from the aerodromes on the south coast, Normandy just met this requirement. Secondly, the invasion area needed to have long

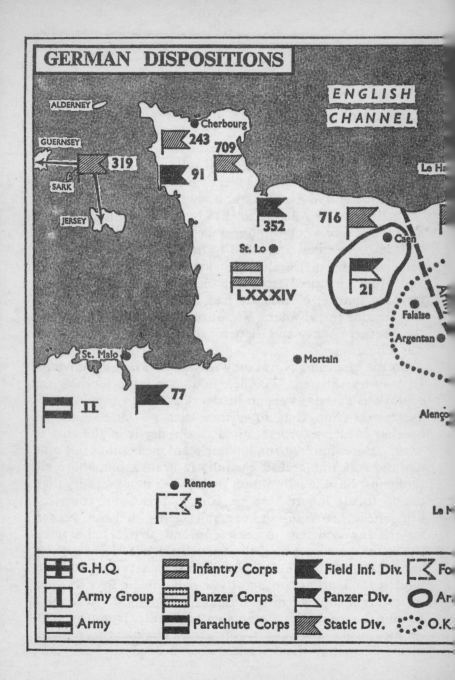

GERMAN DISPOSITIONS

ENGLISH
CHANNEL

ALDERNEY

GUERNSEY

SARK

JERSEY

319

Cherbourg

243

709

91

Le Ha

352

716

St. Lo

Caen

LXXXIV

21

Falaise

Argentan

St. Malo

Mortain

II

77

Alenço

Rennes

Le M

5

G.H.Q.	Infantry Corps	Field Inf. Div.	Fo
Army Group	Panzer Corps	Panzer Div.	Ar
Army	Parachute Corps	Static Div.	O.K.

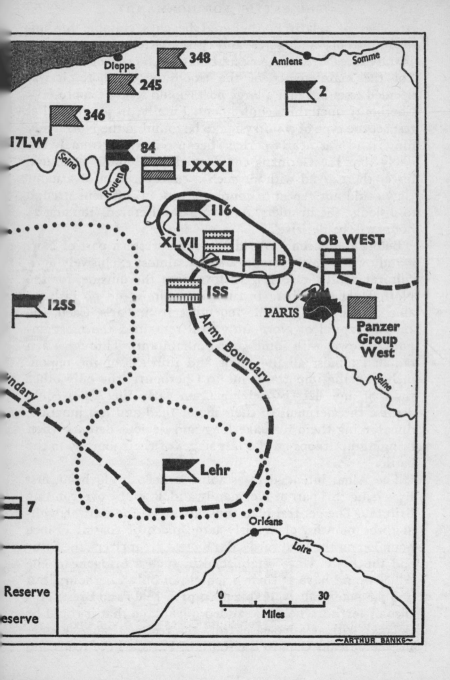

stretches of relatively sheltered beaches suitable for unloading troops and stores, and these existed along the Normandy foreshore, in the western half of the Bay of the Seine.
For the maintenance of the troops once ashore, it was
deemed essential that a large port should soon be captured –
Cherbourg met this requirement. Finally, in another vital
respect the type of countryside to be found in the Normandy
hinterland was nearly perfect, because it was extremely unlikely that the Germans could quickly assemble armoured
forces there. And without such a concentration of armour
they could not expect to counter-attack in sufficient strengh
to dislodge the invaders. As Rommel reiterated, 'the first 24
hours will be decisive'.

Before the Second World War, this western part of Normandy was a fairly remote district, almost exclusively agricultural. It attracted few visitors from the outside, for the
Norman beaches here boasted no casinos and no fashion-
able *plages*. Lying about 100 miles from Paris, Caen, the
ancient capital of Normandy, still remained the most important town, with some 50,000 inhabitants. Through Caen
radiated almost all the roads and railways of the region,
including the important line to Cherbourg, the only other
town of any size. By seizing Caen early the Allies could
deprive the Germans of their major road and rail junction,
thus forcing them to make long and devious detours when
bringing up troops on the last stages of their journey to the
battle.

The Allies intended to establish a deep bridgehead, first
by seizing this part of Normandy and, later, by overrunning
Brittany. The general plan thus envisaged the control, within three months, of a fairly large piece of coastal France
bounded on the landward sides by two great rivers, the Seine
and the Loire. Once established in such a bridgehead, the
Allies would have at their disposal not only Cherbourg, but
also the potentially valuable ports of St Malo and Brest. This
slice of territory held the added advantage that it could be
isolated, with relative ease, from the rest of France. Except
for the Orleans Gap, to the south of Paris, all the roads and

railways to Normandy and Brittany have to cross either the Seine or the Loire; and in this connexion the twenty-four Seine bridges between Rouen and Paris were of outstanding importance. If these vital bridges could either be destroyed or kept permanently badly damaged, German communication with the battlefield would be very severely restricted and it would be difficult for them to reinforce their troops rapidly and on a large scale. In this task of hamstringing the enemy's communications, the Allied airmen succeeded so well that the Germans soon reckoned that the safest and speediest way of getting to battle was by bicycle.

Since most of the fighting in Normandy occurred within a very restricted area, the battle was profoundly affected by considerations of terrain. By about mid-June the Allies had occupied a long narrow rectangular strip of land, and during the following six weeks, they pushed very slowly southwards. The initial shape of this piece of territory was governed by the beaches on the north and the floods on each side.

Throughout the fighting, the easternmost extremity of the battlefield remained unaltered, being anchored on the relatively high wooded ground between the rivers Orne and the Dives. To the east of here the Germans had sealed off this flank by flooding the lower reaches of the river between Cabourg and Troarn. On the western flank, the Germans also had created severe obstacles by flooding. They had let the sea back into the reclaimed marshland in the wide estuary of the Vire and its tributaries. At first, these floods divided Utah from Omaha beaches, but even after the Americans had lined them up, they were still confronted with other formidable inundations which greatly delayed their progress.

Most of the rest of the Normandy battleground consisted of two sorts of countryside. The smaller part was made up of fairly open rolling country, with cornfields and meadows predominating. This pleasant landscape was broken by large clumps of trees, the occasional small wood, and the inevitable apple orchards. Intensively cultivated, and thickly populated, these regions of the Normandy battlefield abounded in what were hamlets, rather than villages, whose houses and farm buildings were solidly constructed of Caen stone. A Scotsman wrote of one, 'It must have been a douce little place once, with its seven or eight big farms and huddle of smaller buildings round them, lying snug behind its fringe of trees like a medieval town within a wall. . . . At sunset it looked like a small green island.'

Typical of this undulating countryside is the part which slopes from just north of the Caen–Bayeux road to the low cliffs and dunes on the coast where the British troops had landed on D-day. Known as the Caen–Falaise Plain, another belt of this sort of country stretches south and southeast from Caen. In so relatively featureless a landscape, some surprisingly panoramic vistas exist. About five miles to the south-west of Caen, the ground rises unobtrusively to a height of 112 metres. From the crest of this small hill, one obtains sweeping vistas across miles of the surrounding country. A couple of miles west of Caen lies the Carpiquet airfield, and though on the map it appears to be on a fairly flat piece of ground, in fact, it overlooks an unexpectedly wide tract of land. Finally a couple of miles south of Caen itself is a ridge about five miles long and from here again one has excellent observation for several miles and in most directions.

Nevertheless to most soldiers, the Normandy battlefields were almost synonymous with the more thinly populated region known as the *bocage*. This is the name given to most of the rest of those parts of Normandy which lie to the west and south of Caen. Nearly fifty miles in depth, it is country ideally suited to defence. In the northerly and more cultivated parts of the *bocage*, there is a profusion of tiny fields separated from one another by earth banks about three feet high on top of which grow dense rows of bushes and small trees. These tree-covered banks thus divide the area into hundreds of little rectangles. Running throughout are innumerable sunken tracks, mostly completely overgrown, and these were to prove of paramount importance in the battle, since they formed natural communication trenches, making it possible for troops to move their position in daylight without being visible. 'Seen from the air the landscape resembled a chess board with thousands of squares; each measured a hundred by a hundred and fifty yards.' Someone compared the *bocage* to a gigantic shrubbery, and the French word means grove, or coppice. The *bocage* is broken by many rivers and streams, running in a northerly direction through steep narrow valleys. It has two important rivers, the Orne to the east and the Vire on the west.

Roughly south of a line drawn from Caen to St Lô, there is a larger and wilder stretch of the *bocage* extending for over thirty miles. Few roads exist here and several quite sizeable forests cover the sharply folded ground. This countryside often resembles Switzerland and is locally referred to as *la Suisse Normande*. In this region of the *bocage*, the ground rises steadily up to a large plateau about 1,000 feet high, and is dominated by Mont Pinçon. From this 1,200-foot hill (some eighteen miles south-west of Caen), it appeared, for over two months, as if the Germans could see into all the Allied positions. Yet this was an illusion. The *bocage* was so dense that the chief problem was to see where one's own side was, let alone the enemy's. When feeling particularly frustrated by the lack of progress in Normandy, Eisenhower, who was visiting the bridgehead, determined to try to see for himself what was happening. He wrote::

It was difficult to obtain any real picture of the battle area. One day a few of us visited a forward observation tower located on a hill, which took us to a height of about a hundred feet above the surrounding hedgerows. Our vision was so limited that I called upon the air forces to take me in a fighter plane along the battle front in an effort to gain a clear impression of what we were up against. Unfortunately, even from the vantage point of an altitude of several thousand feet there was not much to see that could be classed as helpful.

Inevitably the closeness of the *bocage* often made it very uncertain what line was held by the forward troops. Even when this information was supposedly known, in the sense of being marked up on the huge map boards of the higher headquarters, it could prove, in practice, to be unreliable. Sometimes the original map reference might have been in-accurate, but more often the line itself had ceased to be firmly held. German infiltration was always occurring and, therefore, what for many began as a routine journey to visit the front-line troops could only too easily change into a hazardous expedition. Now and again this uncertainty could become so aggravating that more drastic steps had to be taken. Two officers were ordered

to find out whether a certain village over the other side of the Odon was in British or German hands; as nobody could give them a satisfactory answer they had driven to the village in question in their jeep, only to find it lying in no-man's-land deserted by both sides; they had not been in the village for more than a few minutes when shells began to fall; some appeared to be coming from the British lines, others from the German. It was obvious to deduce from this that neither side held the village, but each denied the use of it to the other.

It can be seen therefore, that the nature of the Normandy terrain would give a resolute defender many advantages, especially once an attacking force became enmeshed in the *bocage*. On the other hand, any invader who once secured a firm foothold in this close country would be extremely diffi-cult to dislodge.

2

The German Army

'It is as if life had retreated eastwards. As if the Germanic life were slowly ebbing away from contact with Western Europe, ebbing to the deserts of the East.'
— *D. H. Lawrence*

EARLY IN 1944, the Germans had become convinced that an Allied invasion of Europe was imminent, but their problem was to decide where this landing would take place. By various ruses the Allies had persuaded the Germans that the most likely area was on the Channel coast of France somewhere between the Somme estuary and Dunkirk. Yet, in spite of this conviction, Hitler and his advisers could not afford to stake everything on it, and station nearly all their troops in the Pas de Calais district, since the risk could not be ignored of a landing elsewhere. With utterly inadequate forces, the Germans had to defend themselves against an opponent who had latterly demonstrated such an over-whelming superiority on the sea and in the air that he could land troops almost anywhere from Holland to the Spanish border, a distance of about 1,200 miles.

Indeed fear of this threat began to prey on Hitler's mind. Looking at the large-scale maps with which he surrounded himself in his bunker, he picked on the Normandy–Brittany coast as a probable landing-place and in May 1944 reinforcements were sent there. In June 1944 the consensus of German military opinion nevertheless still firmly believed that the Allied invasion would be in the Pas de Calais, and of the 58 divisions in France and the Low Countries, 17 were in the triangle between the Seine and Loire, whilst 25 were stationed north of the Seine; the remainder, mainly very under-strength, were scattered south of the Loire. (See map, pages 20–21.)

From the German point of view, another very real and disquieting possibility was that the Allies might stage one or more powerful diversionary landings to draw the defenders' troops away from the main invasion area. The likelihood of this occurring had greatly increased when, by the end of 1943, the Allies gained control of the Mediterranean, and could thus, fairly easily, put forces ashore in the south of France. Although the Allies tried to keep the Germans convinced that the invasion proper would be in the Pas de Calais, they naturally encouraged them to believe that diversionary landing(s) would also be attempted.

With a combination of coastal fortifications and troops, the more optimistic Germans hoped to repulse any Allied landings that might be launched. The Atlantic Wall was the name given to a grandiose scheme of defensive positions designed to prevent any invading force from getting firmly ashore. But in spite of all Hitler's authority and Rommel's frenzied efforts during the first half of 1944, the Atlantic Wall remained largely uncompleted, work not having been even begun on nearly half the essential fortresses. In an autobiographical novel, a sardonic German oldier summarized the efficacy of this fortification 'system'. 'Back at home they think of us sitting ever so snug behind the Atlantic Wall. The Atlantic Wall, they quack, it's so solid a louse could not creep through. But if you look at the bloody thing a bit closer you can see that any New York swimming club could land here and walk ashore.' In a rather more conventional manner one of the gloomier generals compared it to a 'thin, in many places fragile, length of cord with a few small knots at isolated points'. Inevitably most of these completed knots, or fortresses, had been concentrated in the Pas de Calais where, by June 1944 the Atlantic Wall did present a very formidable obstacle to any invading force. More especially from April onwards, Rommel had set about frenziedly strengthening the defences in Normandy, but they were fortunately in a less advanced state than those farther north.

If the Germans were to succeed in repelling an Allied invasion in the summer of 1944, they would have to dispose and control their admittedly insufficient forces with the greatest strategic skill and foresight. At the best of times, the disposition and control of large numbers of defensive troops pose strategic problems of great complexity, and it is only too easy to be wise after the event. Yet it is fairly obvious that the system of control of the German armed forces complicated their difficulties during the battle for Normandy. Hitler, for all his enormous powers, had devised neither a logical nor a properly unified system of controlling his armed forces. As the American Official Historian comments:

Until 6 June when the Allied forces stormed ashore, there existed no unified control of the enemy forces in France nor any clear-cut policy on how to deal with the attack. Hitler's absorption with the problems of the Eastern Front, his lack of a consistent policy for the west, and his unwillingness to mark out clearly the authority of commanders in the field were among the factors responsible for this situation.

The German army commanders were often obstructed by this lack of a coordinated authority. They never had undisputed control over the naval and air force units, even when these were supporting the ground forces. This splintering of command resulted in the coastal artillery, the paratroop formations and the anti-aircraft batteries being outside the direct control of Rommel (and later von Kluge), who had to fight the land battle.

Such a ludicrous division of authority on the spot only too easily aroused violent antagonisms. These continued to plague the Germans even until the final stand before Falaise. About this matter a parachutist general stated!

At the beginning of August we sent another forty of these 88-millimetre guns to Colonel-General 'Sepp' Dietrich of Fifth Panzer Army. However, since these guns belonged to the Luftwaffe, they were to be controlled by an air force officer, Lieutenant-General Pickert, rather than an army officer. We had insisted on these guns being controlled by Luftwaffe officers because the army did not know how to handle such equipment. There was always a great deal of argument about who was to deploy the 88s, but Field Marshal von Rundstedt finally allowed us to choose our own localities. This was necessary in order to prevent the army from squandering both men and equipment. We used to say that the German infantryman would always fight until the last anti-aircraftman.

The other side of the story was feelingly expressed by 'Sepp' Dietrich who said, 'I constantly ordered these guns to stay forward and act in an anti-tank role against Allied armour. My orders were just as often countermanded by Pickert, who moved them back into the rear areas to protect administrative sites. I asked time and time again that these guns be put under my command, but I was always told by the High Command that it was impossible.

As will be seen later, the actual gunners were unaffected by the squabbles of their superiors and these 88-mm guns played havoc with the attacking Allied tanks.

Although he realized some of the limitations and frictions produced by this illogical splitting-up of authority, Hitler retained it. As the war went on, he was coming to trust his generals less and thus had no desire to increase their independence of action.

Once the German forces were on the defensive, Hitler's direction of the war was based on one guiding principle, never to yield ground. By thus restricting their freedom of action, Hitler's policy frequently made strategic nonsense to the professional soldiers who had to carry it out, added to which he often issued detailed unrealistic tactical orders when he felt his generals were weakening. He repeatedly interfered with the efficient conduct of the battle, and the task of the German generals in the field was made more difficult than it need have been.

At first sight it is easy to be critical of Hitler's basic tenet of never yielding ground. In Normandy, at any rate, his policy had considerable justification, since Hitler appreciated the political aspects of war far better than did his generals. He realized clearly that any sign of relaxation of the German grip on France would unleash the pent-up fury of the French. The large Communist element and the followers of de Gaulle in the French Resistance Movement could have created chaos in the German rear areas. Hence Hitler utterly refused to consider von Rundstedt's idea of abandoning, at the end of June, the militarily indefensible southern part of France and withdrawing the German army to hold a shorter, and theoretically more attractive, line based on the Seine and Marne rivers.

Another important reason for Hitler's enforcing this rigid doctrine was that most of the ordinary German soldiers still retained an almost mystical faith in the genius of the Führer. Any attempt at a premeditated large-scale retreat could have seriously undermined morale, especially since the success of a move of this sort would have been endangered not only by local sabotage, but also by intensive Allied air attacks.

Moreover by mid-1944, Hitler needed an inflexible type of defence policy. He was determined to buy time. In the later stages of the war he placed what now seem exaggerated hopes on his secret revolutionary weapons, with which he meant to force Britain to sue for peace. The V1, or flying-bombs, were first launched from the Pas de Calais against England on 12 June. Sustained air attacks on the factories and on the launching sites greatly reduced their numbers, whilst their inaccuracy and the smallness of their warheads weakened them as terror weapons. Yet, in more favourable circumstances, the 'buzz bombs' could well have had an important effect on the Allied ability to wage war, especially if large numbers of them had been able to be concentrated on the port areas in which invasion forces were gathering.

Like the British, Hitler over-estimated the effects of aerial terror bombardment on an enemy. Yet the V1 rockets, falling on London and south-east England, did sorely try the morale of the ordinary citizen. The courage and endurance of those who were subjected to this horrible impersonal slaughter, which struck all round the clock, was evidently a factor beyond Hitler's conception. So was the

British humour which coined the entomological nickname of 'doodle bug' for these machines. The V1s did have repercussions on the fighting men in Normandy. They made them anxious about the safety of their families and friends who lived in the danger zone. Particularly amongst those Allied soldiers who had experienced the 'doodle bug' attacks, there was born a new more profound hatred of the Germans and all they stood for. These later arrivals longed to reach the Pas de Calais and drive the Germans out of their launching area.

The more ambitious V2, or rocket bomb, was another weapon in Hitler's armoury in which he had long-term confidence, but it needed more time for production in sufficient quantities. With the schnorkel type of U-boat able to travel under water much longer than the conventional submarine, Hitler planned to decimate Allied shipping. It was providential that production difficulties prevented these vessels, virtually immune from air attack, from sinking shipping in the packed water-lanes between southern England and Normandy. Of these secret weapons the German generals knew little and cared less, but they shaped Hitler's strategic ideas, and Hitler was the undisputed 'boss'.

Finally Hitler's fanatical approach to life coloured his direction of this, and every other, battle in the later stages of the war. He thought only in extremes, and thus refused even to contemplate any alternative other than complete success or utter failure and disaster. No matter what the cost to the German Army, Hitler was adamant that the longer the Allied forces were bottled up in the Normandy bridgehead, the better the chance was of some miracle occurring which would give the Germans that eleventh-hour victory in the possibility of which he still had a mystical belief. Hence, through the OKW,* he would personally intervene whenever he thought his generals looked like weakening in their resolution to hold fast, and at Cherbourg this intervention undermined Rommel's plan for defending the port.

In March 1942, Hitler appointed von Rundstedt Com-

* See diagram, page 34.

mander-in-Chief West. In theory, he should have been Hitler's most trusted adviser in the West, but, partly because he placed no confidence in the idea of the Atlantic Wall, he had forfeited most of Hitler's confidence. By the summer of 1944 the sixty-nine-year-old Field Marshal had become thoroughly disillusioned and apathetic. Though still possessing all the outward trappings of power, he had little control over the forces he nominally commanded. He was not unduly exaggerating his position when he told his interrogator after the war that 'as Commander-in-Chief West my only authority was to change the guard in front of my gate'.

In the autumn of 1943, Hitler made Rommel Inspector-General of Defences in the West. This further reduced von Rundstedt's authority, since Rommel, as a Field Marshal, had direct access to Hitler. At first Rommel's Army Command, known as Group B, contained no fighting troops, being exclusively concerned in analysing ideas for strengthening the coastal defences and for mounting offensive operations against Allied landings. Rommel soon jibbed at only running so nebulous an organization, and he sought more power. This he obtained when, at the end of 1943, Army Group B took over operational control of the 7th and 15th Armies. Rommel thus became responsible for all the defences from the Scheldt to the Loire. Relationships between the two commanders then grew less strained, but Rommel remained, in theory, subordinate to von Rundstedt, though still continuing to approach Hitler directly.

This right of direct access to Hitler was destined to be an ill-omened privilege. On 5 June, Rommel left La Roche Guyon, his headquarters near Paris, to motor to Germany. Significantly he went to see Hitler. Rommel seems to have discussed his forthcoming visit to the Führer with von Rundstedt, who gave the trip his backing. Amongst other things, Rommel probably intended to try to persuade Hitler to devise a less irrational system of command which would give him, Rommel, what he considered the necessary authority to control and station forces in the way he felt best suited to the overall situation. Rommel may also have felt

HITLER
War Minister, Supreme Commander and Commander-in-Chief of the Army

OKW or *Oberkommando der Wehrmacht* (High Command of the Armed Forces)
Chief: Keitel — Chief of Operations Staff: Jodl

NAVY: OKM
(Doenitz)

AIR FORCES: OKL
(Goering)

ARMY: OKH
(exclusively engaged in running the war on the Eastern Front)

NAVAL GROUP WEST [Paris]
(Krancke)

THIRD AIR FLEET [Paris]
(Sperrle)

OK WEST [Paris]
(von Rundstedt)

ARMY GROUP B
(Rommel; responsible for the Low Countries and France to the river Loire)

PANZER GROUP WEST
(Geyr von Schweppenburg; later Eberbach)

ARMY GROUP G
(Blaskowitz; responsible for France south of the river Loire)

15TH ARMY
(von Salmuth)

7TH ARMY
(Dollmann; later Hausser)

1ST ARMY

19TH ARMY

that he must again try to make Hitler find him an adequate strategic reserve. In addition, Rommel may have decided to attempt to cajole Hitler into allowing him to draw on the troops, many of good quality, who were scattered in isolated garrisons, like those in the Channel Islands.

By going on this trip when he did, Rommel was absent when the Allied invasion came. The exact time of his return is not clear, but it could not have been before the evening of D-day. Rommel thus got off on the wrong foot, since he had played no part in controlling the battle during most of the first day, and he had always regarded these first 24 hours as the most crucial period.

Being south of the Seine, the German 7th Army was immediately engaged in the fighting. It was commanded by the somewhat shadowy and ineffectual Dollmann who had last seen action in 1940. He was deeply preoccupied by his own private fears, for he was in Hitler's black books. The cumulative effects of this worry and the strain of the fighting brought on a fatal heart attack at the end of June.

As a whole, the corps and divisional commanders consisted of a tough group of experienced professional soldiers who found themselves fully occupied in their daily and dangerous task of trying to halt the Allied attacks; they were, therefore, little interested in the wrangles of their superiors. Typical of the best of these German generals was the fifty-three-year-old Marcks who had lost a leg on the Russian Front. He commanded LXXIV Corps and was thus responsible for the infantry divisions defending the Normandy coast where the invasion took place. An officer of the old school, Marcks' habits were Spartan. He conscientiously restricted himself to the official rations, and in this he was unlike several of the senior German officers who revelled in the comforts of occupied France. Popular with his troops, Marcks had done his best to train them. He soon met his end in a soldierly manner. On 12 June he was killed in his car by a fighter-bomber near his headquarters at St Lô.

The soldiers forming the German Army were an extremely heterogeneous collection. At the bottom end of the scale were the 'static', or transportless divisions, of which Marcks had three in his corps. The astonishing extent of the German manpower-shortage is well illustrated by an analysis of those eligible to serve in such divisions. One class consisted of men so young that their comrades termed them 'babes in arms'. A second group was drawn from the more elderly, thirty-five being the minimum age for those in this category. The entrance 'fee' for another contingent was that they had to have suffered from third-degree frostbite on the Eastern Front before being accepted. But it was the last group, over 60,000 strong, which presented the most remarkable and colourful characteristics. These were soldiers captured in the Russian campaign, who subsequently 'volunteered' to serve with the Germans, but, it being unfair to ask them to fight on the Eastern Front, they were formed into *Ostbatalliones* and sent to man the Atlantic Wall. In these units the more senior officers were Germans, whilst the junior ones were generally émigré White Russians. The administrative nightmare involved in dealing with such a diversity of races can be judged from their paybooks, which were issued in eight different forms:

    (i) For Russians, Ukrainians and White Ruthenians – Russian paybook.

    (ii) For Cossacks – Cossack paybook.

    (iii) For Armenians – Armenian paybook.

    (iv) For Aserbaijans – Aserbaijan paybook.

    (v) For Georgians (including Adschars, South Ossetans and Abschars) – Georgian paybook.

    (vi) For Adigia, Karbadins, Karatjers, Balkars, Kherkassians, North Ossetans, Ingus, Takjenen, Dagastares (Calmuckes, Awares, Lakes, Dargines, etc.) – North Caucasian paybook.

    (vii) For Turkemen, Usbeks, Kazaks, Khirgiz, Karakalpaks, Tadschiks – Turkestan paybook.

    (viii) For Volga Tartars (Kazan Tartars), Bashkires, Tartar-speaking Taschuwashi, Maris, Merdwiners, Udmuns – Volga Tartar paybook.

Small wonder von Rundstedt remarked that, 'The Russians constituted a menace and a nuisance to our operations in

France.' Indeed one of the few such battalions placed in the front line did run away on D-day.

In the event, the fighting ability of these 'static' (i.e. without transport) divisions varied greatly. Opposing the British and Canadians on the beaches were the 7,771 men of a static infantry division which, contrary to the forecasts of Allied Intelligence, proved itself to be a tough formation. It was well supplied with artillery, chiefly of French, Polish, Russian and Czech origin, and had been strengthened during April and May by units from 21st Panzer Division and from one of the better infantry divisions being posted into its area. On Utah beach, on the other hand, a static division showed far less fight.

It is even harder to generalize about the quality of the German infantry and parachute divisions stationed in the West in June 1944, since France was used as a convenient place in which to rest, re-form and refit divisions which had been decimated on the Eastern Front. As von Rundstedt gloomily remarked after the war, 'Often I would be informed that a new division was to arrive in France direct from Russia or Norway or central Germany. When it finally made its appearance in the West it would consist, in all, of a divisional commander, a medical officer and five bakers.' But perhaps even more frustrating was Hitler's habit of raiding France for the better divisions, once these had been brought up to strength and trained. In spite of solemn promises to the contrary, Hitler, in March 1944, ordered the II SS Panzer Corps, comprising two crack divisions, to be sent to try to halt the Russian winter offensive. Hence, with the exception of the static divisions, the German armed forces in the West were in a constant state of flux.

There were two good infantry divisions stationed in the region controlled by Marcks' corps. One of these was positioned around Omaha Beach and the Americans pitted against it had a very costly struggle before gaining a foothold on French soil on D-day.

The all-important formations in the German defence of the West were the panzer (armoured) divisions, and, in June

1944, Rommel's Army Group B had three excellent ones. In conformity with his principle of trying to place the armour as near as possible to the likely invasion sector, he had in May moved one of these divisions, 21st Panzer, into the Caen area. This division had originally fought with Rommel's Afrika Korps and, after the German defeat there, had been reconstituted with a nucleus of desert veterans. Rommel's two remaining, better equipped and trained, armoured divisions were north of the Seine and thus in the 15th Army's area; these divisions could only be moved from there on Hitler's authority, which had to be obtained through the OKW. Since these vital formations were technically in reserve they came nominally under von Rundstedt as Commander-in-Chief West, who was advised on their employment by Geyr von Schweppenberg. Geyr added a further complication to an already bewildering situation, since Panzer Group West was responsible only for the training, but not for the deployment or the operational control, of these armoured troops. Stationed farther inland in Normandy were two other formidable panzer divisions, 12th SS and Panzer Lehr. As they came directly under Hitler's orders, being in OKW Reserve, Rommel had no authority over their disposition.

With some of the important formations outside his control, Rommel was in an extremely frustrating position. He was further embittered because he mistrusted Geyr's judgement. The two commanders had diametrically opposed views on the best way to deploy the panzer divisions. Geyr believed that this reserve should be stationed well back from the coast. Once the Allies had declared their hand and landed in strength, then Geyr maintained these panzer divisions could launch their counter-attack, protected en route by the Luftwaffe. This made no sense to Rommel who had suffered from the might of the British Air Force in North Africa. With air inferiority, he insisted that the panzer forces would be terribly mauled during their advance to the coast. Thus Rommel argued that panzer divisions should be very close to the coast, but he could never fully persuade Hitler of the correctness of his thesis. Hitler compromised, and the result was a ludicrous compromise which satisfied nobody. Nevertheless, by June 1944, three powerful German armoured divisions had been stationed within 100 miles, or a normal day's movement, of the Normandy invasion beaches. Between them these panzer forces possessed over 500 tanks of superior quality to those of the Allies. With these strong armoured formations and the infantry divisions already positioned on or near the coast, the German High Command considered that any Allied landings on the obstacle-infested Normandy shores would be repulsed. If the German organization had been better or more rationally coordinated this belief would have been much more firmly grounded.

3

The Allied Armies

'There is not much difficulty in posting a British Army for a general action, or in getting the officers and men to do their duty in action. The difficulty consists in bringing them to the point where the action can be fought, and in the exertion to be made afterwards to derive all the advantages which any other troops in the world would derive from victory.'

– *Wellington*

WHILE THE GERMANS were miserably preparing to repel any landing on the coast of France, the Allies had been training and organizing the greatest invasion fleet the world has ever seen. In their hazardous task, the Anglo-American forces held one trump card. Being able to choose the time and place for their attack, they enjoyed an advantage usually only possessed by an aggressor. To exploit this asset fully, the Allies had to assemble a team of Service experts who would direct this vast enterprise both efficiently and harmoniously. In the final analysis, this called for political guidance of the highest order.

By 1944, the Allies had evolved a reasonably unified system of command which normally operated smoothly. Put in its simplest terms, the Allied method was that the Prime Minister of Britain and the President of the USA were advised by their Combined Chiefs of Staff in all matters of general strategy. Both countries retained their own Chiefs of Staff systems, and Churchill and Roosevelt daily conferred with them. The political leaders did not normally interfere with the day-to-day running of the war, though Churchill took a much closer interest in this than did Roosevelt. Each of the major theatres of operations had its own Supreme

Commander who, though working under the general plans formulated by the Combined Chiefs of Staff, possessed very considerable freedom of action.

As the Supreme Commander Europe, Eisenhower had full authority over all the three Services directly involved in mounting and supporting the Normandy invasion. Difficulties cropped up when he tried to obtain the fullest aerial support prior to the invasion. Such a policy meant cutting deeply into the realms of the 'semi-independent empires' which had become firmly established within the Allied air forces. Nevertheless after some months of delay and discussion, Eisenhower did achieve temporary operational direction over both the British and US strategic air forces which controlled the four-engined bomber fleets. Neither Air Marshal Harris, of Bomber Command, nor General Spaatz, of the US Strategic Air Force, were, however, fully reconciled to this change in the programme of aerial warfare. They resented their pilots being switched, even temporarily, from the task of reducing German industry to rubble, a policy which they passionately believed could bring the war to an end on its own, if only it was pursued with sufficient force and selectivity.

From April 1944, the heavy bombers together with the smaller machines of the tactical air forces, were increasingly side-tracked from targets in Germany to immobilizing the vital communication systems of France and the Low Countries. This was accomplished by extremely accurate pinpoint bombing of such targets as bridges and locomotive repair shops. Largely unseen by soldiers on the battlefields, the airmen were thus contributing greatly to the eventual victory in France by continuously preventing the Germans far away in the rear from supplying and reinforcing their troops in Normandy. On D-day itself, the 'heavies' helped soften-up the beach defences. As part of this coordinated plan, the Allied air forces paid special attention to protecting the invasion assembly areas of southern England from German photographic reconnaissance aircraft.

By June 1944, Eisenhower's command embraced the huge

armies of men destined to fight the land battle in France, many of whom were still in the United States or North Africa. His authority also extended, directly or indirectly, over all the aircraft based on Britain. Finally he controlled a vast fleet of assorted vessels which included battleships, monitors, cruisers, and merchant ships, as well as thousands of landing vessels of all sizes. It is indeed hard to imagine a larger, more complex or more variegated but unified command being placed under the control of one man.

A protégé of General Marshall, the American Army Chief of Staff, Dwight Eisenhower's wartime promotion had been extremely rapid. Born in 1890, the third son of a humble Kansas dairyman, Eisenhower had risen to the rank of colonel when the war started. He first came into international prominence when, in 1942, he was chosen to command the Allied landings in North Africa. Early in the following year, he was promoted to be commander-in-chief of all the Allied forces there, including Montgomery's famous 8th Army. So successful did he prove in this role that he was the obvious choice for Supreme Commander Mediterranean when the post was created. It had thus fallen to him to coordinate all the forces which conquered Sicily and later went on to invade the Italian mainland. At the end of 1943, Eisenhower was designated Supreme Commander Europe and thus responsible for the overall command of all three Services. In addition he was appointed commander-in-chief of all the land forces in north-west Europe. He returned to England early in 1944 to set up his headquarters, known as SHAEF (Supreme Headquarters Allied Expeditionary Forces).

Eisenhower's main weakness lay in his almost total lack of experience of commanding troops in battle, and this dual appointment did not meet with universal approval. Brooke, the Chief of the Imperial General Staff, felt strongly about this subject and never showed confidence in Eisenhower. On 15 May, after listening to Eisenhower's 'final runover' of the plans for the cross-Channel invasion, Field Marshal Sir Alan Brooke summed him up as:

A past-master in the handling of allies, entirely impartial and consequently trusted by all. A charming personality and good coordinator. But no real commander. I have seen many similar reviews of impending operations, and especially those run by Monty. Ike might have been a showman calling on various actors to perform their various turns, but he was not the commander of the show who controlled and directed all the actors. A very different performance from Monty's show a few days previously.

Perhaps the most perspicacious verdict is Chester Wilmot's, who argues that Eisenhower did show considerable tactical skill later on in the campaign, but at this stage was 'a military statesman rather than a generalissimo'.

Eisenhower chose as his deputy, Air Chief Marshal Tedder who had commanded the air force in the Middle East from 1941 to 1943 and had then gone on to become Eisenhower's air commander-in-chief in the Mediterranean. The two men had thus worked together and come to know and like each other. From the Supreme Commander's point of view, Tedder possessed two invaluable qualities. In the first place he had shown he could work amicably with both British and American senior officers of all three Services, and secondly he understood the technicalities of coordinating air support on a massive scale.

During the first part of 1944, Tedder found himself very fully engaged in bringing together the full might of the Allied forces for the benefit of the *Overlord* operation. Having brilliantly accomplished this task, there remained little else for him to do. As Deputy Supreme Commander, Tedder had been allocated no staff of his own. His job carried with it no day-to-day routine duties of any magnitude, nor was there any likelihood of his being given an active role in the future conduct of the campaign. It is not surprising, therefore, that when the Normandy battle began, in the airmen's opinion, to develop unsatisfactorily, Tedder felt it his duty to intervene behind the scenes with Eisenhower.

As Allied Naval Commander, the Supreme Commander had the friendly, unassuming British Admiral Ramsay. In all naval matters concerning combined operations he had

had more experience than any other person, having organized the evacuation from Dunkirk and later been in charge of the landings in North Africa, Sicily and Italy. His appointment was universally popular and he managed to run the immensely complicated naval side of affairs quietly, diplomatically and very skilfully.

Air Chief Marshal Leigh-Mallory, the Allied Air Commander, was not Eisenhower's own choice and turned out to be a more temperamental character. As a fighter pilot he had shown himself to be a resolute and aggressive commander, but his obstinacy, his hot temper and his inability to get on happily with the Americans, sometimes made him a difficult comrade-in-arms; in addition, he tended to view the progress of the battle from an airman's angle. Partly because his reputation was essentially that of a brilliant tactical airman, Eisenhower did not press Leigh-Mallory's claims to be granted any control over the heavy bombers. He may have felt this to have been unjust, since he had originally devised the plans, so successfully carried out by the strategic bombers, of smashing the German communications system in France and the Low Countries.

As has been mentioned, no separate post of Allied Commander Ground Forces existed, because Eisenhower combined these duties with those of Supreme Commander. Nevertheless, even by the autumn of 1943 (before Eisenhower was appointed), it had become evident that no one man could hope properly to discharge the bewildering variety of tasks involved in such a double appointment. Thus it was decided that the commander-in-chief of the British 21st Army Group should be 'jointly responsible with the Allied Naval Commander-in-Chief and the Air Commander-in-Chief, Allied Expeditionary Air Force, for planning the operation *Overlord*, and when so ordered, for its execution, until such time as the Supreme Commander allocated an area of responsibility to the first American Army Group'. In non-military phraseology, this meant that the British General in command of 21st Army Group would also act, temporarily, as the commander-in-chief of the Allied ground forces. Also he would remain in this post until the American forces in Normandy were of sufficient size to warrant their being made into an army group (this consists of two or more armies). Thus when Montgomery was picked to lead 21st Army Group, this appointment carried with it the same status and responsibility as the commanders-in-chief of the naval and air forces.

Montgomery's handling of the battle for Normandy marked the climax of his military career. Perhaps more than any other single person, he was to be responsible for the success or failure of this, the greatest invasion the world has ever seen, or is likely ever to see.

In 1907, Montgomery started his 50 years' service with the British Army. He joined the Royal Warwickshire Regiment and served with them in India. His battalion went over to France in late August 1914 and he was soon in the worst of the fighting. When only a platoon commander, he was awarded the DSO for his bravery in an action in which he was so seriously wounded as to be taken for dead. Having recovered, Montgomery spent the rest of the war in operational Staff duties at divisional level. In 1918 he was a lieutenant-colonel; it took him sixteen years before he was promoted back to the same rank.

Reflection on the lessons of the First World War, brought home to him two appalling and interconnected facts, first, the frightful casualties unnecessarily incurred by the Army and secondly, the terrible gulf between those on the Staff and the troops at the front. In his *Memoirs,* he tells the story of Sir Douglas Haig's Chief of Staff visiting Passchendaele Ridge before returning to England. 'When he saw the mud and the ghastly conditions under which the soldiers had fought and died, he was horrified and said "Do you mean to tell me that the soldiers had to fight under such conditions?"' Montgomery never forgot that lesson. He always saw for himself, lived under much the same conditions as the fighting soldiers and made his Staff do the same.

During the first half of the 1920s, Montgomery's military career did not seem remarkable and he could have passed almost unnoticed as one of the more unconventional and outspoken of a small group of 'Regulars' who took an unfashionably keen interest in their profession. Montgomery spent several years instructing Staff officers, first at Camberley and then at Quetta in India. He became steadily better known and had already impressed Brooke, the wartime CIGS, and Paget who became Commander-in-Chief of the Home Forces in 1941.

Moorehead has described Montgomery's precepts and methods at the time. 'He held forthright views about everything and these views were nearly all on the side of innovation. ... But when the details were said and done with he came back again and again to the abstract and unalterable tenets of his creed: morale, morale, morale. Simplify everything. Let subordinates carry out the detail. Stick to the essentials and hang on until you win. ...'

In 1939, Montgomery was sent to France as a majorgeneral. He trained his 3rd Division so efficiently that it was one of the few formations that did not disintegrate on the retreat to Dunkirk. During this most testing period, Brooke had further evidence of the skill and calmness of his subordinate, for he was Montgomery's corps commander. For the next two years, Montgomery remained in Britain and further enhanced his reputation by capturing the imagination of the Army (and the public to some extent) through his intensely realistic large-scale exercises conducted in all weathers.

In the summer of 1942, this highly professional, but somewhat unsociable, soldier was sent to take over the dispirited 8th Army in North Africa. Montgomery revitalized it and soon made the 8th Army one of the most renowned in all British history. As the commander of a victorious army well away from home, Montgomery soon obtained for himself a great measure of independence and wide powers of action. This kind of responsibility ideally suited his autocratic temperament.

When he returned to Britain, he acted as Eisenhower's most trusted adviser on military problems. As temporary Commander-in-Chief Land Forces, Montgomery had his own headquarters quite distinct and separate from SHAEF where Eisenhower presided. With his victorious reputation, his inimitable character and his enormous experience of battle, Montgomery soon became the dominant figure in what may be called the highest *Overlord* circles.

It is most important to realize that Montgomery was only to act as Commander-in-Chief Land Forces for a limited period and then hand over this position to Eisenhower. His permanent post was Commander-in-Chief of the British 21st Army Group, which consisted of two armies, 1st US Army commanded by General Omar Bradley* and 2nd British commanded by General Miles Dempsey who was one of the most senior battle-trained officers brought back from Italy by Montgomery. A friendly, unassuming man, Dempsey had a thorough knowledge of all the aspects of higher staff work and plenty of common sense. Absolutely loyal to his chief, he admirably fulfilled the role of a modest first violin in an orchestra playing a piece conducted by the composer, Montgomery.

At this point, it is essential to give, in outline, the structure of what was officially called the British Liberation Army. This expeditionary force consisted of an army group (21st) which comprised two or more armies. Each army consisted of two or more corps which in turn consisted of two or more divisions. A corps could be switched from one army to another, as occasion demanded, and divisions were similarly transferred from one corps to another.

By the end of the battle for Normandy, about 850,000 British, Canadian and Polish troops, as well as 1,200,000 Americans, had been disembarked. Nearly all the British-controlled troops belonged either to GHQ units and were part of the army group which was responsible for allocating

---

* On 1 August, Bradley was given command of the newly formed US 12th Army Group. On 23 July, 1st Canadian Army, under Crerar, became operational and joined 21st Army Group.

them to a particular army or corps, or they belonged to one of the fifteen infantry and armoured divisions (each corps had a very few units which were solely responsible for the protection of the corps headquarters). The surprisingly high proportion of over half of the whole BLA consisted of GHQ troops, many of whom were in lines of communication or base installation units. But there were also some very important fighting GHQ formations. In a so-called division (79th) had been placed all the specialized armoured vehicles such as the Sherman 'flail' tanks (the 'Crabs'), whose task was to clear the minefields, and the Churchill 'Crocodile' tanks, the flame-throwers. Large numbers of the GHQ (the official term for 21st Army Group troops) and Army troops served in independent armoured brigades, of which there were eight in Normandy. The medium guns (5.5-in.), the heavy guns (7.2-in. and 155-mm), and nearly all the anti-aircraft guns and their personnel were GHQ forces. To obtain quickly the maximum concentration of fire-power these medium and heavy artillery regiments were permanently grouped into organizations called AGRAs (Army Groups Royal Artillery), of which there were six. The Commandos and the Marines were also amongst the GHQ troops. Except for wearing the 21st Army Group's or 2nd Army's arm badge (or 'flash'), the vast majority of the GHQ troops had little idea of what was meant by 21st Army Group or 2nd Army and never visited their headquarters.

The reason for lumping all these heterogeneous units together within 21st Army Group was to achieve the highest possible degree of flexibility. By this system it was found that those planning an attack could easily switch these more specialized formations to support whatever corps or division needed their assistance. Nevertheless many GHQ units did remain in support of the same formation throughout the battle; for instance, each corps retained its own AGRA. The versatility which thereby resulted from the planning staffs having at their disposal so many GHQ units had a further advantage in that it made it more difficult for the German Intelligence rapidly to assess the scale of any attack. Hence flexibility was the keynote of this system of employing formations.

One, often serious, disadvantage sometimes arose from this method of employing GHQ units. With the intensely personal traditions of the British Army, especially amongst the innumerable cavalry and infantry regiments, there was a tendency to conduct operations in a particular way that might vary considerably from the standard drill. Hence a newly arrived GHQ unit might find that its methods of support were not those to which its hosts were accustomed and, in the heat of the battle, disastrous misunderstandings were liable to occur.

In 1944, the organization of the British ground forces was constructed round the division. This constituted the largest single fighting formation whose numbers were constantly kept up to an agreed strength. The division was standardized into two types, the armoured and the infantry.* Although it might temporarily have other units attached to it, the essential feature of the division was that it should remain intact, never being amalgamated with another division and only broken up if, as a last resort, reinforcements could not otherwise be obtainable. Thus for the fighting man the division and his own regiment became the two focal points of his loyalty.

The divisions employed in Normandy fell into two categories, those which had seen action before and those which had been waiting and training in Britain, some since Dunkirk. Three divisions, the 7th Armoured (the 'Desert Rats'), the 50th Infantry (Northumberland) and the 51st (Highland) Divisions had all fought with the 8th Army in the North African desert and then later taken part in the campaigns in Sicily and Italy where they had established a

---

* There was also an airborne division and the 79th Armoured Division. The airborne differed from the standard infantry pattern. It was smaller and being expected to fight only for brief periods before being relieved, was relatively lightly equipped. The term division was a misnomer for the 79th which was designed solely to provide specialized support (for instance, clearing minefields).

brilliant fighting reputation for themselves; two of the eight independent armoured brigades had been similarly battle-trained. In many ways, these divisions and armoured brigades proved a disappointment in Normandy, not always living up to the standard expected of them. Too much was, in fact, anticipated from them. Many of their troops had passed the peak of their fighting efficiency. This was particu-larly true of the 'Desert Rats', where the saying that 'an old soldier is a cautious solder, that is why he is an old soldier' summed up the spirit in which a fair number of these hard-ened campaigners may well have viewed the prospect of yet another round of fighting. To give them their due, the 'Desert Rats' had, as a division, been in action fairly continu-ously since 1941. Some of the soldiers in these three divisions tended to grumble at again having to bear the brunt of the fighting, whilst so many of the soldiers who had not left the shores of Britain were often given an easier role. At the same time, the troops in the 7th Armoured and 50th and 51st Divisions liked to adopt a patronizing attitude to the new-comers who perforce lacked their battle experience. This 'know all' spirit was soon rudely shattered, since the veterans of the desert and Italy unfortunately did not at first appreci-ate that the lessons they had learnt earlier would have to be considerably modified before they could be effectively applied in the terrain of Normandy. To a lesser extent, some of the Germans suffered from the same kind of over-confi-dence. The veterans of the Eastern Front regarded the British and American troops as easy prey after the Russians; they too were soon jolted out of their feeling of superiority by the sustained violence of the Allied air attacks which proved far more devastating than any they had ever en-countered in the East.

In fairness to the 'old soldiers' of the battle-experienced divisions, they had already suffered heavy losses. Only those who have had some first-hand knowledge of this kind of life can begin to appreciate the incessant dangers and discomforts, as well as the cumulative stresses and strains, which the front-line soldier is called upon to endure for weeks or months on end without proper rest. In the Second World War, as always before, the heaviest battle casualties inevitably occurred amongst the infantry, few of whom survived a year in action without being wounded. Being frequently in contact with the enemy, the tank and armoured-car crews and some of the gunners and engineers also suffered quite high casualties. But the rest of the soldiers, well over half the Army, led a fairly safe, if none too comfortable, existence when in action, traffic accidents being the main danger.

To win battles in modern warfare, it is not only essential for a nation to have more troops better trained, led and administered than its adversary, but also for it to have developed and produced equipment which is both quantitatively and qualitatively superior to that of its opponent. By mid-1944, the Allies had achieved a massive quantitative superiority over the Germans in almost all branches of 'hardware', except multiple mortars, of which they had none. The German advantages in these weapons were, however, more than compensated for by the Allied preponderance in all kinds of conventional artillery. Moreover, the Allied gunners controlled their fire-power extremely skilfully and usually being well supplied with ammunition, could bring down enormous concentrations of shells accurately and rapidly, as the Germans freely admitted. Nevertheless, in one very important group of weapons even an enormous superiority in numbers failed effectively to counterbalance a dangerous Allied weakness in quality. The German tanks and self-propelled anti-tank guns proved so much better than those with which the British and Amercans were equipped that it was often to their airmen that the Allied soldier had to turn for protection against the panzer forces. One armoured expert considered that 'but for the 17-pounder Sherman, the close nature of the Normandy battlefield, which robbed the Germans of some of the advantages of their powerful tank guns, and the overall Anglo-US superiority in resources the tank situation might have been critical'.

Soon after the end of the war, when writing of the British armour, Alan Moorehead did not mince his words:

Our tanks were Shermans, Churchills and Cromwells. None of them was the equal of the German Mark V (the Panther), or the Mark VI (the Tiger)....

The Germans had much thicker armour than we had. Their tanks were effective at a thousand yards or more: ours at ranges around five hundred yards. ... Our own tanks were unequal to the job because they were not good enough. There may be various ways of dodging this plain truth, but anyone who wishes to do so will find himself arguing with the crews of more than three British armoured divisions which fought in France. Oliver Lyttelton, the wartime Minister of Production stated bluntly, in his autobiography 'It is, of course, quite true that we did not produce a really good tank until the end of the war.'

The Americans fared no better than the British. They concentrated on mass-producing only one tank, the Sherman, and they built nearly 50,000 of them. But by 1943 the Sherman, though mechanically very reliable, was completely obsolete by German standards. General Bradley had no illusions on this subject and he stated, 'Only by swarming around the panzers to hit them on the flank, could our Shermans knock the enemy out. But too often the American tankers complained it cost them a tank or two, *with crews*, to get the German.' According to Bradley, Eisenhower was equally taken aback by this state of affairs, for, when he heard of it, he remarked angrily, 'Why is it that I am always the last to hear about this stuff?' Indeed for once the Americans were over-impressed by a piece of last-minute British improvization. Hearing that the British were hurriedly fitting their excellent 17-pounder anti-tank gun into some of their Shermans (then renamed Fireflies), Bradley tried to persuade Montgomery to let him have some of these guns to put into the American Shermans to improve their fighting qualities. Owing to a severe shortage of the 17-pounder anti-tank guns, Montgomery could not meet Bradley's request. Nevertheless, in Normandy, the Americans' inferiority in tank quality did not affect them as seriously as it did the

British, since, by design, Montgomery drew the bulk of the German armour on to the British flank and therefore the Americans had comparatively little tank fighting.

This weakness in the quality of the Allied armoured equipment was accentuated by an almost complete lack of self-propelled anti-tank guns in the British Army. The British anti-tank guns were towed behind 'soft-skinned' wheeled lorries and had to be unhitched before they could be positioned to fire. In open country this cumbersome process could be extremely hazardous and also, once in position on the gun site, the crew were quite immobile and therefore vulnerable to enemy fire. The Germans, on the other hand, had mounted many of their 88-mm and 75-mm anti-tank guns on tank chassis. Thus with their greater mobility and longer range, the German anti-tank guns could often destroy the Allied tanks without endangering themselves. The German anti-tank guns were also superior to the British, since they could fire both solid shot, to destroy armoured fighting vehicles, and also high-explosive shells which were effective against both infantry and ordinary vehicles; the British anti-tank guns were limited to firing solid shot.

It cannot be overstressed that the Allies would have been in a critical plight in Normandy had they not been able to call upon their massive artillery and their fighter-bombers and rocket-firing aircraft to aid them against the qualitatively superior German tanks and anti-tank guns. When the weather was fine, the German tank crews found the aircraft their main worry, since as a German historian has written (with perhaps justifiable exaggeration) 'Once a tank was spotted it was done for. Mercilessly it would be dive-bombed or attacked until a bomb or volley of cannon fire (or rockets) had finished it off.' A German novelist, who apparently had first-hand experience, put it more colourfully: 'The planes drop their eggs among the soldiers and circle above them like birds of prey. They are hunting for the German tanks which lurk like fat grubs in the bushes or beneath the trees. They hunt and they find. Their cannons shoot down apple leaves, pine cones....Rockets screech down again and again!'

It must be conceded that the Germans' tanks, too, had their problems and faults. Both the Panther (Mark V) and the Tiger (Mark VI) were prone to mechanical failures (one authority asserts that more of these latter tanks were lost from mechanical breakdowns than from Allied attacks). The Tigers also suffered from a weakness in their turret drive mechanism which was not powerful enough to traverse rapidly the massive 88-mm gun and turret; there were stories of Allied tanks escaping to cover more speedily than the Tiger crew could slowly bring its gun to bear. Having relatively lightly armoured plating on their sides, sometimes the Allied tanks could work round to attack the big German tanks on their more vulnerable flanks and so destroy them; but other tanks had to draw the German fire, and so it usually proved a costly way of knocking out the enemy. Perhaps the greatest single handicap the German tanks had to face was the purely physical one imposed on them by the *bocage*. The dense nature of this country frequently meant that the fighting took place at such close quarters (under 300 yards) that the Allied tank and anti-tank guns were effective. Also, even the largest tanks were highly vulnerable to the small rocket-propelled anti-tank weapons. These were standard equipment in every infantry company, being called Piats (Projectile Infantry Anti-Tank) in the British Army, Bazookas in the American and Panzerfausts in the German Army. Firing a 2½-lb bomb, the Piat weighed only 35 lb and could be easily concealed and fired by one man, but its chief drawback lay in its effective range being about 100 yards. To attack a 25-ton Mark IV tank, let alone a 45-ton Panther or a 55-ton Tiger tank at such close quarters demanded a very cool and skilful operator; all tanks carried, besides their gun, at least one machine-gun, hence, if the first shot did not disable or destroy the tank, retribution was normally swift and lethal. Nevertheless, both sides did knock out each other's tanks with such weapons.

The Germans had devised a good balance between lighter and heavier tanks. About half the tanks in a panzer division were the 45-ton Mark V Panthers, the remainder being an up-to-date version of their well-tried Mark IV which weighed 25 tons;* as a fighting machine, this tank was comparable with the few British Fireflies. Otherwise, the German Mark IVs were unquestionably better tanks than the under-gunned 27-ton Cromwells and the 30-ton Shermans with which the Allied forces were almost exclusively equipped. There is, therefore, no escaping the sorry truth that, in the summer of 1944, the only Allied tanks not obsolete by German standards were the small number of Fireflies. German tank design had to be good, or their forces would never have survived the Russian onslaughts on the Eastern Front, where the Red Army had tanks of excellent quality. The Allies, on the other hand, had not had to fight any serious tank battles since those in the Western Desert in 1942, when the Shermans had proved themselves competent to take on the earlier models of the Mark IV.

Neither Eisenhower nor Montgomery can be criticized for the Allied failure to produce a tank comparable in armoured protection and in hitting power to the Panther or the Tiger, since they had returned, early in 1944, to take over forces already equipped with their tanks. Montgomery, in particular, seemed to have appreciated this weakness in his tank divisions, for he pressed on as rapidly as he could with the conversion of the Shermans into Fireflies. Where, however, Montgomery seems to have been tactically at fault was his optimism in expecting that in the more open parts of the Norman countryside his armoured forces with their poor equipment could decisively defeat the heavier German panzer divisions.

In their family of specialized armoured vehicles, the Allies possessed a great advantage over the Germans. The invention and development of these strange weapons of war was the work of General Hobart and his team of experts. Using Churchill tanks, christened Crocodiles, they had produced a most horrifyingly efficient flame-thrower with a range of 120 yards, which was in great demand for burning the enemy out of unfortified strong-points and woods.

* The Tigers (Mark VI) were organized in separate formations.

Towing a 400-gallon armoured trailer full of fuel, the Croco-
dile-Churchill had a fire-gun in place of its machine-gun and
through this it spurted jets of flame which bounced their
way to a target. The fantastically noisy 'Flails' consisted of
an ordinary Sherman tank whose engine had been adapted
to turn a revolving drum set out a few feet in front of the
tank itself. To this drum were attached large chains which
'flailed' the ground as the tank moved on at 2 mph. The
effect of this flailing was to explode mines harmlessly and
these clanking monsters must have saved thousands from
death or the horrible wounds inflicted by mines. Finally
Hobart's team had devised the AVREs (Armoured Vehicle
Royal Engineers) which were Churchills. They could either
transport a large mortar device for throwing a charge of
high explosive to demolish concrete defences or they could
carry a variety of bridge-building equipment.

To sum up this controversial subject. It is valid to say that
through the combination of air supremacy, immense superiority in numbers of tanks and artillery and the closeness of
the Norman *bocage* the Allied forces eventually managed to
overwhelm and destroy the better equipped German panzer
divisions. For a short time after this when the German tanks
and anti-tank guns were eliminated, the hordes of fast, reliable, lightly armoured Allied tanks came into their own
and proved temporary masters of the battlefield.

4

7 June, the Day after the 'Day'

'It had always been impossible to imagine D + 1.'
– *Norman Scarfe, Assault Division*

THE EVENTS OF D-DAY went fairly well according to plan. The bravery of those taking part in the landings and the skill of commanders directing them had meant that beach areas had been secured in five different places, Utah and Omaha in the US sector, and Gold, Juno and Sword in the British. Though the penetration inland had nowhere been as deep as had been somewhat optimistically forecast, the fact that all the landings had been made as planned seemed to everyone a near miracle, especially as losses had been less than anticipated.

Naturally the spotlight has always been on the brilliant success of the D-day landings, but this has inevitably been inclined to make the next, and less dramatic, stages of the battle seem an anticlimax. In particular, the fighting on D + 1 has seldom been treated as fully as it warrants. The description of the battle on this day is necessarily confusing, since the reader must be ready to share the experiences of both commanders and troops involved in the piecemeal and rather isolated conflicts designed primarily to link up the beachheads.

Before dawn on 7 June, Montgomery arrived off the Normandy beaches. He had crossed over from Portsmouth in the destroyer HMS *Faulkner*, and later that day he installed his Advanced (Tac) HQ in France where he discussed the progress of the battle with Eisenhower, who was paying the first of his many visits to the Normandy battlefront. Earlier on D + 1, Montgomery had conferred with his two

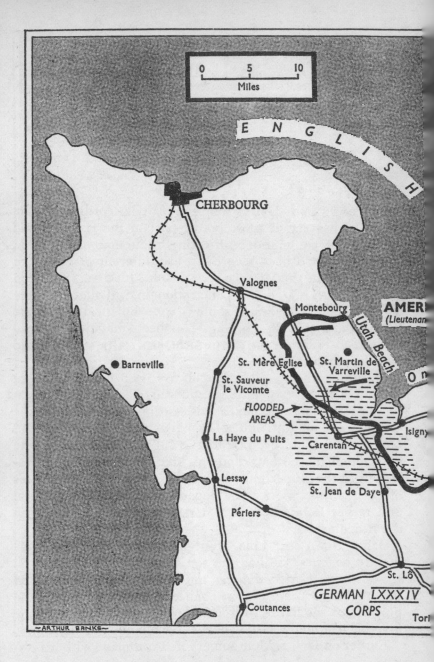

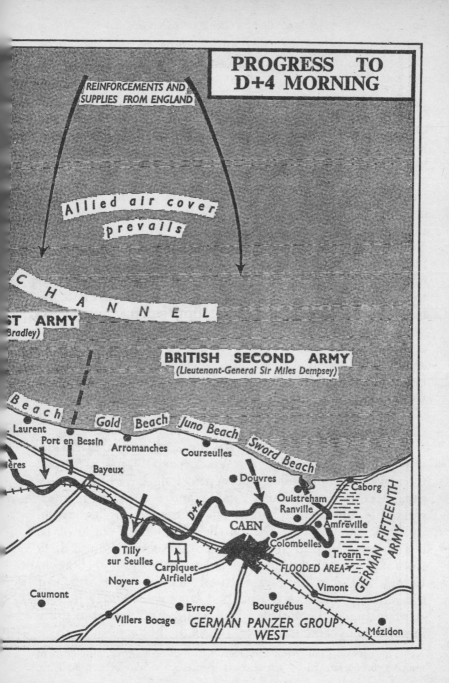

PROGRESS TO D+4 MORNING

REINFORCEMENTS AND
SUPPLIES FROM ENGLAND

Allied air cover prevails

C H A N N E L

ST ARMY
(Bradley)

BRITISH SECOND ARMY
(Lieutenant-General Sir Miles Dempsey)

Beach

Gold Beach Juno Beach Sword Beach

. Laurent
Port en Bessin Arromanches Courseulles
ères Bayeux
Douvres
Ouistreham
Ranville
Caborg
D+4
CAEN
Amfreville
Colombelles
Tilly sur Seulles
Troarn
Carpiquet Airfield
FLOODED AREA
GERMAN FIFTEENTH ARMY
Noyers
Vimont
Caumont
Evrecy Bourguébus
Villers Bocage **GERMAN PANZER GROUP WEST**
Mézidon

army commanders, Bradley and Dempsey, who had spent
the previous night in their command ships moored just off
the beaches.

As he had anticipated, Montgomery saw himself confronted on D + 1 with three main problems. First and foremost, he had quickly to get the separated landing places
joined up to form one continuous and secure beachhead; this
was especially urgent in the American sector where Omaha
and Utah beaches were about ten miles apart. Secondly, he
was determined that the Allied forces should retain the
initiative they had so gallantly gained, and this meant keeping up the momentum of the attack, not only by completing
the D-day tasks, but also, where possible, by pressing on
farther. Such forceful tactics would guarantee that the Germans remained 'off balance'. Finally, he was very conscious
that he had to prevent the enemy from making any successful counter-attacks which might threaten the smooth development of the vast and complex inter-service build-up of
equipment and stores needed to sustain the offensive. The
more long drawn-out and less spectacular administrative
battle of the build-up had now to be begun. In the words of
the Official History, Montgomery on 7 June had 'no need to
issue fresh orders, but only to emphasize the urgency of
these tasks'.

As Scarfe, the historian of the British 3rd Division,
makes clear, the troops who had specially prepared and
trained for the invasion had been so long keyed-up for this
great assault that they were unable (and were perhaps understandably unwilling to try) to project their thoughts beyond
it; 'Sufficient unto the Day is the evil thereof', might well
have been their prayer. Hence, awaking cold, stiff and dirty
from a night of fitful sleep spent in a shallow hole in
French soil – in most cases their first on terra firma for
three days – these men who had landed on D-day had almost to pinch themselves to be assured of the astonishing
fact that they were still alive*. Also, at the same time, these

* The invasion had been far from a bloodless victory, since out of
about 156,000 landed by sea and air, some 9,000 had been casualties.

troops had to make the necessary psychological readjust-
ments quickly. One phase of the battle was now successfully
completed, but to the vast majority of the soldiers on the
battlefield little definite was known of the form the fighting
was now likely to take, except that they had been led to expect that the Germans would recover soon and try to counter-attack. The Allied commanders clearly realized that their
forces must now make every effort to push on well inland.
Yet boldness had to be carefully balanced with caution, since
any advance inland must not be made at the expense of consolidating and strengthening the bridgehead. Above all else,
the Allies must build up their strength more rapidly than
the Germans, otherwise they might be hemmed in and not
be able to break out from this restricted bridgehead. As it
turned out, this latter task was to prove a far more laborious
and costly affair than had generally been anticipated. Nevertheless on that fine blustering morning of 7 June, the most
immediate and unpleasant job for those on the ground was
to resume the fighting, and this they did.

Reviewing the most immediate task, that of linking up
the beaches, the situation in Normandy on D + 1 presented
some fairly sharp contrasts. On the western flank, the Americans on Utah beach had spent D-day busily building up
their strength. Their disembarkation on the lower part of
the Cotentin peninsula had been remarkably successful,
mainly because they had surprised both themselves and the
Germans when they had landed, on a very lightly defended
stretch of the coast, 2,000 yards away from their planned
beach. The main task of the Americans here was to push
on and consolidate their tenuous links with the two Airborne
Divisions (101st and 82nd) which had been dropped farther
inland. In this area, the parachute and glider descents had
gone seriously awry and the airborne troops were now scattered around in numerous small pockets all over the lower
half of the peninsula. But, in spite of this, many of these
highly trained troops had come together and hurriedly organized themselves into battle groups. Some of these pockets
of troops were taking on equally bewildered Germans in the

low-lying regions of marsh and flooded meadow-land at the base of the Cotentin peninsula. Other airborne units had been dropped on to the higher ground and had coalesced into *ad hoc* formations. Nearly everywhere isolated and bitter contests were being waged with the German units stationed in this region.

Almost the only definite information which had filtered through from this sector was the heartening news that the airborne troops had seized, and were managing to hold on to their main objective, the all-important cross-roads on which stands the village of Ste Mère Eglise. It was imperative, therefore, for the more heavily equipped Americans on the beaches to push on as rapidly as they could to join up with these hard-pressed airborne detachments; this juncture was quickly and successfully achieved. During the next few days, the Americans gained the firm footing on the Cotentin peninsula which was essential if the link was to be effected with the neighbouring beach, and the port of Cherbourg be speedily captured.

Returning from the forward positions, an American officer wrote of Utah:

The beach was a terrific thing on the morning of D plus 1, already jammed with vehicles and equipment and with thousands upon thousands of soldiers and vehicles milling about. But the road net made sense. Without asking the way once we went through a maze which the MPs (Military Police) had already organized and suddenly found ourselves running along the dune road behind the beach. The beach itself was still under fire from pillboxes farther up the shore which the infantry weren't able to get at. But these guns, firing through slits, had a narrow traverse and could only cover the edge of the beach itself and a few feet out into the water. Their shells sent high geysers of water up into the air and the DUKWs and the landing craft shuffled in among them.

The air over my beach was full of balloons now and as far as you could see towards England there were the hulls of ships and more ships crowding in. ... The ammunition dump that had been begun on the sand spit was spread out on the beach side of the road. It was already a few small piles of boxes and crates.

The layout of everything was very nicely planned. Right next to the ammunition dump they were laying out the corpses.

Much the most critical position was at the American Omaha beach, where little more than a precarious toe-hold had been obtained on D-day and there had been no link-up with the beaches on either side. On the morning of 7 June, the American troops found themselves still strongly opposed by the best German infantry division on the Normandy front, and had only gained a narrow strip of land nowhere more than 2,000 yards deep. As the day wore on, the Americans, having managed to overcome the resistance and the obstacles, had begun to fight their way inland. Separating them from their compatriots at Utah was, however, about ten miles of extremely difficult country which included the extensively flooded areas of the Vire and Douves estuaries. On their other flank, the Americans could not join up with the British until the well-defended small fishing port of Port en Bessin had been captured. After a day- and night-long battle, in which rocket-firing Typhoon aircraft and naval guns were called in to help, the Royal Marines forced the German garrison to surrender. The actual link up between the American and British occurred very early on 8 June.

In contrast with the comparative peace and order at Utah, an American broadcaster reported that at Omaha:

The German shelling continued steadily at various points up and down the beach. . . . It would work over an area, then move on to another. It was accurate, landing for the most part close to the water's edge, and I saw one small landing-craft catch fire after taking a hit. Men came spilling out of it into water waist-deep.

From time to time there were huge concussions as the engineers set off demolitions; the ground would shake, and the troops would throw themselves violently on the ground.

Making his way towards the higher ground above the beach, he found:

The mines had been marked with bits of paper, and soldiers at the top advised just how to climb so as not to venture into dangerous ground. ...

The column had stopped moving, and I began to step past men following a captain. Suddenly a voice said: 'Watch yourself, fellow, that's a mine.' A soldier sprawled on the bank was speaking; he had one foot half blown off; he'd stepped on a mine a short time earlier. ... I began to make my way down the path again. It was slow work. The soldiers were so alarmed that I would step on a mine right next to them that one man told me to walk on his back rather than step off the path.

The American attempts at pushing inland here were proving painful and costly.

Known as Gold, the most westerly of the three beaches in the British sector came under the control of XXX Corps, and here 50th Division had landed. On D + 1, this division continued its somewhat leisurely advance on Bayeux (originally a D-day objective) which it soon took with little trouble; Bayeux thus had the honour of being the first French town to be liberated and was also almost the only one in Normandy fortunate enough to escape heavy damage. During the rest of the day, other formations of this division advanced at a steady pace and got well astride their D-day objective, a stretch of the Caen–Bayeux road. 50th Division also found no difficulty in joining up with the 3rd Canadian Division on its eastern flank. Certainly this part of the bridgehead seemed to offer the most promising prospects of exploitation, for only minor German opposition was encountered, and the process of consolidation proved a fairly simple one causing few casualties. On 7 June, units of the 7th Armoured Division began to disembark on Gold beach to join their former 8th Army comrades.

3rd Canadian Division had come ashore at Juno beach. Like 50th Division, the Canadians had managed to move five to six miles inshore by nightfall, but they too had failed to reach their D-day objectives. These were to seize six miles of the Caen–Bayeux road and railway line, which here lie parallel to each other. It had also been planned that they should capture Carpiquet aerodrome which lies just south of this railway and is about ten miles from the coast. It had been an ambitious assignment.

As with almost all the Allied formations, the Canadians had passed a relatively peaceful night on 6–7 June. Early the following morning, together with their attached armoured brigade, they resumed their advance, crossing the Caen–Bayeux road and railway in several places just outside Caen, and one unit almost reached the aerodrome at Carpiquet which turned out to be a German strong-point. In the early afternoon, however, the leading Canadians nearest to Caen were almost engulfed by a strong counter-attack launched in conjunction with the 21st Panzer Division, by the 12th SS Panzer Division.

12th SS (Hitler Jugend) Panzer Division rapidly became notorious for 'reckless courage and determination combined with a degree of barbarity found perhaps in no other formation'. Since the Canadians were to fight for so long against these indoctrinated youths, it is worth while to quote more extensively from the pen of their official historian. 12th SS Panzer

had not fought before D-day, but it certainly contained a high proportion of battle-experienced officers and NCOs. The officers appear to have been either hardened Nazis who had distinguished themselves in Russia or professional soldiers sympathetic to the Nazi viewpoint. The NCOs were in part at least selected young veterans of the Russian campaigns, which were waged on both sides virtually as a war of extermination. The rank and file were largely youngsters (aged eighteen) fresh from the military fitness camps of the Hitler Youth and full of the Nazi ideology.

At the beginning of June 1944 the division's strength was 20,540 all ranks ... it was not quite complete in tanks, having 150.

On 7 June, this division had boastfully issued an order which stated it would 'attack the landed enemy and throw him back into the sea'. Kurt Meyer, later commander of this notorious division, was even more self-confident, remarking to Feuchtinger (the commander of 21st Panzer Division) about the Allies: 'Little fish! We'll throw them back into the sea in the morning.' But the Allied airmen were also up and about early on 7 June and so harried the columns of 12th SS Panzer Division that only about one-third of its formations were, in fact, available for this counter-attack. Nevertheless, the Canadians had to give some ground just outside Caen before finally stabilizing the situation; both sides lost heavily in this confused encounter which was much the most menacing the Allies had yet fought.

Given the code-name Sword, the most easterly beach had been allocated to the British 3rd Division. With the Canadian 3rd Division (most confusing this numbering), this formation composed I British Corps which was commanded by General Crocker. The general situation in the British 3rd Division's area gave some cause for anxiety on D + 1. In the first place, the crossing had been a rough one. Then the British, and to a lesser extent the Canadians, had found their landing more strongly opposed than they had expected, with the underwater and shore obstacles more numerous and ingenious than 3rd British Division's out-of-date (taken in August 1943) 'briefing' photographs had shown. These factors resulted in considerable congestion on the beaches, which deranged the carefully timed unloading programmes. This, in its turn, reduced the speed of the division's thrust inland. After breaking through the beach fortifications and clearing the immediate hinterland, there had been fairly heavy casualties on D-day. Moreover, 3rd Division had been the only British formation to have been subjected to a major armoured counter-attack on D-day. Although this had been successfully repulsed, it had somewhat disrupted the division's D-day plans. By first light on D + 1, British 3rd Division's leading troops formed a kind of wedge pointing at Caen which lay some three miles away, but the foremost units had been halted by much more powerfully constructed fortifications than the Intelligence reports had foretold. On the west flank of this division, between it and the Canadians, existed an ominous gap, about two miles wide, stretching from the coast, where several German strong-points still resisted capture, down to Caen itself. It had been along this gap that the tanks of the German 21st Panzer Division had tried, on D-day, to make their way to the sea and divide the British forces.

On his eastern flank, Crocker was growing hourly more concerned about the position of 6th Airborne Division. Although this lightly equipped division was fighting magnificently, the Germans were hurling ceaseless and ferocious attacks against it. Crocker, therefore, felt his corps must be ready to give the highest priority to supporting the hard-pressed airborne troops.

Thus on D + 1, the experienced Crocker found himself in a dilemma. Either he could throw the bulk of British 3rd Division into an all-out attack on Caen, or he could pause and consolidate. Unfortunately he had not the resources to do both these things. Under the circumstances, there can be little doubt that Crocker took a sound decision in pausing, since some breathing-space was essential if the bridgehead was to be firmly secured and the vital link-up between the British and Canadians completed.

Crocker's policy succeeded. The British joined up with the Canadians late on D + 1, thereby finally linking all the British beachheads with one another.

British 3rd Division's advance on Caen was not, however, entirely abandoned. A small-scale attack was made, but this was beset by a series of misfortunes and misunderstandings and ended in utter failure. No one on the Allied side had yet grasped the hard fact that this northern, and direct, approach to Caen had been turned by the Germans into a part of the West Wall fortifications system and was strongly held in some depth. This vital ground did not, in fact, fall to the Allies until a month later when a full-scale corps attack had to be mounted against it. In short, by the evening of D + 1, the Germans around Caen had recovered from their first shock and had brought the situation under some sort of control.

During 7 June, growing concern was everywhere felt about events on the eastern flank. As has already been mentioned,

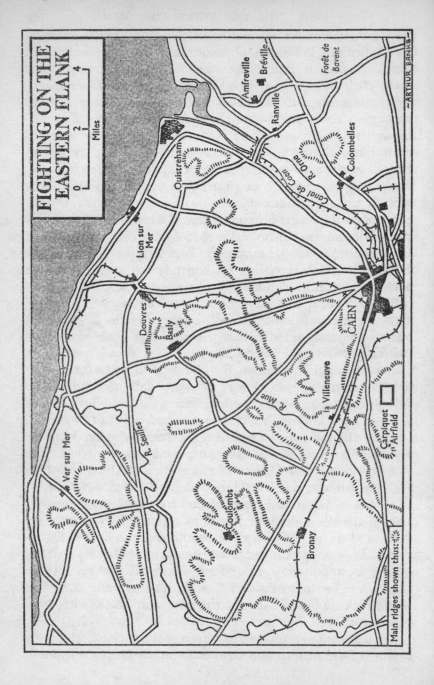

FIGHTING ON THE
EASTERN FLANK

0   2   4
Miles

Ouistreham

R. Orne

Canal de Caen

Amfreville

Bréville

Ranville

Forêt de
Bavent

Colombelles

Lion sur
Mer

Douvres

Basly

CAEN

R. Mue

la Villeneuve

Ver sur Mer

R. Seulles

Coulombs

Bronay

Carpiquet
Airfield

Main ridges shown thus:

~ARTHUR BANKS~

the German counter-attacks here looked most threatening. On D-day 6th Airborne Division had dropped, well concentrated, on to their objectives. In particular they had seized the all-important bridges across the Canal de Caen and the Orne at a small place called Bénouville. Once east of the Orne, they had started to fan-out, but this district, with its woods and villages, offers many excellent defensive positions. The airborne forces therefore soon found themselves pinned down and in difficulties. The Germans, who had always appreciated the tactical value of the ground here, were in a very strong position, since their flanks rested securely on the rivers Orne and Dives. They were especially sensitive to any advance on Caen from the east bank of the Orne, since this would mean their losing an invaluable ridge of high ground just outside the town, known as the Colombelles and Ste Honorine district of Caen. A huge steel works with many high chimneys dominates this ridge, and provides unrestricted observation over large tracts of the surrounding countryside on both sides of the Orne river. By retaining this factory area the Germans could watch all movement for several miles into the British-held area of the bridgehead. Until the capture of Caen, this sprawling factory area was like a thorn in the British side, and all those in the eastern half of the bridgehead had the sinister sensation that their every movement was being noted by German observers perched in these lofty look-out posts.

To the east of the Orne, therefore, the Airborne Division was soon forced on to the defensive. But in spite of almost continuous attacks supported by tanks, heavy guns and mortars, the depleted airborne troops clung grimly to their positions, only giving way a little here and there. These counter-attacks were pressed home with the greatest ferocity in and around the two small villages of Amfreville and Bréville. They are close to each other, and the Germans were extremely keen to recapture them, since, from D-day onwards, they overlooked the masses of shipping unloading troops, vehicles and stores on Sword beach (Sword beach was just west of the mouth of the Orne). If, therefore, the Germans could have held these two villages, they could have directed fire accurately on to this beach where targets were so plentiful that any artillery officer would have been in a seventh heaven of delight. Furthermore, if they could have regained this area the Germans would have closely overlooked the Canal de Caen and the Orne river, where the engineers were busily constructing bridges to take heavy traffic, and it would have been simple to put down such concentrated mortar and artillery fire, that life would have been made unbearable for the sappers.

The gunners came to the rescue of the Airborne Division. Gale, the divisional commander, was convinced that it was the artillery support given him by I Corps which saved the day. Without it, he wrote, 'we should have been unable to hold our position.' In this sector of the front, the Germans had their first taste of the British naval and ground artillery fire. They soon became well acquainted with the speed and flexibility with which the British artillery commanders could switch an enormous volume of the shell-fire on to almost any target.

For the Allied commanders, the land battle was not the only source of anxiety. Throughout D + 1, they kept glancing anxiously back at the beaches. All that fine morning a strong wind whipped up the sea, and it was not until the afternoon that it became calmer. The prolonged German resistance on Omaha beach, the long period of rough weather and a greater profusion of beach obstacles than had been anticipated, all these factors contributed to upsetting the somewhat optimistic schedules of unloading. The rate of build-up had fallen far behind the planned programme. In many cases, men and equipment were being disembarked up to 10 to 12 hours late.

Congestion was also beginning to occur offshore. The convoys, mainly composed of the large 5,000-ton L S T s (Landing Ship Tanks), were arriving regularly from England, but were then often finding it impossible to discharge their cargoes into the smaller ships, known as landing craft. The problems centred round the growing shortage of these craft,

which were designed to tranship stores between the larger
vessels and the beaches themselves; the number of these
craft either lost or severely damaged by the weather and
beach obstacles had so greatly exceeded estimates that a
breakdown in the whole supply and reinforcement system
seemed possible. Under these circumstances, Admiral Vian,
commander of the British Naval Task Force, decided by the
evening that the cargoes were so urgently needed that he
was justified in ordering the LSTs to be beached. The
Americans soon followed suit. Hence these hulking great
vessels came in with the tide, to be left high and dry as it
went out. As soon as the sea had sufficiently receded, the
huge doors of the LSTs were opened and their ramps
lowered. The badly needed vehicles and stores could thus be
unloaded directly on to the shore. Before the invasion, the
suggestion of beaching these vessels had been turned down
for fear of their breaking their backs in the process. Even
though the sight of large ships deliberately grounding themselves and lying apparently stranded always caused considerable anguish in the more orthodox naval circles, the
system worked so admirably and so rarely were the ships
themselves damaged that this method of unloading them
was thereafter accepted whenever delays began to arise in
the normal unloading schedules. By the evening of 7 June,
therefore, the supply problems became much less pressing
on all the beaches except Omaha; also off the British beaches
the first few blockships ('corn cobs') appeared and were
rapidly positioned and sunk to form the beginning of the
invaluable breakwaters that were an integral part of the
artificial harbours and jetties to be constructed during the
next ten days.

On D + 1, the close support of large naval guns greatly
assisted the ground forces in consolidating their positions.
The naval bombardments proved a surprise to the Germans
who had always counted on any allied invasion force
being very short of heavy artillery for the first few days. Instead, they were pounded by fire from huge 15-in. and 16-in.
guns. These were mounted on the British battleships and

monitors, *Warspite* and *Ramillies, Roberts* and *Erebus* (*Nelson* and *Rodney* joined them a few days later). In addition, there were available the 14-in. and 12-in. guns of the US battleships *Texas, Nevada* and *Arkansas*. The smaller guns, mainly of 6-in. or 4.5-in. calibre, of the battleships themselves and of the dozens of cruisers and destroyers, were also frequently called upon. The Germans testified not only to the destructiveness of such naval gunfire, but also to its high rate of fire, accuracy and long range; the biggest naval guns could comfortably shell Caen some 15 to 16 miles inland from their normal ships' stations.

In the early stages, most of the fire control of the naval guns was in the hands of specially trained pilots flying Spitfires, though there were a few naval-trained gunnery observers with the troops ashore. This kind of naval gunfire had a very important administrative advantage, since the warships, by carrying their own guns, personnel and ammunition, made no demands on the heavily committed beach unloading groups, as did conventional ground artillery. The employment of so many warships so close inshore (about three or four miles out to sea) had however its attendant risks. By no means all the well-fortified German coastal guns had been silenced and some to the east of the Orne river and in the Cherbourg peninsula were active, though they caused little damage to the ships.

Like the navies, the Allied air forces too were very busily engaged throughout D + 1. Close-support fighter-bomber aircraft answered many calls that day. Some groups of aircraft attacked targets which were holding up the ground forces, whilst others carried out armed reconnaissance sorties to photograph areas behind the forward positions and report on German troop movements. It was a pity that the most spectacular support for the armies necessarily went on unseen by the soldiers. Three examples will illustrate the direct kind of assistance the pilots rendered the armies by cutting up and demoralizing the German units en route to the battle front. On D-day, Bayerlein, who had earlier been Chief of Staff in the Afrika Korps and was now commander of the 'crack' Panzer Lehr Division, was told to move his division from its billets, near Le Mans, to Caen, a distance of some 90 miles. Panzer Lehr was a most formidable fighting force, having been constituted from training units (hence the German word Lehr for teaching), where it had recruited NCOs of the highest class. With these men, Bayerlein had been able to train his young soldiers with great thoroughness and was very proud of his fine division which must have been almost unique in the German Army for, with its 260 tanks, it was fully up to strength. Panzer Lehr had also greatly impressed the German tank expert Guderian who had told Bayerlein, 'With this division alone you will throw the Anglo-Americans back into the sea.'

Bayerlein, having experienced Allied air attacks in the Western Desert, decided to take every precaution he could, thus he moved on five roads to secure maximum dispersion for his forces. He vainly tried to persuade Dollmann, the 15th Army Commander, to permit him to make the journey under the cover of darkness. Bayerlein later gave a vivid description of what happened on 7 June.

At daylight, General Dollmann, commander of Seventh Army, gave me a direct order to proceed and there was nothing else to do. The first air attack came about half-past five that morning, near Falaise, by noon it was terrible; my men were calling the main road from Vire to Bény-Bocage a fighter-bomber racecourse. . . .

Every vehicle was covered with tree branches and moved along hedges and the edges of wood. Road junctions were bombed, and a bridge knocked out at Condé. This did not stop my tanks, but it hampered other vehicles. By the end of the day I had lost 40 tanks trucks carrying fuel, and 90 others. Five of my tanks were knocked out, and 84 half-trucks, prime-movers and self-propelled guns. These were serious losses for a division not yet in action.

When, on D + 1, an SS division was ordered up to the front, they took it all pretty lightheartedly, for, as one of their Staff officers later recalled:

Everyone was in a good and eager mood to see action again –

happy that the pre-invasion spell of uncertainty and waiting was snapped at last.

Our motorized columns were coiling along the road towards the invasion beaches. Then something happened that left us in a daze. Spurts of fire flicked along the column and splashes of dust staccatoed the road. Everyone was piling out of the vehicles and scuttling for the neighbouring fields. Several vehicles were already in flames. This attack ceased as suddenly as it had crashed upon us 15 minutes before. The men started drifting back to the column again, pale and shaky and wondering how they had survived this fiery rain of bullets. This had been our first experience with the 'Jabos' (fighter-bombers). The march column was now completely disrupted and every man was on his own, to pull out of this blazing column as best he could. And it was none too soon, because an hour later the whole thing started all over again, only much worse this time. When this attack was over, the length of the road was strewn with splintered anti-tank guns (the pride of our division), flaming motors and charred implements of war.

The march was called off and all vehicles that were left were hidden in the dense bushes or in barns. No one dared show himself out in the open any more. Now the men started looking at each other. This was different from what we thought it would be like. . . . Although now we only travelled at nights and along secondary roads rimmed with hedges and bushes, we encountered innumerable wrecks giving toothless testimony that some motorist had not benefited from the bitter experience we had had.

After being bombed during D-day whilst loading their equipment, the battle group of another German division eventually managed to set off on two trains from St Nazaire at dawn on 7 June. A little later one of the trains was destroyed by aerial attacks and the other one had to be abandoned because the railway lines had been cut. The survivors of this division had to continue their journey on foot or on bicycle, since those proved the best way of reaching the battlefield relatively undetected.

The Allied pilots, thus, hit the advancing Germans when they were 20–30 miles away from our troops.

In a less direct manner, the air forces also helped the

soldiers in Normandy, and on the night of D + 1 some of the heavy bombers of Bomber Command resumed their attacks on important railway targets near Paris. They suffered fairly heavy casualties from anti-aircraft fire and from night fighters. In their daylight attacks on the German troops and strong-points, the Allied pilots, too, often paid a heavy price, since their machines were vulnerable to the very efficient German anti-aircraft (flak) fire.

Finally, in conjunction with the navies, the air forces roamed widely across the Channel and the Bay of Biscay, to protect the many convoys crossing from England to Normandy. But, on D-day the anticipated U-boat attacks never materialized, nor did the German light naval torpedo craft (E-boats), try to interrupt the sailings of the build-up fleets. Of the Luftwaffe too there was little or no sign.

By 7 June, therefore, the three Allied Services were already working together as a closely coordinated team, all their efforts bent on the rapid defeat of the Germans in western Europe.

5

A Battle Exists on Different Levels

'To war and arms I fly.'
                        – Lovelace

THIS CHAPTER WILL gather together some eye-witness accounts of how the humbler soldier saw life during the early days in the bridgehead. It will thus be unlike the previous chapter which concentrated on the situation on D + 1, as it might have been pieced together from the information available to those directing the battle.

At its lowest level, a battle becomes difficult to explore and relate. It is partly because those most closely locked together in the actual fighting are normally inarticulate and unliterary men who find it hard to put their experiences down in a readable form. It is also because, for most of those engaged in it, any battle is a kind of untidy blur in which things happen in an alarming and frequently unpredictable manner. Nevertheless, some accounts do exist which managed to recapture the full excitement, horror and boredom which engulfs the fighting soldier so impartially.

On his first day in action, the mind of every soldier tends to be preternaturally alert, with a keen awareness of everything, but for many new soldiers there also exists an unspoken and unspeakable morbid fear: how will he react to the sight of a corpse? Except for those working in hospitals and for undertakers, modern society has managed to conceal the stark reality of death from the normal routine of life, but on a battlefield, when they cannot be buried quickly and reverently, the dead come into their own. On one new soldier, his first corpse, a dead German in a minefield, made a profound impression, for it 'lay on its back, spreadeagled, its helmet tilted in such a way over its ashen face that the dead eyes seemed to be peering up at us as we passed; there was a dead grin on its face and one foot was missing'. The Germans had a nasty habit of affixing cleverly concealed booby-traps to the corpses of their dead comrades which made everyone disinclined to take the risk of burying them.

It is true to say that the nearer soldiers are to the enemy, the more ignorant they tend to be of the wider aspects of a battle. Men in the most forward positions are often not even aware of what is happening around them and few, if any, are competent to give them such information. Though the front-line troops long to get news of events around them, no one is keen to try to tell them. This is not surprising if one remembers that it is an unhealthy occupation visiting the troops who are right forward. Woodrow Wyatt wrote of Normandy:

What impresses me most about the front line is not violence but the absence of it. When the battle was stationary for a while I often drove down to visit the forward units. The approach was always the same. The quick change from the hubbub and noise of the jumbled convoys in the back areas to roads deserted save for an occasional civilian walking very slowly. A few cattle in the fields grazing among the dead and swollen bodies of their fellows, but no farm workers. A complete silence – not even the sound of birds, a sense of being in an unreal world with no life, so that even the people in the villages timidly looking out of their shell-damaged houses don't seem alive. There is no reality because no one is doing his normal job. Even the war does not exist – until you see a notice 'You are in sight of the enemy now' and a little farther on 'Drive slowly – dust causes shells', and then a few steel-helmeted soldiers cautiously poking their heads out of slit trenches to see who is going by. At my destination the same slightly eerie atmosphere would persist. I would park my car very carefully out of sight behind some bushes or a wall and walk across to the Headquarters. There I would find the people I was looking for in a dugout or an armoured vehicle, oppressed by the same feeling as my own and talking quietly as though afraid the enemy across the fields or on the other slope of the

hill opposite might overhear. The opening exchange of cour-
tesies wasn't the weather but 'How many times have you been
shot up today?' followed by a visit to the latest shell or mortar
holes, much as one might go and see how the sweet peas were
coming on in a country garden.

When an attack is going on an agonizing sense of helplessness and loneliness can descend on soldiers. Paradoxically,
a strange bond exists here between the highest and lowest in
a battle, since the most senior officers feel the same sensation
at the same time, for once a battle has started, they become
virtually powerless to direct or influence events, and have
to be content to wait and hope for good news.

On D + 1, a young subaltern, who had never before been
in action, was ordered to take his heavy machine-guns forward to support the attack on Caen. His platoon never made
contact with those they were supposed to be helping. That
night he jotted down in a small notebook his recollections of
this unprofitable day:

June 7th. Wednesday. We stood to at 4.30 for an hour. After
this I handed the rum out. I had to report to Company HQ
straight away before breakfast. We were to support an attack.
To get to the CO while bn [battalion] was attacking I had to
move along the same road as last night. Half-way there a sentry
halted us. He told me that there was a machine-gun sniper in
the wood on the left front. He fired as he spoke and something
sped across the road fifty yards ahead of us. I sent everyone back
except the wireless operators and keeping our heads low we drove
past. There was a burnt out tank in the middle of the road which
made one reduce speed as we came to the crucial spot.
The plans were made for the attack. I moved up the road and
prepared for the occupation. On the hill I took the NCOs forward to show them the ground. We crawled along a long ditch.
This took a little while. At last we reached the right spot. I was
just about to raise my head to look over the crest when there was
a crack and I heard a bullet smack into the earth of the side of
the ditch by my head. It was a sniper and he had missed me by
about half an inch.
After that I was in a dilemma. We were spotted and it was impossible to do a safety shoot [with the machine-guns] without

exposing at least one's head. The only thing was to get the guns in as best we could. It took a long time to do this for they had to crawl a long way very low.

My sergeant opened up with the Bren on the sniper but we never found out whether he got him. There was no more sniping.

By this time it was long past the hour when the attack should have gone in. We could not fire in any case for they had put down smoke and our own troops were advancing.

But I had seen no attack and yet it was well past the time set. I could not fire and yet for all I knew they needed our help badly. I tried to contact them through the 18 [wireless] set. I tried to get my own company commander on the 22 [wireless set]. Neither worked. I think the trees were screening us. I seemed completely cut off from information. There was shelling in the distance. Self-propelled [guns] moved about us in front. But on the whole we were very much alone. An attack on our flank seemed a possibility.

All that day we lay in the hot sun. The men scratched themselves holes which grew into trenches. At mid-day they began to mortar us and when it seemed that they had found our range I began to expect casualties. One landed ten yards from Platoon Headquarters but only killed a couple of cows, spewing their stomach and intestines over the field.

Still activity was vague on the hill in front of us. Then stragglers began to fall back through us bringing tales of strong defences and heavy casualties. Since then I have learnt to disregard most of what one hears on or near the battlefield.

During the day, three attacks went in. I heard nothing of any of them: only noise and more stragglers. The self-propelleds have moved off. I could see tanks over on our left and could not identify them. Morale began to suffer.

In the evening I moved Platoon Headquarters and decided that since the wireless was still no use I must go back with the dispatch rider and find out what was happening. I had had no information all day and felt that I must have some now.

Back at headquarters I could not find my company commander but I met my own CO who told me to pull out and move to a position farther north and then to contact my company commander.

I pulled out and moved on up the road. It was dark; the sky was red in the west and in the distance in front were many blazing houses. The place was deserted yet everywhere was the crack of snipers' bullets and the answering fire. It was all weird and unearthly. It reminded me of a picture by Brueghel.

I could not stop in the suggested position. It was too hot there. I drove on into the village and then lost my way. We were in the heart of the sniping now and drove up the road. Still the snip-snap of bullets and blazing haystacks in the evening light along the roadside.

I got my bearings, rode back to the village and led the Platoon down the right road. This had been D + 1 and it was the worst day that I spent.

The late General Freyberg, vc, is claimed to have stated that 'a little shelling does no one any harm'. Reputed to have been wounded over 20 times in two world wars, men as brave as Freyberg are rare, and the majority of soldiers find it almost impossible to become properly acclimatized to being shelled and mortared. For the newcomer, the impression is that every shell or mortar bomb is aimed at him personally. This sense of being singled out by some unseen, but seeing, eye tends to create a profound mixture of loneliness, helplessness and pure fear. The first time, therefore, a soldier comes under direct enemy fire is an occasion which remains indelibly imprinted on his mind. An officer recalls how, when his party of men were shelled for the first time, he had just ordered them to pack up and move off. He remarks candidly that:

It was one of those moments when an officer feels that he would give anything in the world to be a private soldier; on my decision rested the safety of my men; it is an unpleasant experience to know that within seconds the whole process of reasoning has to be accomplished, the pros and cons weighed up and a decision reached. In the circumstances I had to take the decision that would give us all a chance of survival; I could leave at once or I could stay; I decided to stay. Thirty seconds later the shelling started again; they came whining lazily over, and every one of them landed in the orchard. We lay together like frightened rats in our trenches.

After this spell of shelling had stopped, he decided that all must wait in their slit-trenches for at least ten minutes, since a favourite trick of gunners is to interrupt their shooting briefly, thereby lulling more gullible soldiers into the belief that the shelling is all finished and so luring them out of their holes into the open. Sure enough, three minutes later the Germans resumed their shelling. After a further ten-minute wait they made a dash for it and got away unharmed.

On the German side, their soldiers at all levels shared a common fear, the dread of the Allied fighter-bombers. One who had suffered from the attentions of such aircraft lamented:

Unless a man has been through these fighter-bomber attacks he cannot know what the invasion meant. You lie there, helpless, in a roadside ditch, in a furrow on a field, or under a hedge, pressed into the ground, your face in the dirt – and then it comes towards you, roaring. ... You feel like crawling under the ground. Then the bird has gone. But it comes back. Twice. Three times. Not until they think they've wiped out everything do they leave. Until then you are helpless. Like a man facing a firing-squad. Even if you survive it is no more than a temporary reprieve. Ten such attacks in succession are a real foretaste of hell.

During the week or so following D-day, the build-up of troops continued apace. Some of the more fortunate ones flew in, and a pilot of one of the small Army Auster observation aircraft has described what it felt like on such an occasion. It was D + 4.

I circled the airfield in England once at 1,500 feet and then set course. A Walrus [a slow naval amphibian aircraft] leading the party. After ten minutes I ran into some heavy sea mist and lost sight of the others in front, added to which my wireless went 'off net' after the first 'checking of signals', so I jus* flew on the compass, hoping everything would be OK. Just after we had taken off, I saw below me, anchored on the sea just off the shore, dozens and dozens of huge concrete blocks, each looking like a block of flats. I found out later that they were the caissons of the prefabricated 'Mulberry' harbour.

After about three-quarters of an hour the mist cleared and I saw the others about half a mile ahead. Down on the starboard side, 2,000 feet below, I saw streams of ships coming and going from the beachhead along the lanes swept by the minesweepers. We had orders to keep fairly close to these in case we were attacked. Then we could dive down to seek cover from their guns, or if the worst came, 'ditch' close to a ship. After about an hour the French coast materialized. Le Havre on the left and the Cherbourg peninsula way over to the right. As we passed over the protecting screen of warships at 2,000 feet (to be clear of the balloons), the Navy opened fire at us with Bofors guns. One shell burst between Alec and the Walrus! Someone fired out the recognition colours and the Navy shut up! We passed over the coast at Arromanches, which looked a bit of a mess! Everywhere seemed to be on fire and the occasional shell kept bursting in the water amongst the thousands of large and small ships which were hurrying backwards and forwards, showing that the enemy were not completely silenced.

The Walrus flashed out 'Good Luck' in Morse and turned for home. I looked down and there was a winking green Aldis lamp coming from a field near a small village.

Once on the ground the most striking immediate impression was of the all-pervading fine white dust. The first French fighter pilot to land in Normandy wrote of his arrival, 'Two commandos whose eyes only were visible under a crust of dust and sweat, with Tommy-guns slung on their backs, helped me to jump down from my plane and laughed when they recognized my uniform. "Well, Frenchie, you're welcome to your blasted country!" '

Even by D + 5 the RAF airstrip was still a dangerous place as the same author found out:

A Captain from the Canadian division stopped in his jeep on his way past to warn us. 'No straying from the airfield. No crossing from one side of the track to the other. Don't touch anything. Avoid areas marked by cloth strips, they are still mined. The Huns have left mines everywhere and only half an hour ago a man was killed and the others wounded by a German sniper hiding in a wood half a mile away who has got telescopic sights.'

Throughout the period of the bridgehead fighting the

Germans usually sent over a few aircraft every night, and these could hardly fail to hit something with their bombs, for the place was packed tight with troops, vehicles, ammunition dumps and equipment of all sorts. The several hundred anti-aircraft guns of various calibres concentrated in this small area were plentifully supplied with ammunition, and it was hard to get a good night's sleep. As the gunners fired at the unseen enemy, the air soon became filled with shell fragments which rained down to slice open tents, tear branches off trees and to clang and bang on the lorries and other metal objects, so that it all seemed like a violent and prolonged thunderstorm from which emerged vast, fiery hailstones. Thus with the front line still so close to the coast all those in the early days of the Normandy bridgehead shared, to some extent, common dangers and hardships.

The vast majority of the participants in this battle arrived by sea. The troops were usually packed tight into the transports which varied in size from the 7,000-ton 'Liberty' ships to the small landing craft. When the sea was stormy the usual miseries of sickness were accentuated by the very cramped quarters; to avoid sickness on an LST was anyhow no easy matter, since it was reputed to have a 'capacity for rolling all ways at once which fortunately is unrivalled by any other sea-going vessel'. Other unforeseeable hazards existed even before arriving offshore, as when two ships became locked together in the swell. The officer on one of them recounted that:

From the other ship, which was British, came a weary voice, whose sorrow was magnified by the megaphone through which it was forced. 'I should keep away from me if I were you. I've got seventy tons of high explosives on board; and if we keep on bumping each other anything might happen.' Unfortunately, by this time, our screw had become entangled as well, and we appeared firmly hooked to this other ship and its unfortunate cargo of high explosives. We freed ourselves, after half an hour's hard work with saws, crowbars and other means; and, during all that trying period, not a soul either on the American ship or the British lost their temper; a truly remarkable feat.

When the weather was fair, the two- or three-day crossing took on the air of a kind of bizarre cross-Channel cruise, all passengers being issued with one-way tickets. Delays in disembarking were welcomed, because they gave everyone their first, and usually last, opportunity to watch the incredible activity off the beaches, where it seemed 'as if all the ships in the world were concentrated'.

An excellent account describes how this scene affected the officers and men of a Seaforth Highland battalion on D + 1:

We had to disembark next morning at 0700 hours, so reveille was at 0430. As was customary on such occasions, we did in fact disembark at 1430, after hanging about on crowded decks for hours; but for once no one grumbled. It was not a day for boredom. No one who saw the Normandy beaches that morning will ever forget them. It was an even more impressive sight than the Sicilian landing. We came gently in to landfall and dropped anchor four miles offshore. Ahead was a low ridge with a small town below it, fat farming country, neat and peaceful, like the coast of Devon before the war. Only on the sea did the picture fit our preconceived ideas of D-day. Ships were everywhere. None of us had ever seen so many ships. The whole sea crawled. There were battleships and tiny landing craft, channel packets and ocean-going liners, ducks and hippos and all the other contrivances designed for this day, some going, some coming, some anchored; and this monstrous regatta, this mass of some five hundred vessels, was spread over seven miles of a bridgehead already more than fifty miles long. Beyond, out of sight, were thousands more. As close as the next bay, a bare five miles away, was a tangle of masts and funnels which must have represented a fleet as great as the one we could see spread out before Courseulles; and astern of us the sky was black with the smoke of more and still more convoys creeping over the horizon.

On disembarking, the same author again draws a vivid picture, this time of the way in which the average infantryman was festooned with equipment.

The Jock, as he prepared to go ashore, was a sadly burdened creature. First, as a basis, he wore boots, battledress, and a steel helmet. Next came his web equipment, to which were attached ammunition pouches, two waterbottles, a small and bulging haversack slung at the side, a bayonet, and an enormous pack round which a blanket had been bound with pieces of string. Next, on top of all that had gone before, were a respirator [gas mask] and a lifebelt. If he were lucky, he carried a rifle; if unlucky, a bren gun, a two-inch mortar, or a load of two-inch mortar bombs done up in sacking and worn round his neck like a horse-collar. If any man had gone overboard he would have sunk like a brick, lifebelt and all. And to all this was added the invasion wader, a garment of repulsive design and doubtful utility, elephant-waisted and duck-footed, made of green oiled cotton, and (we found) extremely liable to split. As the seat was so cut as to admit the small haversack and the two waterbottles as well as other necessary portions of the wearer, the invasion wader must go down as the least becoming garment in history.

The more frivolous compared their apparel with the White Knight's outfit in *Through the Looking-Glass* and remarked that he at least had 'a plan to keep it from falling off'.

There were normally two ways of reaching French terra firma which depended on what kind of ship one happened to be on. Those on conventional passenger and Liberty ships had to transfer to smaller craft. For anyone with a poor head for heights this could prove a nerve-racking process, since it meant climbing over the side of the ship and working one's way down a large broad piece of rope netting, known as a scrambling or clamber net, which had been secured to the rails. With the distance from the deck of a Liberty ship to that of a landing craft being about 25 feet, the drop was considerable. Cluttered up with all their equipment, the soldiers' gymnastic powers were fully tested. If there was a strong swell, the boat alongside might be bobbing up and down half a dozen feet, and on the last part of the descent, when to let go of the piece of swaying rope netting called for precise judgement and timing. The climber also might have to withstand a suddenly added hazard, the noise and blast of a near-by warship firing salvoes. This could be almost unendurable for those waiting on the decks of neighbouring ships, but for anyone clinging precariously to the side of the ocean-going ship, it was most unnerving.

Those who had been treated to the sick-making propensities of an LST could bless their luck when the time came to go ashore. Frequently these ships were beached, and the disembarkation was normally a fairly simple matter. First of all, one by one, the three rows of ten tanks would come crawling out of the belly of these whale-like monstrosities. The sight of the tanks, grotesquely prehistoric and very noisy, cautiously edging their way down the steep ramp to the shore had, a year earlier, made the Sicilian peasants run in panic; this almost apocalyptic vision (how Hieronymus Bosch would have revelled in it), always strangely affected everyone who witnessed it. Once the tanks were cleared, lifts brought the lorries down from the upper deck of the LSTs.

Vehicles were waterproofed by an ingenious system of sealing up all the vulnerable parts of the engine, and by carrying up the exhaust pipe and the carburettor air-intake above the roof of the machine; in theory, this permitted all the vehicles to be driven through the water with only the driver's head appearing just above sea-level in the cab. In the first few days, when the unloading was seriously falling behind schedule the JSTs would sometimes start unloading before the water had receded fully from the ramp. If all went smoothly they could discharge their cargo in 20 minutes and, having left their anchor farther out to sea, they could winch themselves off the flat Normandy foreshore, get into deeper water, catch the tide and save an eight-hour delay on the beach. Now and again, however, the unloading operations might start a little prematurely and the troops on the surrounding vessels would be entertained by an exciting spectacle, as in this case when

a lorry slithered down the ramp into the water; and, amidst a cloud of steam, ploughed slowly towards the land; we watched its progress with interest, for the water was lapping away from it in a tidal wave and the driver's cabin was dim with steam.

'Accelerate! Accelerate!' we shouted.

If she slowed down she'd stop; the bonnet dipped as she began to push her way through the deeper water of a dip in the
sands; she was moving slower now, chugging painfully along;
the cloud of steam almost obliterated her from sight; then,
with a final burst of steam, she stopped and all was silent; we
could just see the driver and his mate cursing and lifting their
feet, as the sea found its level in the cabin; a bulldozer tank
came charging out from the beach; this was not the first vehicle
that had come to grief in that particular dip. It edged forward
to the stricken vehicle, taking a devious course around the edge
of the hollow. Shouts were exchanged, tow-ropes were lugged
into position and the truck was quickly dragged away and on to
the beach.

Though urged on by the impatient beachmaster and by
military policemen, most soldiers turned back before leaving
to have another look at this far-flung naval regatta so busily
at work off the beaches. For the majority this would be their
last view of it, for, unless wounded, there was rarely either
the opportunity or the need to revisit the beaches.

Even during the first week after D-day, the countryside
immediately behind the coast looked fairly peaceful, the
most prominent sign of war often being the German notice-
boards with the black skull and cross bones and the words
written across them – ACHTUNG MINEN. As the forward assembly area was approached, the traffic would thin out in an
almost miraculous manner and a mixture of tenseness and
quietness would become evident, for on the evening of D + 1
2nd Army only held a strip of coastline about twenty-two
miles long and from five to ten miles deep: most inland
places were, therefore, within easy range of the German
guns and mortars.

Naturally during the first few days after the landings in
Normandy, some confusion arose over the unloading of the
ships. One story illustrates how individual resourcefulness
made light of this problem. An American skipper had
landed troops on D-day and

was sent back to the Solent, where he received orders to load

British troops. ... Having done so he awaited orders, but none came. Observing a convoy of Landing Craft Infantry making up the Solent he decided to join it, lest his passengers run out of food while waiting. As he was passing the Isle of Wight a signal station blinked to him, 'Where do you think you are going?' to which the skipper replied, 'I don't know!' After an interval came the answer, 'Proceed!' Upon his arrival at the far shore a British beachmaster told him where to land the troops, and everyone was happy. By 10 June most of the initial confusion had been cleared and unloading proceeded smoothly, though not yet up to schedule.

Those who had landed during the first few days after D-day soon settled down to the strange life in the bridgehead. For instance all felt a striking sense of solidarity, since, with the narrowness of the bridgehead, the 'base wallah' just did not exist. When Churchill visited Montgomery on 10 June, he asked him how far his château was from the front and Montgomery replied, about three miles, and had to admit, under further cross-examination, that there was then no continuous line. To Churchill's query as to what there was to prevent 'an incursion of German armour breaking up our luncheon?' Montgomery could only rather lamely reply that he did not think that the Germans would come. Having found out that the château where Montgomery had his headquarters had been heavily bombed the night before, Churchill strongly advised him not to take avoidable risks.

The knowledge that all, from the Commander-in-Chief downwards, were in the same 'boat' had a remarkably tonic effect on the morale of the fighting soldier. A general aura of optimism permeated the Normandy battlefield during these early days; the troops were gratified with the publicity they were getting at home, and the feeling tended to be that, having pulled off the invasion so successfully, it could not be long before the Germans were driven back; then, with the help of the new Russian offensive in the East, the war must end. During the week or so after D-day, the visible and audible proofs of the tremendous efforts by the Navy and the RAF in support of the Army further helped to buoy up the expectations of the campaign being soon over. Perhaps the most heartening of all the sights was the endless columns of troops, vehicles and stores arriving. By 15 June about half a million men and 77,000 vehicles were ashore and in the bridgehead. It really seemed inconceivable that the Germans could long resist such apparently overwhelming odds. One soldier summed up the general opinion when he said: 'I'm glad I'm here, I'd hate to miss what is probably the biggest thing that will ever happen to us.'

6

Extending the Bridgehead

'He who holds Hill 112 holds Normandy.'
 – A local saying

THE DOZEN DAYS from D + 2 to D + 13 (19 June, the beginning of the Great Storm) mark a definite phase in the Normandy battle. On the western (American) flank significant and encouraging progress was made in extending the bridgehead. In the British sector, on the other hand, the territorial gains were disappointingly meagre.

Before considering the Allied plans, it is useful first to review the enemy policy. Much the most difficult problem facing the German High Command was to determine whether the Allied landings in Normandy constituted the main invasion effort, or whether this was only a large-scale diversionary raid designed to draw off forces and weaken the defences of the 15th Army in the Pas de Calais before another and greater assault was launched there. Believing the Anglo-American strength to be so much greater than it was, and still fooled by the Allied deception plans, the German High Command decided that the real invasion would be mounted in the Pas de Calais. As a result of this appreciation, Rommel's forces had a twofold duty. In the short term, they had to keep the Allies confined in as small an area as possible. Their second task was to concentrate a powerful panzer force as rapidly as possible. Only thus could they smash any dangerous Allied thrust, and be strong enough eventually to dislodge the Allies from France altogether.

The whole success of the German plan in Normandy depended on the rapid and regular arrival of men and equipment. From D-day to 18 June, the German casualties amounted to about 26,000 men. This would not have been regarded as excessive, if only replacements had been arriving sufficiently quickly and regularly to enable the line to be maintained, as well as strengthened in its weaker places. As it was, the German troops who made their way into Normandy usually appeared in unpredictable numbers. They frequently lacked much of their heavier equipment, since, to avoid being destroyed en route by the continuous aerial attacks, they had to travel by side roads and during the short hours of darkness. One extremely important result of this slow and intermittent arrival of supposedly fresh troops was that they had to be pushed into action almost as soon as they appeared on the scene. One unit having bicycled over sixty-five miles without halting, was shoved into the line an hour later, only to be captured almost straight away. Moreover so great was the shortage of troops that once they were engaged in the fighting, it proved almost impossible to withdraw any formations without seriously jeopardizing the security, not only of that particular sector, but of the front as a whole. Hence the highly trained panzer divisions were securely tied up and could not, without risking a major collapse, be brought back to be formed into a properly co-ordinated force. Rommel was thus committed to the expensive and wasteful policy of using his potential strategic reserve to plug the holes in his lines. On the other hand Montgomery was fulfilling his policy of keeping the German forces 'off balance'. Furthermore it also soon became clear that the Allies were winning the all-important 'build-up' race. Their forces were, in fact, arriving in the bridgehead at a faster rate than the Germans could move available new formations into Normandy. By 18 June, Montgomery had about twenty divisions ashore (approximately half a million men all told) whilst Rommel was quite well aware of the dangerous implications inherent in such a state of affairs. One of the first orders he issued, on 9 June, made it absolutely plain that the German forces must concentrate on two things. First and at all costs, they must retain the small town of Carentan. Situated at the base of the Cotentin peninsula,

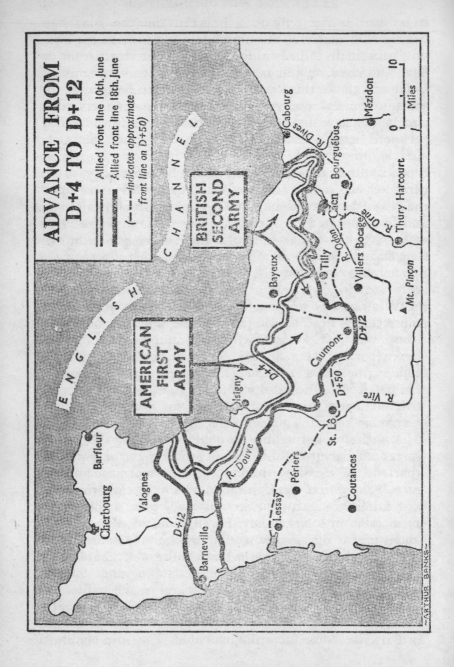

ADVANCE FROM D+4 TO D+12

Allied front line 10th, June
Allied front line 18th, June

(——— indicates approximate front line on D+50)

ENGLISH CHANNEL

AMERICAN FIRST ARMY

BRITISH SECOND ARMY

Cherbourg
Barfleur
Valognes
Barneville
D+12
R. Douve
Lessay
Périers
Coutances
St. Lô
D+50
R. Vire
Caumont
D+12
Isigny
D+4
Bayeux
Tilly
Villers Bocage
Mt. Pinçon
Caen
R. Odon
R. Orne
Bourguébus
Thury Harcourt
Mézidon
Cabourg
R. Dives

0   10
Miles

—ARTHUR BANKS—

it lay astride the only road between the two American beaches. Obviously, if the Germans could prevent the link-up of the main Allied bridgehead with the smaller one at Utah (on the Cotentin peninsula), they stood a chance of isolating it. Once this was done it might then be possible for them to concentrate enough forces to nip out Utah completely, which would greatly reduce the size of the Allied perimeter, and the Germans would thereby lessen the frontage that their over-extended forces were trying to hold. Secondly Rommel emphasized that the Germans must not permit Cherbourg to fall into Allied hands. He appreciated the Allied desire for a major port through which to build up and sustain their forces. It was, however, one thing to decide what ought to be done, but quite another thing to do it. The German 7th Army's war diary of 10 June ruefully admitted that precise military calculations were rendered largely academic by the violence of the Allied aerial attacks. As if to rub this point home, that evening the Allied airmen pinpointed and attacked the headquarters of Geyr's Panzer Group West. This organization was, somewhat optimistically preparing plans for a great armoured thrust to split asunder the Allied invasion front. Except for Geyr himself, this attack wiped out almost the whole senior headquarters' Staff of Panzer Group West and deprived Rommel of several of his more able tank officers.

Adversity brought von Rundstedt and Rommel together. On 11 June they decided to submit separate, but very similar, reports to Hitler. Both these documents spoke gloomily of the way in which the German Army was being forced to fight a defensive battle, and complained of the serious shortage of infantry so urgently required if the armoured formations were to be relieved and freed for an offensive role. Their reports also stressed the devastating effects of both the aerial attacks and the naval gunfire, stating that the one 'will paralyse all movement and control of the battle, and make it impossible to conduct operations', whilst the effect of the other is to make 'any advance into this zone dominated by fire from the sea impossible. The sole crumb of comfort offered to Hitler was von Rundstedt's well-merited praise for the manner in which the German troops were resisting these onslaughts.

By now grown well accustomed to disastrous news from the Eastern Front, Hitler replied characteristically that 'every man shall fight and die where he stands'. He specifically forbade any withdrawals, however limited, to more easily defended lines. Nevertheless he did promise reinforcements, ordering that the II SS Panzer Corps, two divisions strong, be transferred immediately from the Russian front to help Rommel. Hitler was quite out of touch with the extent to which sustained aerial attacks could disrupt movement timetables, and it was not until July that one of its divisions arrived in Normandy. This division had spent longer crossing 400 miles of France than on its 1,300-mile journey from eastern Poland to the French border. The snail-like pace of the latter part of this trip was grim evidence of Allied air-power.

A few days later, Hitler announced that infantry replacements would be sent, but these troops would be drawn exclusively from units in Norway, Denmark and Germany, since the formations in 15th Army, stationed close at hand in northern France and Belgium, were to be kept intact. Like most of the senior German officers, Hitler still insisted that the Normandy landings were a bluff to suck troops away from the Pas de Calais area.

Perhaps influenced by Churchill's visit to Normandy on 10 June, Hitler decided, on 17 June, to go and meet von Rundstedt and Rommel personally. For the German generals it proved an abortive conference, with Hitler holding forth for much of the time on the war-winning capabilities of the V1 rocket attacks which had just begun on England. When, the next day, one of the V1s went off course crashing close to the bunker near Soissons, where the conference had taken place, Hitler decided to return immediately to his main headquarters in East Prussia. After that none of the German generals dared argue with him and suggest he should visit the troops in Normandy. Hitler never set foot in France again, and this was the nearest he ever got to the Normandy front.

Between 8 and 18 June, the developments on the western half of the bridgehead were satisfactory. On 12 June, after some particularly bitter fighting, the Americans took Carentan. They had thus linked Omaha beach with Utah, and the Allies now controlled over fifty miles of the invasion coast. By reaching the sea at Barneville on 17 June, the Americans had sliced the Cotentin peninsula in two; they thereby isolated those defending Cherbourg from the rest of the German Army. Even more spectacular was their advance inland from Omaha beach where the German resistance suddenly collapsed and enabled the Americans to push on some twenty miles to form a deep salient around the small town of Caumont.

In contrast to the events in the American sector, the British had little or nothing to show for their hard fighting during this time. All Montgomery's efforts to take Caen came to nothing. He had originally planned an elaborate pincer movement, one arm of which would close in on the city from east of the Orne river, whilst the other would come round, in a much broader and wider sweep, from the west. At the crucial moment a British airborne division was to be dropped behind the German lines to strengthen these two encircling thrusts. The whole plan never looked like materializing.

On the eastern flank of the British sector, across the Orne, a very violent battle raged from 10 to 12 June. The Germans made repeated efforts to dislodge Gale's Airborne Division from its tenuous foothold here. The climax of this conflict occurred on the evening of 12 June, when Gale in a perfect piece of timing threw in the last pitiful remnants of his reserve. He took the equally exhausted Germans completely by surprise and captured the key village of Bréville. The parachute battalion who carried out this feat of arms started with only 160 men and they had sustained 141 casualties by the end of their attack. The German losses were proportionately as high. This magnificent display of valour settled the

issue and in Gale's own words: 'Neither in the north nor in
the south were we ever seriously attacked again.'

The other division on this exposed flank was the 51st Highland. The Scotsmen, with their attendant tank brigade, were
earmarked for the pincer movement to outflank Caen from
the east. Inevitably some of their units had to be diverted
to help the Airborne in their crisis. The Highlanders did,
however, make a series of thrusts southwards, to the east of
the city. In thick country with the defending Germans
alerted, the veterans of the Western Desert made very little
progress. The Scottish division suffered heavily in its first
action in Normandy. By 13 June this prong of the pincer
movement round Caen had to be abandoned. It had never
properly got under way, nor had it posed a major threat to
the well-prepared Germans.

South and south-east of Bayeux, the other (western) arm
of the pincer movement fared no better. The British were
confronted with the difficult countryside around the Aure
and the Seulles valleys, and all their frontal attacks on the
crack Panzer Lehr Divison were repulsed. The veterans in
50th Division and 7th Armoured Division were here having
their first taste of fighting in the shrubberies of the Norman
bocage and, after the Desert, they were finding it claustro-
phobically unpleasant. On 11 June, this operation was temporarily called off, since it was obviously not penetrating
anywhere near its main objective, the small town of Villers
Bocage.

The easy American advance towards Caumont, however,
seemed to open up the far more promising opportunity of
working round to the rear of Panzer Lehr's positions and
taking Villers Bocage this way. To exploit this, 7th
Armoured Division was thus ordered to wheel behind 50th
Division and strike southwards. It would thus be moving
parallel with the Americans advancing on Caumont. The
division was then to turn sharply east and take Villers Bocage. At first, everything went smoothly. On the morning of
13 June, some units had passed the town and begun to push
on along the main Caen road. Suddenly they were con-

fronted by five of the 55-ton German Tiger tanks. The 27-ton British Cromwell tanks were completely outclassed and soon the whole advance guard was lost. In the town itself, the British troops put up a much more dogged resistance and a day-long, house-to-house struggle ensued. A British account shows how this confused close-quarter fighting appeared to the men in one detachment of Cromwell tanks:

Turning into the main street the crew of the leading tank saw a [German] Mark IV [tank] twenty yards away, while behind were two alert Tiger tanks, the foremost of which started to swing its gun to engage them. The gunner quickly shot up the Mark IV which burst into flames, and the driver reversed the tank into a side street with commendable celerity.

The German tank men dismounted to peep round the wall at the British tank, and a game of hide-and-seek began. Armour-piercing shells were fired at our tank through the intermediate buildings, fortunately without effect. . . .

After a time the Huns seemed to consider our tank had been knocked out and one of the Tigers started up. As the hull appeared at the end of the street, the gunner fired one shot which put the tank out of control and it crashed into a building. . . .

In the meantime the troop commander had entered a house overlooking the Tiger, and seeing the tank was shut down and that there was no sign of activity, he assumed that the crew had baled out. He collected some petrol, poured it over the tank and was about to set it alight, when to his surprise, the tank moved off.

The Cromwell tank-gunner, mentioned earlier, then claimed to have destroyed the Tiger as it crossed the end of his street.

A German version of the details of this struggle differs somewhat from the British, claiming that their tanks:

broke into Villers Bocage and destroyed the Cromwell tanks. Still in the town, in vain did the commander of the British anti-tank detachment try to avert disaster. One of his guns was firing out of a narrow side-street. The Tiger swung towards it. It rammed the house on the corner. The house collapsed. The gun was buried under the masonry. The Tiger merely shrugged off the rubble and the beams and, moving into reverse, rumbled back to the main road.

Only one of the British anti-tank guns he claims made a lucky hit in blowing the track off a Tiger.

Judging the position to be untenable, the commander of 7th Armoured Division ordered his forces to pull out of Villers Bocage that night. On the 15th, the British withdrew still farther back to occupy the ground beside the Americans to the east of Caumont. A little earlier, on 14 June, a further attack by 50th Division in the Tilly sur Seulles area again failed to make any impression on the German line. Therefore, in spite of all these somewhat expensive, sustained offensives, the German hold on Caen had not been weakened.

Inevitably this inconclusive fighting in the British sector, and particularly the somewhat ignominious retreat from Villers Bocage, was regarded in some circles as a setback. It came as an especially severe shock for those who had predicted a quick break-out from the Normandy bridgehead. After the exhilarating success of the first days of the invasion, this 'inch-by-inch' type of offensive seemed a dreary anticlimax.

This fighting showed up some weaknesses in the British forces, notably a chronic inability for the infantry and armour to cooperate closely and spontaneously. Yet, the overall picture was brighter than many critics would admit. In particular, the permanent shortage of good German infantry formations meant that in the British sector Montgomery was sucking in and tying down the German panzer divisions whose tanks were having to be misemployed as armoured 'pill-boxes'.

A German historian has told how the crews of four Mark IV tanks (part of Panzer Lehr Division) spent their first fortnight in action against the British: 'It was like a game of Red Indians – only deadly serious – this business of hide-and-seek to evade the sharp eyes of the fighter-bombers. ...' The tank skipper 'got out to reconnoitre along a sunken lane. He crawled through the hedges. He inspected every inch of ground. He had moved up and down the lane about a dozen times. "You'd think he was choosing a building plot" remarked one of the crew to which the other replied "Better a building plot than a tomb." ' The tanks

were concealed in sunken lanes, in orchards, and in hayricks. The infantrymen around them were camouflaged by bushes, sheaves of oats, and broken-off branches and twigs. . . .

The first few hours were spent in camouflage. Branches and twigs were carefully cut out of a hedge, and the tanks decorated with them until they seemed to have been spirited away. Time and again a man would go off to see whether the camouflage looked genuine. . . .

Next, the tank-tracks in the field of oats had to be obliterated – or they would be a clear signpost for any fighter-bomber. Laboriously each blade was bent back again and made to stand upright.

The first two days were tolerable. Water for washing and hot food were not yet missed. The men in the tank were not yet getting on each other's nerves. . . . Mentally they surveyed their whole field of fire. They became familiar with the distances. In an emergency they would not have to spend long calculating.

On the third day the long-awaited British offensive began. Other attacks followed almost daily and were usually accompanied by a very heavy preliminary bombardment in which naval guns were sometimes used, but always the strength and depth of the German defences foiled the attacker. By the eighth night, still camouflaged, the crews found life in the constricted bowels of the tank almost intolerable; they had ceased to be amused any longer when one of their number asked to be handed the shell case which acted as a chamber pot. By enduring this incarceration for fourteen days, by careful camouflage, by knowing every foot of the ground in front of them, by never relaxing their watch, and by the effectiveness of their guns, these highly trained and brave German tank crews broke the momentum of the 2nd Army's attacks.

Nevertheless, the cost was high, since through the

misemployment of their tanks in tactics of this kind, the Germans steadily eroded their strength, both in men and machines. During the prolonged and inconclusive battles round Villers Bocage the crack Panzer Lehr lost about 100 tanks. Bayerlein, its very experienced commander, reckoned that this fighting had so weakened his division that it could no longer contemplate staging an armoured thrust towards the sea; the Germans had hoped to drive a wedge between the British and American Armies by pushing their tanks to the coast. The Germans also staged several small counterattacks, especially in the Tilly sur Seulles area, and these had proved almost as costly as the comparable British attacks.

By 19 June, a fortnight after D-day, the first phase of the fighting in Normandy may be said to have ended. Montgomery was well satisfied by the way in which the German armoured strength was being steadily eroded. But the failure to capture Caen and advance towards Falaise was beginning to cause considerable anxiety in some quarters, especially amongst the most senior RAF officers.

7

The Great Storm

'This damned weather is going to be the death of me.'
— General Omar Bradley

EVERY YEAR SOME part of the world is hit by the worst storm in living memory. On 19 June (D + 13), the Normandy coast was suddenly struck by the most severe June gale in forty years. For over three days, NE–NNE winds, gusting from 25–40 mph, raged against the bridgehead beaches which were particularly vulnerable to bad weather from this direction. A gale from this unexpected quarter resulted in steep waves six to eight feet high being built up and these followed each other in very rapid succession pounding relentlessly against everything in their path. Unfortunately, the meteorologists were caught unawares and the shipping lying off the beach received little or no warning. This ferocious sea wrecked much of the shipping in the area. It seriously damaged the uncompleted floating piers, as well as those pieces of the Mulberry harbours which had been got into position. Very high tides during these three days further increased the damage because helpless vessels were swept far inshore.

On the shallow Normandy beaches, flat-bottomed landing craft were especially vulnerable, since they were anchored by the stern and incoming waves easily swamped their engine-rooms. Some landing craft which got clear of the shore and then tried to ride out this storm failed to do so, since, with their engines running continuously at full speed, they exhausted their fuel before this prolonged gale had blown itself out. Once they had got out of control the larger ships became a menace to other shipping. Drifting helplessly, they behaved like floating battering-rams, smashing into the piers and generally causing havoc to anything in their way. One eye-witness reported that at the height of the storm 'Ships were now dragging their anchors and parting their cables. ... As night fell a big coaster grappled by two tugs bore down on us. Next came a signal: "If the ship on your port bow is No. 269 she contains 3,000 tons of ammunition", but the tugs held her like terriers all night, and she was saved.'

The most exposed beach was the American one at Omaha and here huge portions of the uncompleted Mulberry harbours also broke loose. But more devastating were the floating steel breakwaters, 2,400 feet long. Even when these had snapped into sections of 200 feet, they still proved terribly destructive. At Omaha, some of the enormous concrete breakwaters (know as caissons) for the Mulberry harbours had already been positioned on the sea-bed. The caissons suffered particularly badly when repeatedly battered by such massive steel objects, and parts of their concrete walls soon gave way; great waves surged through the gaps, transforming previously relatively tranquil waters into rough seas.

The most sheltered spot was the British Mulberry harbour off Arromanches. At this beach, the main breakwater, a line of sunken merchant ships together with concrete caissons, remained more or less intact and held back the worst of the gale. Inside this large protective breakwater 500 vessels sheltered and some unloading was at times possible.

About a dozen concrete-filled ships had also been carefully positioned and sunk off each of the other four unloading beaches. Known as 'Gooseberries', none of these breakwaters had disintegrated during the Great Storm. They were absolutely invaluable in lessening the worst impact of the waves before these reached the shore. The most magnificent of these vessels was the aged French battleship, *Courbet*. In her devotion to duty, this proud old warship seemed to resent such an ignominious ending to her career and she waged her private battle against the elements and the German foe.

The last episode of her life has been movingly related. Alone of the blockships, she had to be towed across the Channel because:

her engines and boilers had been removed and replaced by concrete She had given much trouble to her tugs but eventually came to rest on an even keel in the 'Sword Gooseberry'. This was the most easterly of the sunken-ship breakwaters and with within range of the German guns around Cabourg. Proudly flaunting a large tricolour and the flag of the Croix de Lorraine, she continued to present the appearance of a fighting ship, attracting many shells and bombs from the puzzled Germans who failed to grasp her true purpose; twice she was torpedoed, but this only made her a better blockship.

By 22 June, the Great Storm at last abated. When the damage was assessed, 800 craft of all sizes and shapes were found to have been driven ashore, besides dozens which were sunk at sea. Almost as distressing was the terrible damage done to the floating piers and parts of the Mulberry harbours. When an American naval engineer went to survey Omaha beach, the worst hit, he could hardly believe his eyes. He gazed on 'wrecked landing craft in every direction and on such destruction as I could not have imagined possible from any cause – either from the fury of man at his worst or from nature at her most violent. Inshore lay a beach strewn with wrecks.' On a lesser scale, the same kind of scene was repeated elsewhere all along the bridgehead beaches, and everywhere 'at the water's edge came in a vast flotsam of wreckage – and of dead men'. Even weeks later visible evidence of the Great Storm obtruded itself. Newly disembarked troops were always taken aback to see men living in quite large ships stranded well inshore, like the landing craft which lay, 'so high above any sign of high water in that vicinity that except by building launching ways under her and sending her down that incline, it was hopeless to expect ever again to get her back into the water'.

In three days, the Great Storm had destroyed more vessels than all the German guns, mines, E-boats and bombs managed to harm in the course of this whole campaign.

Without a steady flow of stores and equipment, and especially ammunition, the 600,000 troops ashore would soon be helpless. The navies fully realized this peril. As soon as possible the unloading of vessels began again. In this emergency, the little amphibious DUKWs came into their own. They had not been caught by the storm, as they had crawled out of the sea before the weather had really deteriorated and had been driven inland to safety. Like strange insects, directly the sea was smooth enough they returned to the water. Their crews worked day and night ferrying cargoes from the ships offshore to the beaches. A simple but most effective system had been devised for loading the DUKWs. Two tons of stores were placed in a large net which was lowered from the ship on to the DUKWs which immediately sailed away with their load; on arriving at the beach, they climbed out of the sea to draw up beside one of the mobile cranes; these then transferred the load on to a waiting lorry. Carrying only an empty net, the DUKW returned for its next load.

Salvage and repair work began almost immediately. Fortunately, the situation was not quite as catastrophic as had been first imagined and, by the next very high tide on 15 July, 600 of the 800 stranded vessels had been repaired and refloated. The uncompleted American Mulberry harbour had, however, suffered such destruction that it was decided to abandon it and, using all the available parts, to build only the British one. This was completed early in July.

Nevertheless, in spite of these almost superhuman efforts, the effects of the Great Storm did make themselves felt for several weeks, In the first place, it was estimated that the delays directly due to the gale deprived the Allied forces of 140,000 tons of stores and 20,000 vehicles. Secondly the long-term effects were to slow down the rate of the build-up because so many vessels were either lost or damaged. Not until the very end of June did the daily average tonnage unloaded creep back to the same figure as on 18 June.

The Great Storm had presented the Germans with a unique opportunity for attacking a harassed enemy. After it had lasted three days, Rommel must have realized that the British and Americans would everywhere be running dangerously short of ammunition, as indeed they were. But the truth was that Montgomery's forces had already gained such an ascendancy over the Germans that the latter could no longer exploit unexpectedly favourable events of this nature. Instead of attacking, the Germans remained on the defensive and employed this breathing-space in strengthening their positions and bringing up reinforcements and supplies. In addition to reducing the arrival of supplies to a trickle, the atrocious weather also grounded Allied aircraft. For the first time, therefore, since the invasion the Germans had a prolonged chance to move freely by road in daylight and they made the most of this respite from aerial attention to strengthen their defences.

Besides delaying the Allied build-up, the Great Storm forced Montgomery to postpone two offensives he had planned to launch on or about 20 June. The first of these was to have been in the American sector where Bradley was to roll up the German positions in the Cotentin peninsula and capture the port of Cherbourg. This offensive was only put off for a few days. It began on 22 June and after some stiff fighting on the outskirts of the town itself, Cherbourg was captured on the 27th. By the end of the month all German resistance had ceased in this region of Normandy.

The rapidity with which this important victory was won so soon after the Great Storm had a most heartening effect on the morale of both those in Normandy and at home. But some of the fruits of the victory proved disappointing. The Germans had done such a thorough job in mining and demolishing the harbour and its installations that it was several weeks before Cherbourg could be fully used. In spite of the capture of this major port, the Allies had to depend on all their supplies being unloaded either precariously over the open beaches with their floating piers or through the single and vulnerable Mulberry harbour. This handicap was not, however, anything like as serious as those at the time felt it to be, and Ramsay and his staff regularly met all the major demands made upon them. With quiet efficiency, the convoys of ships steamed back and forth between the English ports and the Normandy beaches. They crossed the Channel along lanes that had continuously to be swept to keep them clear of mines which were the biggest menace to shipping. Since Normandy of itself could supply the troops with none of their requirements, the Great Storm had brought sharply home to everyone how dependent they were on this vital life-line.

The end of June is a convenient time to pause and take stock of the situation. It was becoming evident that a new, bloodier, and less dramatic phase in the Normandy campaign was now about to open. But before describing this second stage in the battle, it is helpful to try to see the earlier events in perspective.

On the credit side, the Allied forces had a most impressive list of successes during June. First and foremost they had consolidated their D-day gains and had established themselves firmly on French soil. Looking back today, it is clear that the greatest tragedy would have been if the Allies had merely managed to gain a tenuous foothold in Normandy and had then been repulsed, forced back to the beaches and compelled to flee back to England from whence they had come: a sort of Dunkirk in reverse. None of those responsible for the invasion dared to consider such a terrible possibility, but this nightmare-like prospect must have haunted them during the early stages of the battle. It is, now, only too easy to forget that a seaborne invasion on this scale, involving landing on and being supplied over open beaches, had never previously been attempted. The only comparable event in the First World War had been the Dardanelles landings and these had proved a costly failure.

In 1944, the German Army was still a very formidable fighting force and for over two years had been preparing to repel just such an invasion. From many points of view, therefore, both the idea of the landing itself and the initial advance inland must be regarded as tremendous acts of faith. By the end of June, this first phase of the campaign had, to a considerable extent, been successfully accomplished. Proof of this had been the failure of the Germans to exploit the effects of the Great Storm. Indeed, within ten days of the end of this appalling natural affliction, two major offensives had been launched by the Allies. No general as careful and as calculating as Montgomery would have acted in such a manner unless he had felt certain that the rate of build-up for his forces was satisfactory, and by the end of June the disembarkation of men and equipment had almost got back into its stride again. Therefore, three weeks or so after the initial landings had been made, the Allies were not only securely ashore, but they were also winning the longer-term battle for the build-up of men and equipment. Daily they were becoming more powerful than their adversary. All this had been achieved under Montgomery's personal leadership. He is the undisputed hero of this epic.

Montgomery's tactical wisdom had also been triumphantly vindicated. Before the invasion, a most important decision had been radically to alter the original assault plan. This step had been taken primarily at Montgomery's insistence, though he had at all times been given the unqualified backing of Eisenhower. At the end of 1943, Montgomery had been shown the provisional invasion plan which had been based on an initial descent on the Normandy coast by three sea-borne divisions, plus two-thirds of an airborne division, the latter to be dropped on the easternmost flank. Montgomery's first reaction had been to disagree with the scale of the landing. In his own words, he emphasized that; 'the initial landing is on too narrow a front and is confined to too small an area'. He was adamant that the landings should be on the widest possible frontage, otherwise, he maintained, with the practical experience of Sicily and Italy behind him, that there would be, 'the most appalling confusion on the beaches, and the smooth development of the land battle would be made extremely difficult if not impossible'. Montgomery had got his way. Early in 1944 the plan was modified. The frontage of the initial assault was widened, with five, as opposed to three, seaborne divisions being employed in the first assault; in addition it was agreed that two airborne divisions were to be dropped, on one flank, and one airborne division on the other.

Not everyone had been convinced by the soundness of Montgomery's reasons for altering the original plans. Yet, by the end of June, the correctness of Montgomery's decision in this matter could hardly be seriously questioned. Although the greater dispersion of forces in the assault stage had had its dangers, the larger beachhead had undeniably resulted in troops and equipment being deployed much more rapidly and smoothly than would otherwise have been the case. Furthermore, this wider frontage had meant that the Germans straight away found their forces embarrassingly over-extended. Where they might have hoped to bottle up the Allies' troops opposing them on a relatively narrow front of 25 miles, as originally planned, the Germans had not the resources at hand to do this on the wider front of nearly 50 miles which Montgomery's revised plan had entailed. Thus Montgomery's far-sighted decision had contributed immeasurably to the safety and success of the Allied armies during the first critical period. Within a fortnight of the landing, the major front was over 90 miles in length and there was a subsidiary front of about 20 miles on the Cotentin peninsula held by Germans drawn up to protect Cherbourg. In these circumstances and with the battle of the build-up going in the Allied favour, the Germans could not manage to launch a concentrated armoured counter-attack which was their only hope if they were to repulse the invasion forces.

With the capture of Cherbourg, Montgomery had also successfully completed the *Overlord* naval plan. This meant that all the coastal areas of Normandy promised to the Navy had been taken. As far as Montgomery was concerned, he had fulfilled his promise to the Navy and he could leave them to make the best use of the coastal waters under their control. Thus Montgomery and Ramsay had no serious mutual problems and throughout the campaign there was little friction between the Navy and the Army.

In some quarters, these evident successes were felt to be more than counterbalanced by Montgomery's failure to take Caen and expand the bridgehead according to plan. And already several very influential officers felt misgivings about the way the battle was developing.

At this stage, Montgomery's main critics were the very senior airmen. The most important of these was Tedder, the Deputy Supreme Commander to Eisenhower at SHAEF and the most powerful airman in the Allied command; the other was Coningham who, as commander of 2nd TAF (Tactical Air Force), was in charge of the RAF units actually supporting the British Army in Normandy. There has been a widespread tendency to sweep aside Tedder and Coningham's misgivings as being unreasonable. This is an unjust use of historical hindsight. Both these airmen had had very considerable experience in army–air cooperation in the Western Desert where they had worked amicably with Montgomery. In Normandy their complaints against him were neither frivolous nor animated by personal dislike.

Put at its simplest, the airmen wanted more space. They claimed this as of right. As a result of the high-level conferences held before D-day, a fairly precise timetable for the advance into France had been drawn up, and was called the Phase-Line Plan. This predicted that the Army would advance inland at a fairly steady rate, once the initial landings had been accomplished. On the predictions in this timetable, all the three Services had drawn up separate, but interlocking, plans for their part in tht development of the battle. Nevertheless, although the whole Normandy campaign was a most intricate piece of joint Service planning, everything depended on the Army. In the final analysis, the soldiers alone could conquer the territory without which the plans of the other two Services were unrealizable.

As has been mentioned, with the conquest of the Cotentin peninsula at the end of June, the Army had fulfilled its promise to the sailors, who had possession of the necessary beaches and the port of Cherbourg. On the other hand, the Army had fallen seriously behindhand on its own timetable. 21st Army Group's own plan had been based on the forecast phase lines which had predicted a fairly constant rate of progress inland. It had been assumed that Caen itself as well as the large aerodrome at Carpiquet would both be in British hands by the end of D-day and specific orders had been issued to this effect by Montgomery. This somewhat ambitious programme had been finalized in April when it stood a fair chance of success. But thereafter the Germans greatly strengthened their defences and reserves in Normandy. Although advised of this, Montgomery decided to adhere to his original orders. Montgomery would have been wise to have emphasized more forcefully, at this stage, that the capture of Caen was bound to be a much more difficult enterprise than had originally been anticipated. Four weeks after D-day, both Caen and Carpiquet had resisted onslaughts and were still firmly held by the Germans. Not only here, but everywhere, the predicted rate of advance had fallen far behind schedule. The British sector merely consisted of a narrow rectangular strip of territory. It had a front of about forty miles and tapered from a depth of about fifteen miles on its western border to about five miles on its eastern end. From the airman's point of view, insufficient space existed for the airfields which had been planned.

Particularly frustrating for the airmen had been the failure of 2nd British Army to gain territory south of Caen. Between that city and Falaise stretches the one large area of flat open country in this region. The Caen–Falaise Plain, as it was known, was ideally suited for airfield construction, and it should have been in Allied hands well before the end of June. On 14 April 1944 Montgomery had specifically stated that he intended 'to assault west of the river Orne and to develop operations to the south-east, in order to secure airfield sites ... in the Caen–Falaise area'. On 15 May, he had again stressed the need for deep armoured penetration inland south of Caen to gain airfield sites. None of this had happened. The air plan had thus been seriously distorted. By the end of June, out of the fifteen airfields which had been planned in the British sector, only ten had been com-

pleted. Furthermore none of these was an all-weather
airfield. The majority were earth strips bulldozed out of
cornfields. In wet weather the ground soon became very soft
and the fairly heavy aircraft got bogged down easily; a
Typhoon loaded for operation weighed over seven tons. In
dry weather conditions, the aircraft propellers raised vast
clouds of dust and so bad was this that the machines had to
be fitted with desert type air filters. Admittedly, some air-
strips had been constructed of bumpy, mesh-netting runways which enabled aircraft to operate even in wet weather.

The airmen were disturbed by other technical factors.
First, the pilots' safety was being jeopardized by the closeness of the airfields to each other. Touching down at about
100 mph, a Second World War fighter needed a minimum
of runway length of 1,200 yards before it could be brought
to rest. On take-off a fighter-bomber (a fighter carrying a
2,000-lb load of bombs or a rocket-firing Typhoon), took the
best part of a mile before becoming airborne. In addition,
airfield circuits ought not to be very near one another, since,
during the crucial period of taking off and landing, the pilot
wants at least 1,000 yards clear of other aircraft at either end
of the runway. This is because once a pilot has begun to make
the last part of his descent his machine is flying near to its
stalling speed and thus he cannot safely or quickly alter
course; a pilot is similarly handicapped just after taking off.
The British sector being so narrow, all runways had to face
roughly in an east-west direction, otherwise, during part of
the critical taking-off and landing periods, the pilots would
have found themselves flying directly over the German
lines, making their aircraft very vulnerable to anti-aircraft
fire. In the other direction, over the sea, the Navy had balloons aloft which were a serious hazard to low-flying
machines. Airfield circuits in the British sector were thus
dangerously close to one another, and anyone who flew over
the bridgehead in Normandy must have retained vivid
memories of fighter aircraft, twin-engined Dakotas (used as
ambulances) and the small Austers all milling about in a
horribly confined airspace. The perpetual risk of collisions

greatly increased the strain on the pilots who had to fly from the bridgehead.

The Auster pilots, at any rate, suffered several casualties from the shells of our own artillery. On a very narrow front, with a high density of artillery, pilots were often forced to fly through their own shellfire. With a gun firing at a normal range, a shell rises to over 5,000 feet at the top of its trajectory, and so pilots, especially when taking off and landing, were sometimes caught in an air space filled with artillery shells. A hit from any one of these was almost certain destruction.

A further cause of concern to the airmen was that all the airfields lay within range of the larger-calibre German artillery. Since they were very susceptible to damage by shellfire, the dispersion of aircraft had to be carried out more widely than was the normal practice. And to do this the RAF had to have a lot of ground. With nearly half a million men ashore, over 100,000 vehicles and tens of thousands of tons of stores to be dispersed, the Army also devoured space. Hence both the Army and the RAF had to compete for the limited available room and some friction was inevitable.

The airmen were also extremely anxious about the defence at night of the bridgehead, and it was impossible to protect such a narrow strip of territory. The Germans were known to have about 200 bombers stationed in north-west Europe, and had these machines been used to lay on a series of sustained night attacks they could not have missed hitting something. The bridgehead was stuffed with excellent targets. The German pilots only needed to have spent about five minutes over the area and then could have flown back relatively unmolested to collect more bombs and make a return trip. As it was the Germans only sent over very small numbers of aircraft every night. They were fired at by hordes of anti-aircraft guns, but were not noticeably dissuaded and very rarely brought down.

In short, the senior airmen felt most keenly that these cramped conditions prevented Allied air-power from being fully exploited. It is indeed possible that the German Army might have been broken earlier if there had been more room for the close-support aircraft in Normandy; the Spitfires, Mustangs and Thunderbolt fighter-bombers had soon shown themselves to be the most effective weapon against the German armour.

In fairness, Montgomery's case must now be examined. Though it is true he had committed himself to a fairly rigid timetable for the advance into Normandy, he had, to some extent, been forced to accept this concept from the COS-SAC* planners and frequently had expressed doubts about this aspect of the *Overlord* plan. On several occasions, he had warned SHAEF that he expected there might be delays for about a fortnight after D-day, when he anticipated reaching the thickest part of the *bocage*, roughly on a line just south of Mont Pinçon. Nevertheless, before the invasion, XXX Corps (which landed on D-day) was briefed on the phase-line plan; the air planners understood it to be the basis on which they were to build up the air-component and the SHAEF staff had geared all their administrative arrangements on its fulfilment, as had the Navy.

It may be recalled that the *Overlord* planners had been primarily, and perhaps almost too exclusively, interested in making a success of the seaborne landing. The suitability of the beaches was inevitably the most important feature in determining where to stage the invasion. An important, though secondary, consideration was the terrain immediately inland from the beaches. Ideally, it had to be the kind of countryside which would prevent the Germans from being able rapidly to mount a large-scale armoured counter-attack, since this type of action posed the greatest danger to any newly landed force. The Normandy countryside, around Caen and the Cotentin peninsula, admirably fulfilled this requirement, since there were few good roads and the belt of thick *bocage* combined with the marshy estuaries of the Dives and Vire were insuperable obstacles to mechanized

* 'Chief of Staff to the Supreme Allied Commander' was the title given to the organization set up early in 1943, to prepare the preliminary plans for the invasion.

warfare on a large scale. But the Normandy countryside inland from the beaches was to become a double-edged weapon. Both then and later, many ignored the extent to which this hinterland would also assist a resolute defender in sealing up any invading force which might land here.

Early in 1944, Hitler had premonitions that the Allies might choose the Normandy beaches. Rommel, too, thought it quite possible that the invasion might be here. For some time, the Germans had, therefore, taken an increasingly professional interest in this part of France, and were well aware of the innate defensive potentialities of Normandy, both on the beaches and farther inland. In particular, long before D-day, the German staff were fully alive to the supreme importance of retaining Caen, since this town was the strong-point controlling the communications system of the district, as well as being the key to the one open piece of countryside hereabouts, the Caen–Falaise Plain.

With German thoroughness, all the possible approach routes to Caen had been carefully surveyed. By June, the more obvious strong points on the outskirts of the city, such as Lebissy Wood and the large Carpiquet aerodrome, had been incorporated into the West Wall which hereabouts was a fairly formidable affair. Furthermore, the Germans had fully appreciated the commanding views obtainable from the Colombelles steel works. It would not be far from the truth to say that, before D-day, the Germans had already turned Caen into a stronghold. After the invasion they redoubled their efforts to improve the fortifications around the city. With its very defensible approaches, Caen and its environs were converted into something approaching a fortress.

In retrospect, the Allies surprisingly underestimated the tactical grasp of the Germans. It should have been apparent that if they were strengthening the beach defences, they would do the same to Caen. Yet nearly everyone connected with the invasion planning assumed that Caen would be taken on D-day or very shortly afterwards. Only Crocker, commander of I Corps, whose troops were set the actual

tasks of seizing Caen and Carpiquet on D-day, had been
sceptical about the possibility of these places falling so easily.
Montgomery's optimism about the speedy capturing of
Caen did his reputation great harm; as Bradley shrewdly
observed, the town became a symbol and the 'Allied newspaper readers clamoured for a place called Caen which
Monty had once promised but failed to win for them'. The
disgruntled airmen joined in the chorus.

Equally surprising was the very sanguine way in which the
Overlord planners imagined that the Allies' troops would
advance inland at a steady and pre-determined pace. The
expectation that the thickets of the *bocage* and the swamps
of the Dives and Vire estuaries would do little to hold up
the invading armies is almost unbelievable, especially to
those who have seen this kind of territory. Such plans were
enshrined in the phase-line maps with their dated forecast
lines of what would be taken and the D-day forces were
briefed on these predictions. Later, somewhat unconvincing
attempts have been made to pretend that the phase-line
maps were purely administrative guides.

It was not long before Montgomery modified the original
21st Army Group plan for the development of the Normandy campaign and devised a much more flexible one on
which to conduct operations. He retained his main policy of
sucking the bulk of the German armour on to the eastern, or
British flank, and keeping it pinned down there. Also, once
he had gained sufficient strength in the build-up, he intended to break-out on the western or American flank, as he
had always planned. But to fight such a battle and to adhere
to a meticulous timed schedule of advance was clearly impossible. Only the man on the spot, Montgomery, could
judge when the opportune moment had arrived. Nor, in
these circumstances, was Montgomery prepared to worry
unduly about territorial gains, however upsetting this might
be to the airmen. His major purpose had to be to avoid
heavy losses to his troops. When, therefore, these attacks on
Caen proved too costly he felt quite justified in calling them
off. Montgomery was certain that he was right to pursue

such a policy, even if it meant breaking his pre-invasion pledges to the airmen that he would seize the Caen–Falaise Plain for them very early on in the campaign.

Understandably, it proved extremely difficult for the senior airmen and some of those at SHAEF to see it at the time, but there can be little doubt now that Montgomery's policy was the correct one. Although Montgomery may legitimately be criticized for the casual manner in which he explained his modified plan to the airmen and to SHAEF, his senior subordinates certainly understood it. Thus Bradley was perfectly happy about his role and the part the British were playing.

Brooke, the CIGS, also trusted Montgomery, who had hastened to inform him of his revised plan. On 14 June he wrote to Brooke explaining his intentions which were '(a) to increase and improve our own build-up through the beaches. (b) To do everything possible to hamper the enemy build-up. (c) To pull the Germans on to the 2nd British Army and fight them there so that 1st US Army can carry out its task the easier.' At the beginning of the same letter Montgomery had stated that he had decided 'to be on the *defensive in the Caen sector* on the front of I Corps, but aggressively so'.

Montgomery was an autocrat. He expected to be trusted implicitly and left in peace by Staff officers and airmen to get on with the battle in the manner he saw fit to fight it. This was what had happened in the Western Desert. He knew he would defeat the Germans in Normandy, but he was not prepared to say exactly when this would happen, nor was he ready to be tied down to a detailed plan. In short, once in Normandy, Montgomery behaved rather as if he were the Supreme Commander, answerable only to Brooke. It was asking too much of Eisenhower and the rest of SHAEF to concur and accept the passive advisory role in which Montgomery had cast them. Hence the next four weeks were loaded with tension about the direction of the Normandy battle.

8

Epsom, *The Battle for the Odon River*

'This type of country uses up the infantry with astounding rapidity.'
— *Hastings, History of the Rifle Brigade*

To win any major campaign there has usually to be at least one blood-bath. This is because a time comes when a determined and well-prepared enemy can only be broken by a series of hard, unspectacular offensive actions. In such circumstances, relatively heavy casualties have to be expected and accepted, and the infantry always bears the brunt of these.

At this stage of the battle, the skill of the commander is most fully tested. The fundamental problem is one of timing. Only an expert commander can weigh up a situation accurately enough to determine when it is most opportune to begin this period of attrition. But even more difficult, only a truly great commander can judge if, and when, he ought to call off an offensive of this nature; should he abandon his offensive too early, he may throw away a victory which is just round the corner; yet if he continues it for too long, he can permanently weaken the fighting capabilities of his army. In this kind of warfare, the criterion of success lies in causing greater proportionate losses to the enemy than to one's own forces. Directly this ceases to happen either the offensive must be stopped or a new and less costly technique adopted.

As Montgomery knew from personal experience, the British Army in 1917 had continued its offensive too long, and had never fully recovered from its terrible losses. To find the large army which was sent to Normandy, Britain had already stretched her manpower almost to the limit. Montgomery therefore was determined not to repeat the mistakes of the First World War and refused to contemplate another Paschendaele.

By the middle of June, he realized that the battle was fast entering a second phase. A bitter slogging match was developing. The Germans had got themselves well dug in and their resistance was everywhere proving tenacious. Except in the Cotentin peninsula, opportunities for relatively easy territorial gains no longer existed. The Great Storm clinched matters. Inevitably a dreary battle of attrition had to be waged. The Germans had to be worn down and exhausted. Only thus could the Allies hope to break out of the bridgehead.

On 26 June, Montgomery launched the first major British offensive, which lasted five days. It was called *Epsom*, presumably because it had originally been planned to take place during Derby Week, but it had to be postponed because of the Great Storm.

Territorially the prize was Caen. This time Montgomery intended to capture the city by crossing the rivers Odon and Orne to the west of Caen, hoping thereby to cut off the Germans holding the city from the rear. The other object of the *Epsom* offensive was to suck the bulk of the German armour on to the British flank, easing the way for an American break-out on the western flank. Montgomery fully succeeded in drawing the German armour on to the British sector, but failed to threaten Caen very seriously.

Like most bitter infantry struggles, the *Epsom* offensive proved to be a grim rather than a spectacular battle, but it typified the fighting to which those in the bridgehead were now condemned. The Allied armies had run up against deep and carefully constructed German defences and these stretched across the whole front. With their experiences on the Eastern Front, the Germans had become past masters at delaying actions All the resourcefulness, skill and thoroughness of the German commanders had been, for some time, concentrated on producing a series of interlocking fortified positions, and the terrible task facing the British and American soldiers can only be appreciated by describing, in some detail, the sort of defences the Germans had now adopted.

By 1944, the Germans had devised a fairly standardized defensive lay-out. Usually, it consisted of three belts of fortified posts which stretched back some seven to ten miles behind the front line.

The foremost defensive belt was normally called the Battle Outposts. These would start about a quarter of a mile away from the forward Allied positions. In a large attack, the battle outposts were regarded as expendable, but soldiers' manning them were expected to delay the attackers for as long as possible. All the local natural features, such as sunken roads and hedgerows as well as the stone farm buildings and village streets, were incorporated into the battle outposts; intercommunicating trenches and camouflaged weapon-pits were dug to form part of the system. Whole segments of the battle outposts were interconnected laterally and vertically, so that the troops in them could be reinforced if necessary, and they also had a fair chance of making good their escape when overrun. The Germans would spend weeks in strengthening such maze-like positions. Sometimes a few tanks and self-propelled guns might be stationed in the battle outposts acting as armoured pill-boxes. But the main defence was concentrated in the well-sited machine-gun nests. Naturally all the likely avenues of approach had been reconnoitred so that for the attackers surprise was hard to achieve. The more obvious targets were pinpointed and thus heavy artillery and mortar fire from farther back could be brought down very swiftly and accurately.

The battle outposts stretched back for about half a mile. The camouflage was almost unbelievably effective. An unwary soldier could step on a covered dug-out before seeing it. Another hazard was the mines. These were profusely scattered, especially on the roads and paths. As may be imagined, breaking through the battle outposts was an expensive and laborious task and was made even worse in the thick *bocage* where, at the base of hedgerows, there were often six-foot thick banks. It was naturally very easy to get lost in such very close country and this often deprived the attacking soldiers of their own artillery support, as well as rendering close air support difficult and usually abortive.

The battle outposts had one more unpleasant characteristic. Their maze-like construction made it hard to be sure that all the defenders had been driven out or eliminated. The Germans always ordered some snipers to lie low and let the Allies pass through them. A day or so later these soldiers would begin to pick off the Allied officers and attack the supply columns. To reinforce those left behind, other Germans would infiltrate back into the captured battle outposts after dark. Great caution was, therefore, needed when going through newly taken German positions, and considerable time had to be expended by reserves in eliminating this menace.

The second defensive belt was known as the Advance Position. This was normally situated rather over a mile behind the battle outposts and was protected by fairly elaborate wire entanglements and extensive minefields. Grouped here were considerable numbers of infantry, as well as tanks, self-propelled guns and mortars. The soldiers and their weapons were all disposed with great care and in mutually supporting positions about a mile in depth. The Germans in the advance position might either be ordered to sit tight and defend their ground stubbornly and so wear down the attacking Allies, or they might be ordered to counter-attack if the situation in the battle outposts seemed to warrant it. Whatever happened the Germans in this second belt were never expected to retreat.

Finally, the Germans had a much more flexible third belt of defences, called the Main Position. This might be sited some three miles or so behind the advance position and included vital bits of high ground which thus enabled the Germans to observe their artillery and mortar fire over most of the battlefield. Here were stationed all the available reserve troops, as well as the more specialized heavy equipment, such as the huge Mark VII Tiger tanks and the larger nebelwerfer mortar batteries.

The Germans never held the battle outposts in strength all the time, but relied on getting sufficient troops into the threatened advance positions as soon as they had calculated the axis of the Allied attack. In this the British were normally most obliging. In *Epsom* they heralded their attack by an enormous artillery barrage of about 500 guns, including naval ones, lasting several hours. This gave the Germans the vital information they needed to send reinforcements to the endangered areas; on the first day of *Epsom* the Germans were further helped by the atrocious weather which grounded the Allied aircraft.

About 60,000 British troops were employed in the *Epsom* offensive, and most of them had never been in action before; they were the new army which had been training in Britain for three years. Their arrival in Normandy had been delayed by the Great Storm and many had endured a ghastly Channel crossing. They had embarked just before the Great Storm and had had to remain at sea until it blew itself out. But the sea was not the only peril. In one of the big LSTs some of the tanks snapped their holding chains during the height of the gale. The rolling and pitching of the vessel made the tanks charge and slither about like enraged and encaged steel monsters. With their 30-ton bulk they battered through the inner shell of the vessel and then began to plunge into the crew's quarters, situated in the fairly narrow space between the inner and outer skins of the ship. Unless the tanks were retethered very rapidly the ship would be holed and sink. Volunteers were called for, and a small group of them went down into the dark and horribly noisy hold where the tanks were crashing about. After a terrible struggle, the tanks were caught one by one and secured. Though the ship was saved for the time being, everyone still feared that the tanks might break loose again, but in fact their retaining chains held.

Another ship-load of troops had a less trying if somewhat

demoralizing experience. The storm kept their vessel at sea four days longer than usual and the only reserve of rations consisted solely of 'Compo Pack F'. These 'compo packs' were tinned rations packed in wooden boxes and were lettered A–G so that on each day of the week the diet could be varied. Normally the system worked well, but unfortunately in this case there was nothing for it but only to eat Pack F. Pack F consisted of the usual things like tea, sugar and milk all mixed up together in powder form, jam, biscuits, margarine, tinned bacon, and, here was the rub, the main dishes were tinned salmon, Russian salad and tinned treacle pudding. Four days of this unchanged diet was hardly the most inspiring preparation for men going into action for the first time after a very rough sea-voyage.

For the *Epsom* offensive Montgomery was employing fresh, and as yet untried, formations, but the men in them were fit and young, their average age being twenty-three. They were keen to get into action and intended to show the 8th Army veterans that they could fight as well as these more experienced soldiers. They did not have long to wait before being put to the test.

This offensive was organized by VIII Corps which had three divisions under its command, 11th Armoured, 15th (Scottish) and 43rd (Wessex). The main attack began on the morning of 26 June. It was preceded by a huge barrage of land and naval artillery which poured tens of thousands of shells on to the German positions; unfortunately low cloud and rain meant that the air support had to be called off. As the infantry moved in on the wake of the barrage, they found that the enemy came quickly to life; many of the Germans had been so well dug in that they had survived the shellfire. For the first mile or so, the advance was through open corn fields, but soon the troops reached the deep intricate defences of the German advance positions. They were now enmeshed in the close *bocage* countryside which so greatly favoured the defenders who had had weeks to prepare for this attack. The British troops struggled on through the network of strong-points constructed in hedgerows, orchards and stone farm-buildings. Landmarks were few and in the strain of advancing it was only too easy to get lost, and this deprived the soldiers of their own artillery fire. At other times they were so intermingled with the Germans that they could not safely call for support fom their own guns.

In this kind of warfare, the Crocodile flame-throwing tanks came into their own. Even though they were helping the attackers, those watching them operate found it a pretty horrifying experience:

The Spandaus were blazing away cheerfully enough, and then one of these horrors came waddling up. It gave them a burst of machine-gun fire and then quietly breathed on them. It was all very methodical and businesslike, just a thin jet of flame which fanned out as it shot along, low to the ground, until it arrived on the target as a great blazing cloud. Bushes caught fire everywhere. There was a pause. Again the jet of flame, the spread, the billowing cloud. The Spandaus stopped. Men ran out, burning.

Despite the most stubborn resistance, the men of the Scottish Division had, by the evening of 26 June, punched a small salient about three miles deep and two miles wide in the German defences. Yet they had not yet crossed their first main obstacle, the narrow steep-sided valley of the Odon stream.

The next day the attack was resumed. The troops reached the Odon. They captured, intact, a bridge across it. The Germans were now throwing everything they possessed into halting this offensive and it became desperately hard to push on up the well-fortified slopes beyond the far bank of the Odon valley.

Snipers became a pest. One of those who took part in this battle wrote about it.

At night snipers crept in through the positions, to open fire in the morning with rifles and machine-gun on parties coming up from the rear. Dozens of bloody little battles were fought behind the forward positions. The snipers were everywhere.

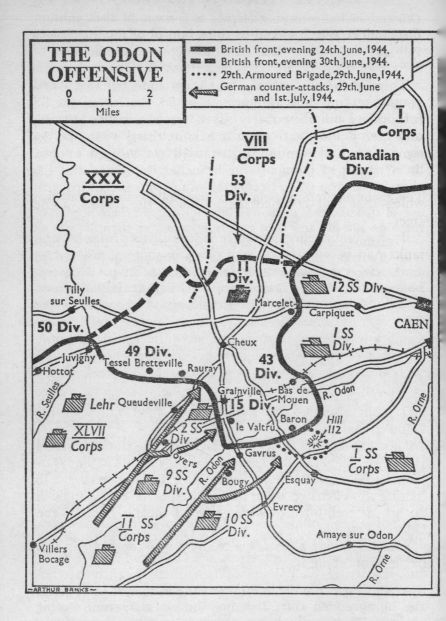

THE ODON OFFENSIVE

0   1   2
Miles

British front, evening 24th. June, 1944.
British front, evening 30th. June, 1944.
29th. Armoured Brigade, 29th. June, 1944.
German counter-attacks, 29th. June
and 1st. July, 1944.

$\overline{I}$ Corps

$\overline{VIII}$ Corps

3 Canadian Div.

53 Div.

$\overline{XXX}$ Corps

$\overline{II}$ Div.

12 SS Div.

Tilly sur Seulles

Marcelet

Carpiquet

CAEN

50 Div.

Cheux

$\overline{I}$ SS Div.

Juvigny

49 Div.

Tessel Bretteville   Rauray

43 Div.

Hottot

Lehr   Queudeville

Grainville   Bas de Mouen

R. Odon

R. Seulles

$\overline{XLVII}$ Corps

$\overline{15}$ Div.

Baron

Hill 112

$\overline{2}$ SS Div.

le Valtru

Gavrus

$\overline{I}$ SS Corps

R. Orne

oyers

R. Odon

9 SS Div.

Bougy

Esquay

Villers Bocage

$\overline{II}$ SS Corps

10 SS Div.

Evrecy

Amaye sur Odon

R. Orne

—ARTHUR BANKS—

Officers, their chosen prey, learned to conceal all distinguishing marks, to carry rifles like their men instead of the accustomed pistols, not to carry maps or field glasses, to wear pips on their sleeves instead of conspicuously on their shoulders.

These snipers were nearly always indoctrinated Nazi youths, seventeen to eighteen years old, serving in the SS formations and they rarely asked for, and never showed, any mercy. Now and again a nest of them would be destroyed when a Crocodile tank squirted its flame into a copse. 'In a matter of moments the branches were bare and the charred remains of 20 Germans swung from the straps with which they had fastened themselves to the trunks of the trees.'

By a supreme effort on 28 June, the British infantry and tanks had battered their way forward another mile or so. They seized the northern slopes of their principal objective Hill 112 (metres), so named from its height. Hill 112 soon became a legendary spot. A wayside calvary stands by the road that traverses its crest. Though it may seem an insignificant place on the map, this bare hillock with its gentle top gives its possessor a panoramic view over the surrounding countryside. (Anyone desiring to get the 'feel' of the Normandy battlefield must visit this spot.) Looking northeast from Hill 112 one can see into the extensive Carpiquet aerodrome with its big hangars and long concrete runways; at this time it was still occupied by the Germans who rightly regarded it as a vital strong-point in their network of defences protecting Caen. A little farther away and more to the east lies Caen itself, the tantalizing object of so many British offensives during June and early July; over the top of Caen the great chimneys of the Colombelles factory area are plainly visible from Hill 112. To the south of Caen one obtains a sweeping vista across the Orne and into the flat and featureless Caen–Falaise Plain, then urgently needed by the airmen. Finally, turning to the west, one can survey the hilly wooded area all round Villers Bocage and out of the corner of one's eye see the inevitable summit of the 1,200-feet-high Mont Pinçon. In short, Hill 112 gives a remarkable commanding view over a wide tract of territory nearly all of which was then under German control. It was a great prize. The Germans realized this and were determined to deny Hill 112 to the British.

O'Connor, who commanded VIII Corps, was expecting a violent and concerted German counter-attack. This came on 29 June. The day was fine and the rocket-firing Typhoon planes and the fighter-bombers were out in strength. Some of the hundreds of German tanks which had been massed into their main positions to repel the attack were knocked out even before they reached the battle area, others were hamstrung through petrol shortages since so many of their fuel-carrying lorries were destroyed by the RAF. Nevertheless, over 200 German tanks were eventually engaged against the British and they attacked the salient from three sides. Several of these tank attacks were broken up by the concentrated artillery fire; the guns on shore, as well as on the vessels out to sea, had an extremely busy day.

In spite of this support from land, sea and air, much of the fighting continued to be at such close quarters that it proved impracticable to call for outside help. Now the ideally defensive nature of the *bocage* told in the British favour. Even the most powerful thrusts by the SS panzer divisions could make little progress against the stubborn resistance of the British. Furthermore, the almost point-blank range at which the antagonists were fighting largely nullified the superior armament and armour of the German tanks. The little infantry anti-tank weapon, the Piat, came into its own and did much damage to the German tanks.

Ceaseless counter-attacks combined with almost non-stop shelling and mortaring began to cause intolerable losses to the British infantry and tanks clinging to the slopes of Hill 112. Particularly lethal was the mortar fire from the six-barrelled nebelwerfers; fifty of these horrifying contraptions were pouring their bombs on to Hill 112.

Hardly anybody got accustomed to being subjected to the attentions of the fearsome big 'Moaning Minnies', as the electrically-ignited mortars were nicknamed. One's first

experience of these nebelwerfers remained a vivid and in-
delible memory. This is how one officer, at the 'receiving-
end', recalled his baptism by this kind of fire. 'Pig-like
squeals came from the south.' These came from a bitch the
unit had acquired.

We were puzzled and stopped eating to listen.... A few
seconds later a howling and wailing grew until it filled the sky,
rising in pitch as it approached, and ending in a series of shatter-
ing explosions all round us. Blast swept in past the bafflewall at
the end of the tunnel and blew us sideways. There was a pause.
We congregated in the centre of the tunnel. Then more squeals,
the same horrible wail, and another batch of thirty-six bombs
exploded astride us, so that the pressure came first from one side,
then from the other, then from both at once. There was silence.
We breathed again.

Nebelwerfer fire was infinitely worse when it descended
on those unprotected by any overhead shelter, since the
fragmentation effect of these bombs was very great. Even
the Germans themselves found the noise frightful and
one of their historians wrote that 'Whenever a camouflaged
mortar battery went into action everyone ran in terror for
cover.'

During the night of 29 June, those still surviving on the
slopes of Hill 112 were withdrawn. From now on, neither the
British nor the Germans could occupy this hill, so murder-
ous and sustained was the fire to which it was subjected by
both sides. The ground was literally ploughed over by bombs
and shells.

By 30 June both sides were exhausted. So heavy had been
the casualties in the narrow Odon Valley itself that the
stream had sometimes been dammed by the piled-up
corpses. The British had, however, driven a small but significant wedge into the German positions and held on to
most of the ground they had seized south of the Odon.

The *Epsom* offensive had ended. So had yet another
attempt to capture Caen. From the British point of view the
result of *Epsom* was, superficially, disappointing. Except on a
large-scale map it was hardly possible to see any progress,

so little ground had been taken. Yet in fact the offensive had achieved a notable success, but one which was only comprehensible to the few who could both follow the battle in its wider implications and were prepared to accept Montgomery's modified plan for destroying the German army in the beachhead area. But, as Bradley sagely commented, Montgomery 'left himself open to criticism by overemphasizing the importance of his thrust towards Caen. ... For Monty's success should have been measured in the panzer divisions the enemy rushed against him.... Instead, the Allied newsmen clamoured for a place called Caen, which Monty had once promised but failed to win for them.'

To halt the threat to Caen, Montgomery had compelled the Germans to switch most of their tanks from the American flank. He had also caused Rommel to send straight into action on the Odon the newly arriving panzer divisions which were coming up from the south of France and from the Eastern Front. On 30 June, Montgomery estimated that there were only 140 tanks opposite the Americans, whereas 725 were engaged on the British flank around Caen. This state of affairs was particularly galling for Rommel who had been planning to make a powerful armoured counter-attack farther to the west in the Caumont area where the British and American fronts met; this point of junction of two armies is normally the weakest place in any front. The Official British History has summed up the wider effects of *Epsom*, stressing that it 'had in fact forestalled and spoiled the last German effort to break the Allied front that could be made while there were still some fresh armoured divisions with which to attempt it; from then on, much armoured strength was gradually frittered away as it had to be used to plug holes in their own defences'.

The newly arrived British troops had certainly shown their mettle in their first battle. Indeed, very soon, the consensus of opinion amongst the critical and experienced press correspondents, like Chester Wilmot and Alan Moorehead, was that these new soldiers were, in Normandy, superior to the desert veterans. Being fresh they learnt quickly

Infantrymen rushing forward along a country lane near Le Tourneur

Tanks moving up towards Ondefontaine

Tanks and infantry pushing forward south from Escoville

British troops making their way through the chaos of Caen, 9th July, 1944

Tiger Tank

Captured British

Nebelwerfer – 'Moaning Minnie'

German mortar teams in action

German anti-tank – Panzerfaust – team

British troops limbering up an anti-tank gun which had been in action from a point by the roadside near Vire

The Crocodile flamethrower in action

Flail tank, Red Cross vehicle and (*left*) Firefly wait to move off

Preparing to cross the Souleuvre during the advance to Vire

Bren carriers of the Rifle Brigade, south of Le Bény Bocage.
The German positions were on the high ground in the distance

and were generally more adaptable, but their chief weakness
was a fault common to most British formations, a ponderous approach to any problem. This may have been due to
their being over-trained, since they always tended to organize their movements according to the text-book and official manuals. A whole series of elaborate conferences, often
starting at the divisional headquarters and going down
through brigade to battalion level, tended to be organized at
every opportunity. This consumed valuable time and was
much too reminiscent of training schemes at home.

In a fierce battle such as *Epsom,* it is often the unexpected
difficulty that can suddenly undermine the morale of new
troops, and the problem of finding the wounded might have
brought about a situation of this kind. It may be recalled that
the opening stages of this offensive were fought in fields
of corn, about 2½ feet high. A soldier who is hit when advancing through corn of this height will fall to the ground
and then often be invisible to stretcher-bearers who are
looking for him. His comrades know this, but they have to
go on with the advance. They are also well aware that a
wounded man may die if he is left untended for any length
of time. Added to this knowledge, the sight and sounds of
the wounded can create tensions too great for soldiers un-
used to battle. In *Epsom* the simple, but very effective, solution, which had been practised in the First World War, was
employed. When a man was hit, a comrade stopped briefly,
took his rifle and bayonet and stuck it in the ground beside
him and placed his seel helmet on top of the rifle butt. The
stretcher-bearers could then be guided to the wounded
man and get him back to the doctors as soon as possible. This
drill soon became almost universal. After any battle, nevertheless, it was always a poignant sight to gaze on these
rifles surmounted by their tin helmets, looking like strange
fungi sprouting up haphazardly throughout the corn
fields.

The losses amongst the infantry in *Epsom* were grievously
high. For example, the 15th Scottish Division was in action
for about 325 days during this whole campaign and in the

five days between June 26 and 30 June they suffered 25 per
cent of their total casualties. In deciding to call the offensive
off, Montgomery was influenced by the severity of these
losses. The British could not afford for long to suffer losses on
this scale, though admittedly so far replacements had kept
pace with their casualties.

The Allied casualties from 6–30 June were as follows.

	Killed	Wounded	Missing	Total	Remarks
British and Canadian	3,356	15,815	5,527	24,698	The considerably higher
American	5,113	26,538	5,383	37,034	American casualties were largely the result of the
Totals	8,469	42,353	10,910	61,732	very bloody fighting at Omaha beach on D-day and D + 1. Some of the missing would be prisoners of war. The figures do not include the casualties amongst the naval and air forces operating in support of the fighting.

In this period the Allies had landed in Normandy over
850,000 men and nearly 150,000 vehicles of various types.
The stores put ashore amounted to more than 570,000 tons,
almost all over the open beaches. In this vast enterprise, the
shipping losses caused by the enemy had been very light,
23 naval vessels and 28 merchant ships and auxiliaries
having been sunk, over half of these sinkings caused by
mines.

By 7 July, the German losses amounted to 80,783, but this
included a much higher proportion of prisoners, many of
whom were taken in and around Cherbourg.

The fighting during the *Epsom* offensive reached a sustained intensity rare even in the Normandy campaign.

On other parts of the fifty-mile British sector many formations inevitably found themselves, for days and weeks on
end, in a fairly static role. In the small salient which had
been driven into the German positions to the east of the
Orne river, the troops of the famous 51st Highland Division
had settled down by mid-June to a fairly regular, if unpleasant existence. Captain Borthwick describes the scene
as his unit took over from the Airborne Division

This place we found was the highwater mark of the airborne
advance. The whole story was there on the ground – the little
hand-carts full of ammunition and stores, hidden in a hedge; the
German armoured car, brewed-up with its crew dead around it;
the sixty corpses, German and British, in the corn between the
hedge where the fight began and the outskirts of the village
where it had ended. There was a pond near the hedge. One airborne man had dragged his helpless comrade there for shelter
and, fearing he would drown, had tied him by the arm to a tree
which grew on the bank, so that he lay half in the water and
half out of it. Then he himself had been killed, barely a yard
away. They lay there still. We went out that night and buried
them.

The author's battalion was soon ordered to take over another position:

It was not quite dark when we went in. We waded waist-deep
through the corn, following the white tape (this marked a pas-
sage through a minefield); and every now and then there was a
bald patch in the corn, perfectly symmetrical, with the flattened stalks radiating precisely from the centre where a mortar
bomb had fallen. The standing corn hid the dead, but the smell
of death lay in little pools along the way. The craters grew
thicker. The tape swung round by a wall, and we were under
trees, picking our way through broken branches. Some trees
were blown in half. Others were split down the centre. . . . It was
now dark, and muddy and we were heavily laden. We went
slithering along the track, not knowing where we were but following the muddy tape, until it brought us to a sea of mud, and
dim trenches, and sandbags, and corrugated iron. The 2nd
Battalion was suspiciously glad to see us. . . .
We were to occupy villages where the shelling was heavier and

the material damage even greater, but never one which had to such a degree the power to depress. The French were good at hanging on, but this had been too much for them. There were no housewives drawing water under fire, or men ploughing among the the minefields. The village had been abandoned completely, and fast ... the contents of the houses were ragged heaps where pigs rooted. . . . Nothing lived among the ruins except cattle and hundreds of hens. As many more had died: the Germans had been firing airburst, and that is a terrible thing for cattle. There were nineteen dead cows in one farmyard and eleven in another, all killed by shrapnel. They had lain there in the sun for twelve days. The less fortunate ones had been wounded, and these were shot. Hens were plastered on to the walls like pats of mud. ... In the end they sent us a bulldozer, and we scooped forty-seven beasts and countless hens into three gigantic graves.

It was a nagging sort of warfare. There was nothing big or decisive about it; but every night their patrols were prodding at our defences and every day they shelled us. On the night of our arrival, a man in 'A' Company was wounded by a grenade thrown into his trench and was being dragged away by three Germans when he was rescued by the rest of the platoon.

The next place they occupied proved almost claustrophobic and life very unheroic, though dangerous

the Boche were practically in the next field.

... Our own defences were in a tight square in country where the fields were so small and the trees in the hedgerows so numerous than it was almost a continuous wood. Visibility, except westwards out into the plain, was nowhere more than fifty yards, and to cover every gap in country so close the Battalion had to be concentrated into an area less than four hundred yards square. . . .

Our opposite numbers, the 858th Grenadier Regiment, were by all accounts low in manpower, weapons and spirits, a fact we could readily believe after hearing their evening serenade. Every night at dusk they appeared to become convinced that they were being attacked by the entire British Army, and loosed off countless rounds of Spandau and rifle fire at the empty air. No one was ever hit by these bullets. No one ever found out what they were aimed at. We just used to sit outside our doovers (roofed dug-outs), watch the Verey lights climbing frantically into the sky, hear the odd bullet clip through the trees thirty feet above us....

Their artillery, however, was a different matter. They had a great deal of it, and it was accurate. When it opened up (which it did several times a day, sometimes for hours on end) no one lingered, but dived into the deepest recesses of his doover and stayed there.

We came to know the 858th Regiment quite well. Deserters used to drop in to see us nearly every morning. ... Before long we knew almost as much about the German positions as we did about our own, because deserters as a class are talkative persons and in any case no one in the German Army then or later had the least idea of security. These men who came in were all Poles or Russians, each protesting that he was in the Wehrmacht against his will, and anxious to prove his good faith by giving his friends away down to the last detail. The Russians were unable to do this, because no Russian ever learned to speak anything but Russian; but the Poles were better linguists. They gave our gunners some beautiful targets.

The enemy strength was between 300 and 350, of which 60 per cent were German, 25 per cent Polish, and 15 per cent Russian; and all the Poles and Russians, said our prisoners, were anxious to desert.

The morale of the Highlanders had fallen. Gone was the elation born of the victories of Alamein, the Western Desert, North Africa and Sicily. Now they were poked away on the apparently forgotten flank of the Normandy front, and they were not strong enough to attack with any prospect of success. It seemed hard to have been brought a thousand miles for this. Nevertheless even in these depressing circumstances the canny Scots found some compensations.

Egg-hunting was the only sport possible in Ste Honorine, and it was pursued so diligently by the garrison that some claimed eggs were snatched before they even touched the straw. All the hens certainly had a harassed look. The great thing was to find half a dozen which habitually laid away from the others in some odd corner, and then visit them three or four times every morning. This would bring you three eggs a day. Failing that, you had to follow the hen into the henhouse and sit staring it out of countenance until it had laid, because if you took your eyes off it for a second someone came in and robbed you. So we poked about the ruins, foraging here and there, and were absurdly delighted when we added to our store. There were strawberries in the garden of M. le Maire, too, for early risers. In these small ways we made ourselves at home.

Looking back now, it seems we were in Ste Honorine for a long time. In actual fact we were there only five days and never returned.

Just north of the Highlanders were the men of the Airborne Division. Though sorely depleted in numbers, these hardened and hand-picked fighters kept up their morale by specializing in forest warfare. They soon became extremely skilful in it, so much so that they got the upper hand of the Germans. They practised their stealthy craft in the Forêt de Bavent which stretched like a no-man's land across their sector. Their Regimental History takes up the account of the fighting in this forest which it defines as being a most unpleasant place, and might well have been confused with a mild type of jungle:

for there was a dense profusion of undergrowth and it was impossible to see more than a few yards in any direction, except down a ride; this impression is amply confirmed by the evidence of many other witnesses who passed their nights, and not a few of their days, probing its silent and far from friendly depths. Here amid the loud hum of mosquitoes, occurred many encounters with an enemy engaged in similar pursuits. . . . This gaining of patrol ascendancy was an interesting game, and was tackled systematically with great enthusiasm by all concerned. The Intelligence section . . . prepared a large-scale map of the whole battalion area. Known features were given code names for easy reference; many of them were unprintable. . . . In daylight the battalion snipers waged their private war and would disappear to the east for the whole day, with their packs stuffed with chocolate and biscuits, and return in the evening with several new notches on their rifles.

Largely on account of the *Epsom* offensive, on 3 July, Hitler sacked von Rundstedt from his post as Commander-in-Chief West. This dismissal marked the climax in a series of disputes between Hitler and those running the war in Normandy. The Führer continually interfered with the day-to-day details of the battle. He closely controlled the disposition of the German forces, even countermanding orders given by von Rundstedt or Rommel when they tried to switch a division from one part of the front to another. All this Hitler did from his headquarters some 600 miles away!

Hitler had an obsession for counter-attacks. He completely ignored the fact that all the armoured troops needed to mount one were fully committed. He was particularly determined that such a thrust should be directed against the Americans during their offensive against Cherbourg; even after the capture of the port, he bombarded von Rundstedt's headquarters with plans for a counter-attack against the American flank. It was an utterly unrealistic idea, especially once the *Epsom* offensive had started, and all the available German armoured troops had to be sent to the British flank to stop the break-through across the Odon.

As a result of these infuriating directives, von Rundstedt was stung into demanding from Hitler, 'a free hand to order even extensive adjustments to the front'. He asserted that he and Rommel needed such freedom of movement at once, so that they could withdraw their forces back to a more favourable line. Otherwise, von Rundstedt insisted, the German troops in Normandy would soon be encircled.

Hitler's reaction to this request was rapid. Early on 28 June, both the field marshals were summoned to Berchtesgaden in Bavaria. Although the *Epsom* offensive was at its height, they departed at once. Because of the danger from air attacks, the two men had to travel separately and by car. The conference began on the evening of the 29th and it was attended by many leading figures, including Goering. Hitler monopolized the stage, but little definite emerged from the deliberations. A new directive was, however, promised. By 30 June von Rundstedt and Rommel had returned to their own headquarters, having motored almost 1,250 miles in three days at Hitler's behest. The new directive awaited them. It said little of importance.

Whilst he was away, reports had been sent to Rommel about the general situation. One came from Hausser, temporarily in command of the 7th Army (Dollmann had died, on 28 June, of a heart attack brought on by worry). The other emanated from Panzer Group West whose commander, Geyr von Schweppenburg, was acknowledged to be the expert on tank warfare. In their reports, both these generals stressed that the only hope for the German forces lay in their being allowed to fight in a more flexible manner. As a start, they advocated pulling the line back beyond the range of naval guns, which meant abandoning Caen. Rommel accepted their views, and so did von Rundstedt who ordered Rommel to prepare for such a limited withdrawal. On 1 July, von Rundstedt informed Hitler's headquarters of this decision and, requesting support for his order, he tried to strengthen his case by sending Hitler these reports which he had received from his subordinates in the field.

Hitler's response was instantaneous. Late the same afternoon a terse message arrived stating categorically that 'the present positions are to be held'. Immediately von Rundstedt cancelled his orders for the limited withdrawal.

The following day, one of Hitler's adjutants appeared at von Rundstedt's headquarters and presented him with another decoration. He also brought a letter telling the elderly and gloomy Field Marshal that he had been sacked, though officially he was supposed to have retired at his own request. A few days later Geyr von Scheweppenburg was dismissed, Eberbach being put in his place. Contrary to Rommel's recommendation, Hausser, an SS general, retained command of the 7th Army. To Rommel, undoubtedly the most humiliating aspect of these changes was that an outsider, von Kluge, should have been appointed Commander-in-Chief in the West over his head. But Hitler had made it obvious that he had lost a lot of confidence in the way Rommel was handling the battle.

On 3 July, Field Marshal von Kluge, bursting with self-confidence, arrived to take over. As an army group commander, he had had experience on the Russian front and, like most of those who had fought there, he considered that the war in the West would be a much softer affair. Hitler's new favourite confronted Rommel. The meeting soon became so angry that all Rommel's staff were ordered out of the room. A two-day inspection of the battle front, however, completely revised von Kluge's ideas. He came round to Rommel's point of view and, thenceforward, gave him a free hand in conducting the fighting.

When he appointed von Kluge Commander-in-Chief West, Hitler also regrouped the German forces in Normandy. Until the first week in July, the 7th Army had been responsible, under the direction of Rommel's Army Group B, for the whole area. Hitler divided up the front. Hausser's 7th Army was now given only the American sector in Normandy. Opposite the British, Panzer Group West was made into an active fighting formation, whereas previously it had been little more than a planning organization under Geyr von Schweppenburg. Its new commander, Eberbach, took a firm grip on the situation and immediately began to construct defensive positions in great depth which were soon to cause the British very considerable trouble. Rommel continued to command Army Group B and coordinate these two forces.

Although four weeks had elapsed since the invasion, the bulk of the German 15th Army remained north of the Seine. It now seems astounding that some 250,000 trained soldiers could have been allowed to sit like passive spectators while a tremendous battle was being waged little over 100 miles away from them. The whole affair becomes even more remarkable when it is remembered how badly these soldiers were needed, because in the 15th Army were grouped the majority of the good quality infantry divisions. This desperate shortage of infantry in Normandy compelled Rommel to continue to misemploy the German armour which had to be deployed there in a purely defensive role.

The causes for the eight-week delay before the German 15th Army intervened in Normandy form one of the strangest stories of the whole Second World War. Hitler and his advisers must share the blame for the tardiness in appreciating the Allied intentions. Nevertheless, the most outstanding part of this story lies in the brilliance of the Allies' deception plan and in the skill with which it was carried through for so long.

To understand the German reluctance to move the 15th Army south of the Seine, it is necessary to go back to events before the invasion. With commendable success, the Allied Intelligence Services had persuaded the Germans that the main landings on the coast of western Europe would take place somewhere in the Pas de Calais region. As a further part of this subterfuge, the Germans had been led to believe that this major descent on France would not occur till about mid-July. To reinforce such an elaborate piece of deception, considerable physical military preparations were made in south-east England by such ways as constructing new railway sidings, putting dummy gliders on air-fields and improving ports and beaches. Most of this activity was concentrated in Kent, and very many of the build-up formations for the invasion were also stationed there, including Patton's 3rd Army and most of the Canadian forces. Naturally these troops remained there some time after the landings in Normandy had taken place. These important pieces of evidence were noted by those few German aircraft which penetrated the British defences. Even when these troops had been gradually moved out of Kent, heavy wireless traffic continued and was picked up by the Germans, thus sustaining their misconception. Hence, well into July, apparently incontrovertible evidence confirmed the German General Staff in its belief that the Normandy landing was still only a feint to draw off the troops from the Pas de Calais area, where the major invasion would soon take place.

The Germans had another reason for accepting the truth of the Allied deception plan, since, in most quarters, it was firmly believed that 70 divisions had been assembled in England for the invasion. Yet even by mid-July, the German Intelligence had been unable to identify half this total in Normandy. Therefore, it seemed obvious to them that the other half of this huge Allied invasion army was just awaiting an opportune moment before descending on the Pas de Calais.

In reality, the Allies only possessed 37 divisions in Britain, and this was well known to some of the senior officers in the O K W (the body responsible for the conduct of the war on all the fronts, except the Russian). Such a state of affairs may seem fantastic, but it becomes less crazy when the difficulties of the OKW are understood. Hitler's main preoccupation was the fighting on the Eastern Front and this was run by the other, and rival, organization to the OKW, called the OKH. The Eastern Front was a bottomless pit as far as troops were concerned. The staggering losses suffered against the Russians meant that the OKH was always short of men. Inevitably, the OKH spent much of its time trying to persuade Hitler to let troops be taken from garrison duties in western Europe to fight on the active Eastern Front. Since crises on the Eastern Front occurred with monotonous frequency, the OKH was often able to raid the troops, under the control of OKW, who were sitting in western Europe ready to repel the invasion. In an emergency in April 1944, three first-class panzer divisions were temporarily whipped away from France to the Eastern Front – of these only the Panzer Lehr was back by the time the Allies had landed. The only way the OKW could hope to keep sufficient troops in western Europe was, therefore, to inflate the number of Allied divisions in Britain; they could then lay a better claim with Hitler to retain a reasonable quantity of troops in the West with which to defend the so-called Fortress of Europe.

By June, however, the senior officers of OKW had become the victims of their own conspiracy. With the risk of dismissal and possibly of death, they dared not admit that they had been duping the Führer. They had thus to continue to support the thesis that the Allies still had enough troops in Britain with which to stage another major landing on the west coast of France. Most of the 15th Army was thus chained to the Pas de Calais on guard against enemy forces which did not exist, except in the German imagination fed by Allied propaganda.

On 5 July, the millionth Allied soldier disembarked in Normandy, whereas by this date the Germans had only committed about 400,000 men to the battle. In addition to the 250,000 men of 15th Army north of the Seine, about another 150,000 soldiers were occupied in defending the south coast of France where, rightly, Hitler anticipated a new landing, though this did not come till mid-August when the fighting in Normandy was almost over. Finally, there were a further 100,000 German troops available in the vicinity of Normandy who took no part in the battle. Some were on police duty subjugating the French, others were locked up in ports like Brest, St Nazaire, L'Orient and La Rochelle, whilst in the Channel Islands a division of good-quality troops did nothing during the whole war.

Even six weeks after the Normandy invasion, the Germans had, therefore, only thrown in about half their available soldiers. Looking back today, it appears almost a miracle that the Allied deception plans could have succeeded so well.

9

Goodwood: 'The Summer of our Discontent'

'If we do not push inland shortly, we shall have to build
skyscrapers to accommodate everyone.'
— *Bridgehead witticism*

DURING MOST OF JULY, the Allies derived little tangible
comfort from their success in fooling the Germans
into thinking that another landing in the Pas de Calais was
imminent. Instead, this period proved a peculiarly frustrating one for the Anglo-American forces. The weather was
often atrocious. Casualties mounted steadily. The advance
came almost to a halt, indeed it needed a careful examina-
tion of a large-scale map to discover the places where territorial gains had been made. A sense of despondency and
frustration was in the air. The Germans seemed capable of
delaying the Allies indefinitely, and talk of a break-out
appeared wildly optimistic and quite unrealistic. More and
more openly, fears were being voiced that the battle in Normandy would degenerate into a stalemate in which there
would be a return to 1914–18 trench-warfare conditions. Less
gloomy prophets predicted that the bridgehead would be
sealed off for many months, as had happened earlier in the
year at Anzio in Italy.

On the American, or western, flank, everything looked
unpromising. From the last week in June until 25 July the
Americans made little progress. Bradley, the commander
of the 1st US Army, had hoped to be able to drive southwards directly Cherbourg had been taken, but bogged down
in the flooded marshes south of Carentan and entangled in
the thick hilly *bocage* north of St Lô, his forces spent a
month inching their way forward.

The key to this area was St Lô, for it commanded the main road out of the region, in much the same way as Caen did farther eastwards. The Germans had always realized the importance of St Lô and stubbornly resisted all attacks on the town, contesting every yard of ground. Only on 18 July, after three weeks of very costly fighting (with 11,000 casualties), did the Americans capture this shattered market town. They then required three days in which to re-form before launching their great break-out offensive known as *Cobra*. The weather turned against them and they had therefore to postpone *Cobra* until 25 July.

Like the British 2nd Army, the American 1st Army had its teething troubles. Bradley had to replace a few unsatisfactory divisional commanders. He also had to retrain some of his troops who were not coping with the kind of fighting imposed on them by the conditions in Normandy. Nevertheless, Bradley's steadfastness at this time would alone entitle him to be ranked amongst the greatest of American generals.

In the British sector, the sense of stalemate was even more acute. Thirty days after the invasion, Caen still remained in German hands. It became like a huge ulcer poisoning the atmosphere. It seemed to defy all attempts at capture.

On 30 June, Montgomery issued an important directive addressed primarily to Bradley and Dempsey. Where the general situation was concerned, this directive emphasized that the fundamental requirement was to retain the initiative, and it was stressed that this could only be accomplished by offensive action.

Translating this directive into concrete terms, the Canadians were ordered to take the large Carpiquet aerodrome which, it may be recalled, lies to the north-east of Hill 112 where the *Epsom* offensive had been halted. For two days, 4 and 5 July, the Canadians tried to drive the enemy from his well-fortified positions, but, in spite of great gallantry, they always failed to gain complete control of the aerodrome buildings. They had to call off this attack having suffered heavy casualties.

At the height of this bloody conflict a very strange incident occurred. As a chaplain was going forward in his jeep carrying a load of hymnbooks, he lost his way. To everyone's consternation he was next seen driving across the open concrete runways of the Carpiquet aerodrome passing through a veritable wall of small arms', mortar, and artillery fire. Realizing that he had made a mistake and was in the wrong place, he turned round and drove back through this lethal barrage. Miraculously he emerged, shaken, but otherwise unhurt. The more cynical asserted that this event caused a religious revival amongst the Canadians. It was also rumoured that all padres were temporarily withdrawn to be given a brief, but intensive, course in map reading.

The next offensive on the British sector was an all-out attack on Caen. Montgomery accepted the offer of Bomber Command to help blast a way through the city. On the evening of 7 July, 276 heavy bombers dropped over 2,500 tons of bombs on the northern outskirts of Caen. It was the first time that the troops in Normandy had watched such a raid and the effect on morale was electric. Soldiers got out of their trenches to cheer. The sight of waves of these majestic aircraft put new heart into the watching troops, many of whom had come to feel almost helpless after prolonged and apparently abortive efforts to smash the tight-knit German defences.

Unfortunately, the effects of this raid proved disappointing. For the sake of safety, the bomb-line had been drawn about three miles clear of the forward troops. This, combined with the raid having taken place at dusk, meant that the ground attack could not begin until early the next morning. By then the Germans had had time to recover. Also, as at Monte Cassino where the same tactics had been employed, the attackers found themselves hampered by the prevailing destruction. Everywhere craters held up the advance – whole streets were reduced to rubble and maps had no meaning. For two days street fighting continued in the ruins of the city. By 10 July, the Allies had gained all the town north of the Orne river, but the Germans were firmly entrenched on the high ground to the south and it had become too costly to contemplate probing across the river and on to the Caen–Falaise Plain. During the same attack, Carpiquet aerodrome had been captured, but its nearness to the Germans rendered it valueless to the RAF. The whole operation had caused heavy losses to the three infantry divisions involved; for instance, in these two days' fighting for Caen, the Canadian division had suffered higher casualties than on D-day.

When captured, Caen itself presented an unforgettably tragic sight. Roads had to be bulldozed through the enormous piles of dust into which the stone houses had been pulverized. That there were less than 400 French casualties was partly the result of prior evacuation of the area to be bombed, and partly because the bombing was extremely accurate. Miraculously, the great Abbaye aux Hommes was untouched. It had been transformed into a hospital for the old. An American, who went inside the building just after it had been liberated, reported that he:

blinked, standing at the door, and listened to the scuffle of children's feet on the great stone floor, now strewn with straw. High overhead there was a large, gaping shell-hole. The sunlight streamed down through it, like a powerful amber searchlight, piercing the religious gloom.

Then, as his eyes grew accustomed to the darkness, he saw that the church was crowded. The inhabitants of the city, or those who had not fled and not yet died, had assembled here, numbly looking for protection under God, waiting to be taken away behind the lines. The first impression was that he was in a gigantic religious home for the aged. Stretched out on the floor on litters and on blankets and on straw heaps were what seemed like dozens of wrinkled, almost evaporated, yellow-faced, fragile octogenarians.

No sooner had one attack been ended than the British put in another. The pressure was relentless. The salient across the Odon, won by the *Epsom* offensive at the end of June, was chosen for the next blow. On 10 July, a further attempt was made to seize the by now notorious Hill 112.

Although a foothold was gained by the men of the 43rd Wessex Division they could not hold the summit. Nor could the Germans. This normally inoffensive feature began to remind the First World War veterans of places like Hill 60, High Wood and Vimy Ridge. Only on 22 July did the Germans pull back from its southern slopes.

Beginning on the night of 15 July, and continuing until the 17th, all the British troops west of Caen hammered away at the German positions. They gained little ground and 3,500 casualties were incurred. This almost non-stop series of attacks was primarily to divert German attention and resources from the area east and south of Caen, where the massive *Goodwood* offensive was scheduled to begin on 18 July.

Here a short digression is called for, otherwise these repeated descriptions of our losses may strike some as unduly depressing. It is imperative to remember that the Normandy battle had now well and truly entered into its second stage. It had become a full-blooded war of attrition. To neglect this fact is to distort the whole picture of the fighting. Purposively, Montgomery was wearing down the Germans. In the prevailing circumstances, no other way of achieving victory existed, except by this harsh and costly slogging match. Most of the commanders on the spot, but probably few of the fighting men, understood this. Whilst some of the junior officers may have grasped the situation, many found it hard to see the battle in its proper perspective and to explain convincingly to their men why, if the British effort was drawing most of the German tanks on to their front, the long-promised American break-out was so slow in materializing.

At times, there must exist a gulf between those directing a battle and those fighting it. To the ordinary soldier in Normandy, higher headquarters was a world completely apart where red-hatted generals lived with their staffs; here were neat rooms showing unintelligible dispositions marked in coloured chalks on huge maps, plans were hatched in words that had little or no meaning to the average man, whilst the comforting communiqués which were issued and appeared daily in the Press seemed all part of a ritual so remote that it might have been invented for the inhabitants of another planet. Anyhow, nobody ever invited the ordinary fighting man (or officer) to spend a day watching the conduct of a battle from a divisional, a corps or an army headquarters. Even if such an invitation had been made and accepted, it is unlikely that most soldiers would have gained much. Fighting a modern battle is a highly technical and professional affair. There was no bitterness about this in Normandy. The commanders and their staffs were generally trusted to an extent unparalleled in the First World War. This was because it was almost universally realized that most of the senior officers and their staffs had themselves fought as front-line soldiers and thus knew personally what the fighting soldiers were being called upon to endure; also seeing their commanders so frequently visiting the forward areas, the troops felt a sense of unity with them. Risks were being shared.

To the ordinary fighting man the narrow confines of his part of the line dominates his mind. What one young officer jotted down in his dairy on the evening of 8 July was fairly typical of life for the infantry in the battles at this juncture. He had just moved into a new position;

I still had to find my bearings. This involved a good deal of running about. I saw quite a few sights – men torn in half, guts lying around, arms and feet, bodies lacerated in one form or another. They all had that stiff waxiness. There was a smell of blood.

We got the guns and began to dig. Mercifully there was half an hour's break in the shelling. The shelling started. I have never known anything like it. My batman and I had managed to scrape a little hole in the bank. We crouched in that. I had put the [machine-] guns forward of the line of the wood on the opposite side of the wall. The stuff landed all around and I had one which landed just off the lip of my own hole. There was a wave of hot air, one's whole body was jerked and showers of earth fell in on us. Fortunately it was a mortar [their shells were less lethal than artillery ones].

They kept it up all day. I had only one casualty.

A parcel came up in the evening, I thought this was a pretty good effort.

The arrival of the post was one of the highlights in any fighting soldier's day.

How does the infantry soldier keep going? Discipline together with a profound sense of comradeship, these are what sustain men in battle. Yet some did crack. As an experienced officer said of the strain: 'There's only one way to fight it, strength; you must be strong with yourself, with your men, with everything; never weaken; never show that you're afraid. Everybody cracks up in the end, of course, but you hope something will have happened by then.'

For those who are fighting, it is hard to realize what is happening on the 'other side of the hill'. As someone wisely remarked, for those conducting a battle and assessing their sources of information, 'the reports on casualties are encouraging. To the men on the scene the casualties are never encouraging.' When after days and weeks of battle, the enemy still fights on, the soldier can be forgiven if sometimes he finds it hard to believe that the plan is effective. Yet in Normandy the plan was working. By the first week in July, one German division had lost 75 per cent of its men, the vicious 12th SS Panzer Division was almost equally reduced in strength, and the same story could be repeated for almost all the German formations engaged in the Normandy battle. Nevertheless, in spite of these fantastic losses the Germans fought on as ferociously as ever.

To return to the main stream of events, by 10 July, Montgomery reckoned that the struggle in Normandy was entering into its final phase. The Allies, he judged, had won the battle for the build-up, and the war of attrition had been brought to an end. The climax of the battle was rapidly approaching when the concerted might of the Anglo-American armies would enable them to break out of their bridgehead.

Montgomery now reckoned the time was ripe for him to launch the two massive offensives with which he had planned to smash through the German positions. The first of these, called *Goodwood*, was to be mounted by the British on the eastern flank. This attack was primarily conceived as a means of keeping the bulk of the German armour pinned down in the Caen area, but was also aimed at 'writing down' the German armour by engaging it in battle. In his directive about the *Goodwood* offensive, Montgomery implied that it would lead to the British armour being able to push down as far south as Falaise; he had always envisaged armoured columns penetrating deep inland, but so far the Germans had obstructed these plans.

The second great offensive, *Cobra*, was supposed to take place two days later. In it, the Americans were to burst through the German defences on the western flank and were then to drive southwards out of Normandy and into Brittany.

Goodwood was the most powerful attack launched by the British in the Normandy battle and employed about half of the 2nd Army. More heavy bombers were used in support of the ground troops than in any other offensive in the war. Unfortunately, the results of *Goodwood* were to cause deep disagreements among the senior Allied commanders.

Although the detailed plans for *Goodwood* were complicated, the broad outlines of the operation were relatively straightforward. Three armoured divisions, the Guards, the 7th and the 11th, were to be injected into the small salient east of the Orne river, where the front, held by the 6th Airborne and 51st Highland Divisions, had been virtually static since D-day. With their 750 tanks, these armoured divisions were then to press forward quickly, punch a hole through the German defences and come round the back of Caen from the east. Once the German lines had been shattered, it was envisaged that the tanks would be able to debouch on to the Caen–Falaise Plain in considerable strength. Whilst the armour was advancing, infantry divisions would mop up the Germans on both the flanks thus broadening the axis of the attack. These infantry divisions would have a further 350 tanks to assist them.

A gigantic aerial bombardment was organized to soften up the German defences. 1,600 heavy and 400 smaller aircraft were not only to blast a gap in the enemy positions through which the tanks could pass, but also to knock out known German reserves stationed farther back. The lesson of Caen had been applied. This time the ground attack was to follow the bombing without any delay. In addition to the bombers, nearly 750 guns were to provide a supporting barrage. This was to be stiffened by fire from heavy naval vessels. Finally some 2,500 fighters, fighter-bombers and Typhoon rocket aircraft were to be engaged in *Goodwood*.

Yet despite these elaborate preparations, this bold plan was a perilous one. The main weakness of *Goodwood* lay in the fact that the British could hardly hope to achieve surprise. Perhaps the most disquieting aspect of the plan was that as long as the Germans still retained the huge Colombelles factory area (north-east of Caen) they could overlook a wide sweep of the countryside on both sides of the Orne valley. From its inception, the *Goodwood* offensive was thus bedevilled by the great problem of crossing unobserved the Orne and the equally large Canal de Caen. These waterways run parallel with each other from Caen to the sea, and there were only three bridges across each of them; since all six bridges lay within three miles of the Colombelles factory site, any movement on or around them was easily visible to the Germans. The best chance of surprise seemed to be to keep the armoured divisions some miles away from the Orne and out of sight of the Germans until the last minute. Nevertheless, the noise of assembling more than 750 tanks could be picked up miles away and this, combined with the unwonted activity around the bridges, led the Germans to anticipate a large-scale attack east of Caen, several days before *Goodwood* began. Dietrich, the Panzer Corps commander, confirmed these rumoured movements by a simple trick he had learned in Russia; he put his ear to the ground and 'the cavernous limestone of the Caen Plain acted as a sounding board' enabling him to hear the distant rumbling of heavy tracked vehicles on the move.

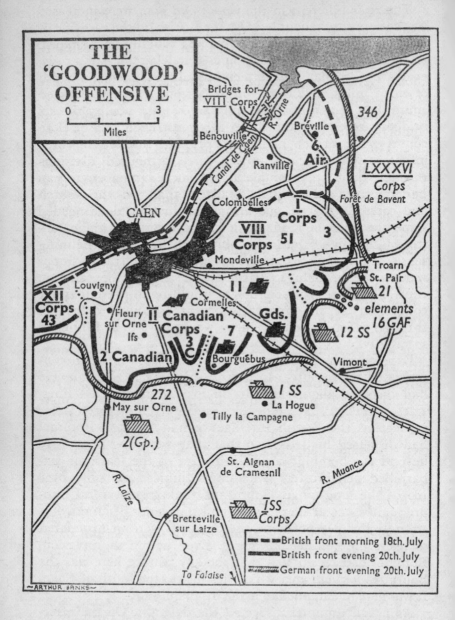

THE 'GOODWOOD' OFFENSIVE

0   3

Miles

Bridges for VIII Corps

R. Orne

346

Bréville

6

Air

LXXXVI Corps

Forêt de Bavent

Bénouville

Ranville

CAEN

Canal de Caen

Colombelles

I Corps

VIII Corps

51

3

Mondeville

Troarn
St. Pair

21

elements
16 GAF

II

Louvigny

Cormelles

Gds.

12 SS

XII Corps

43

Fleury sur Orne

II Canadian Corps

7

Vimont

2 Canadian

3 C

Bourguébus

Ifs

272

I SS

La Hogue

May sur Orne

Tilly la Campagne

2 (Gp.)

St. Aignan
de Cramesnil

R. Muance

R. Laize

I SS
Corps

Bretteville
sur Laize

━ British front morning 18th. July
━ British front evening 20th. July
━ German front evening 20th. July

To Falaise

~ARTHUR BANKS~

The risks inherent in the *Goodwood* plan were increased by the very tiny salient held by the British on the east side of the Orne. This parcel of ground was roughly pear-shaped. At its top or northern end it tapered to less than half a mile, even at its broader, southern end it only extended to a width of three miles, and from top to bottom its length was no more than four miles. The only access to it was by the six bridges already mentioned. In this constricted area of close country, the British had to supply and manoeuvre three infantry divisions, and inject three armoured divisions through them; the complexity of such a manoeuvre can be conceived when it is realized that, on the march and correctly spaced, one armoured division alone needed some 100 miles of road. In such circumstances, traffic control of the highest order combined with an overwhelming sense of urgency would be essential if all these troops were to be brought to battle in the right order and on time. The most crucial problem would be to prevent traffic congestion at the approaches to these narrow bridges through which so many vehicles would have to be funnelled so rapidly.

Expecting the attack to be on 17 July, Rommel had concentrated his resources to defend this very vital sector. He had disposed them skilfully on five interconnected lines. These stretched back ten miles, and were thus three times as deep as the British Intelligence had forecast. Rommel had dispersed his troops so that they were dug in, mostly beyond the bombing areas. With 272 of the fearsome six-barrelled nebelwerfers (Moaning Minnies), probably over 100 of the long-range 88-mm anti-tank guns, several hundred tanks, 200 artillery pieces and thousands of infantry in strongly fortified positions, the Germans were well prepared to resist the coming onslaught. Even before the invasion, Rommel had recognized that the key feature here was the Bourguébus ridge area which lies just to the south of Caen. It was here he intended to make his main stand.

As usual, Rommel inspected the defences. On the afternoon of 17 July he set out to return by car to his headquarters beside the Seine. A German officer, who accompanied him, has told what happened during this journey

We had to be careful of enemy aircraft, which were flying over the battlefield continually and were quickly attracted by dust on the roads.

All along the roads we could see transport in flames: from time to time the enemy bombers forced us to take to second-class roads. About 6 pm the Marshal's car was in the neighbourhood of Livarot. Transport which had just been attacked was piled up along the road and strong groups of enemy dive-bombers were still at work close by. . . .

We saw above Livarot about eight enemy dive-bombers. We learnt later that day that they had been interfering with traffic on the road to Livarot for the past two hours. Since we thought that they had not seen us, we continued along the main road from Livarot to Vimoutiers. Suddenly our spotter warned us that two aircraft [Spitfires] were flying along the road in our direction. The driver was told to put on speed and turn off on to a little side road. . . .

Before we could reach it the enemy aircraft, flying at great speed only a few feet above the road, came up to within five hundred yards of us and the first one opened fire.

The Field Marshal and his driver were hit by fire from the aircraft. The car overturned. The unconscious Rommel was eventually brought, gravely wounded, into the nearest village, called, by a curious coincidence, Ste Foy de Montgomery.*

Almost two years earlier Montgomery had first met Rommel in battle. The struggle between the two had now ended, conclusively in favour of the British general. Rommel's brilliant handling of German troops during the fighting in the Western Desert led many to expect him to display a similar talent in Normandy. The desert had, however, presented ideal opportunities for Rommel's genius, which lay in the exploitation of surprise, in improvization and in speed. But the situation in Normandy was very different. Here he had

---

* Although he eventually recovered, Rommel took no further part in the war, and in October committed suicide rather than face a trial for being implicated in the 20 July Plot.

to conduct a campaign of an essentially defensive nature in the very constricting circumstance of the *bocage*, thus his talents were largely wasted. Furthermore he now had to fight on his own doorstep which meant that Hitler closely supervised him and continually interfered with his arrangements; nor was Rommel helped by having the elderly and time-serving von Rundstedt as his superior for so long.

Nevertheless, Rommel's failure must be largely attributed to the acute insight of Montgomery who, sizing up his chief opponent, wrote, in May 1944, of Rommel's plans:

> It is now clear that his intention is to defeat us on the beaches. . . . He is an energetic and determined commander; he has made a world of difference since he took over. He is best at the spoiling attack; his forte is disruption; he is too impulsive for a set-piece battle. He will do his level best to 'Dunkirk' us. On D-day he will try (*a*) to force us from the beaches; (*b*) to secure Caen, Bayeux, Carentan. Thereafter he will continue his counter-attacks. . . .

Up to this point, Montgomery's predictions about his opponent's reactions had proved remarkably accurate, but his own policy had not gone according to plan. His intention had been that: 'We must blast our way on shore and get a good lodgement before he can bring up sufficient reserves to turn us out. Armoured columns must penetrate deep inland and quickly. . . . We must gain space rapidly and peg out claims well inland. . . .' Montgomery's concluding sentence has a prophetic ring. He wrote: 'the air must hold the ring and must make very difficult the movement of enemy reserves by train or road towards the lodgement areas.' From 1942 onwards, Rommel had always openly expressed the greatest respect for the striking power of the Allied air forces. It was, therefore, perhaps fitting that he should have been knocked out of the struggle by an aerial attack.

On 18 July *Goodwood* opened with a dawn bombardment. One thousand heavy British bombers dropped their loads on targets which included the Colombelles factory area. To those watching on the ground the scene was awe-inspiring. The aircraft:

came lounging across the sky, scattered leisurely, indifferent. The first ones crossed our lines, and the earth began to shake to a continuous rumble of falling bombs. There were no individual explosions, just a continuous rumble which lasted for three-quarters of an hour; and at no time during that period were fewer than fifty planes visible. The din was tremendous. We could see the bombs leaving the planes and drifting down almost gently, like milt from a salmon, and as they disappeared behind the trees the rumble rose a little and then sank to its old level again. The Jocks were all standing grinning at the sky. After weeks of skulking in trenches, here was action; action on a bigger scale than any of them had dreamed was possible.

This raid lasted 45 minutes. Almost immediately afterwards the lighter American aircraft appeared. They dropped their smaller bombs (to prevent cratering) mainly on the German front-line defences, but unfortunately smoke and dust blanketed many of their targets and these were not properly neutralized.

The time was now 7.45 am. The leading armoured division, the 11th, had reached its starting line as had the flanking infantry divisions. They began to move forward behind the barrage from the ground artillery which on this day fired one and a quarter million shells. At first all went well. The Germans seemed dazed by the weight of the attack and offered little resistance. The first major obstacle, the embanked railway line running east out of Caen, was reached and crossed without much difficulty. In about two hours, a wedge about three miles deep had been driven into one of the most strongly held parts of the German line.

By mid-morning, however, the advance was checked. As the tanks went forward towards their second major obstacle, another embanked railway line, they went beyond the range of most of their own artillery. This was inevitable, since the British guns were firing from the far side of the Orne and could not be speedily moved over the bridges and into the tightly packed territory east of the river. As the morning wore on, the deficiencies in the bombing also became apparent. German strong-points on the flanks of the salient had survived the bombing or had been missed. These came to life and shot up the densely packed columns as they edged forward to reach the battle. Fire from these strong-points also held up the infantry who were trying to broaden the salient. Huge traffic jams soon resulted. The congestion grew cumulatively worse, especially at the six bridges, which became bottlenecks. None of the senior officers on the spot appeared unduly perturbed by these hold-ups and the urgently needed infantry were allowed to sit phlegmatically in their trucks which edged forward at a snail's pace. The 7th Armoured Division, at the tail of the tank column, took little or no part in the first day of *Goodwood*.

Out in front, the leading tanks were counter-attacked as they approached the second railway embankment. Hereabouts a surprisingly high proportion of German tanks and anti-tank guns had escaped destruction, whilst the bulk of enemy armour had been kept far enough back to be comletely clear of the bombing zones. By midday, these powerful forces were being deployed against the Sherman and Cromwell tanks. The Germans made full use of the Bourguébus ridge (nick-named 'Buggersbus' ridge) which overlooks this railway embankment. They also skilfully exploited the cover obtainable from the fortified hamlets situated hereabouts. From these vantage points, the German tanks and guns played havoc with the British tanks. The 88-mm guns mounted in Tiger tanks were particularly lethal, being able to knock out the Shermans and Cromwells at up to 2,000 yards, whereas these lightly armoured tanks with their low-velocity guns could do little damage against the thick armour of the Tigers unless they were at almost point-blank range. The German Panther tank was also very much superior to the Allied tanks both in its gun (a high-velocity 75-mm.) and in the thickness of its frontal armour, and only the Typhoon rocket-firing aircraft could easily penetrate it. The pilots of these aircraft spent a busy afternoon, but were hampered because their ground-control officer had been wounded when his tank had been knocked out early in the attack. Nevertheless, by the mid-afternoon of 18 July, the progress looked fairly encouraging.

This is how one tank officer summed up the first day of *Goodwood*

I rather enjoyed the first few minutes as I think most of us did. There was very little opposition and one had a wonderful feeling of superiority as many Germans, shaken by the preliminary shelling and bombing, gave themselves up. As time passed though, they grew more aggressive, having overcome the effect of shells and bombs. . . .

The objective was Falaise and it seemed that at the rate we were going we would reach there comfortably. But we did not hit the crust of the enemy, the 21st and 12th SS Panzer Divisions. . . . It was just as the leading tanks were level with Hubert Folie [a fortified hamlet] when the fun began. . . . I saw Sherman after Sherman go up in flames and it got to such a pitch that I thought that in another few minutes there would be nothing left of the Regiment. . . .

By nightfall a small group of tanks had managed to get beyond the second railway embankment. To sum up, on the first day of *Goodwood*, about 200 tanks had been lost and 1,500 casualties incurred. The Germans were thoroughly alarmed since the 2nd Army had carved a good-sized hole in their front and had penetrated to the east and to the south of Caen, which was now completely liberated from the Germans. With their troops driving southwards through Caen itself and moving round to the east of the city, the way seemed opened to the British to push on to Falaise. This town was now, however, to replace Caen as the tantalizing prize and for the next month the British and Canadian forces were to strive unceasingly to capture it.

Although the tank losses had been heavy, their crews had suffered comparatively lightly. On the night of 18–19 July, however, fairly severe casualties were inflicted when German aircraft hit a large detachment of tanks crews. An officer who was badly wounded on this occasion has given a vivid picture of his journey back. His account will be quoted fairly extensively, not only for its own sake, but also because it illustrates so well the high standards of medical care provided by the doctors.

He was helped to the Regimental Aid Post (the most forward medical station) which was in an 'open lean-to tent slung against a truck'. As the orderlies cut his shirt off, he watched the spare wheel of a blazing lorry

revolving like a catherine wheel against the darkness of the night. . . .

They were still thumping away at my back and side; I could feel the blood running down my back and into my trousers; it felt like tears running slowly over my skin; 'Spit,' said the Medical Officer, materializing suddenly from nowhere. He thrust the white palm of his hand close to my mouth; 'into my hand,' he said sharply; I spat; there was some blood in his hand now. 'Blood,' I said, and left it at that.

'This man must not be put on a stretcher,' said the Medical Officer, 'he must remain seated.' His face came down to mine. 'Remember that,' he shouted as if I were deaf; 'don't let them put you on a stretcher.' . . .

They brought us hot tea, but I was only allowed to moisten my lips with it and spit it out again; nevertheless the sweet taste of sugar on my lips was refreshing.

The Medical Officer moved from stretcher to stretcher, untiring, magnificent; a word, a smile, a few tense orders, cigarettes, a pat on the back; they were the cards he played in order to keep up our spirits; we responded warmly, grateful for what he was doing for us.

An hour later the ambulance arrived, but the driver naturally did not know this newly conquered part of the front, and it was very dark. With some more wounded, he set off 'bumping and jerking in the darkness, in a little world of our own; driven by a man who did not know the way, among the orchards and woods east of the Orne; only the night before an ambulance had driven straight into the German lines and had never been seen again'.

They arrived safely at their destination.

I found myself being lifted out by tough-looking men, on whose shoulders were the bright flashes of the Airborne Division.

'Good old Airborne,' I shouted out in my relief at feeling their confident strength around me : 'Good old Airborne.'

They grinned back and carried me into a large bare room bright with glaring lights.

The Medical Officer and his assistants were standing by a table; they were in shirt sleeves and they leant back against the table, with their bare arms resting on its rough edge; they stared at us through tired eyes, stamped out their cigarettes and came slowly forward.

'Who put on these bandages?' asked the Medical Officer quietly.

'At the RAP,' I said.

'Good work,' said the MO. . . .

The doctor then promised him he would be back in England within 24 hours.

Captain Watney continues:

I was laid on a stretcher and the MO put a cigarette in my dry mouth; but before he could light it the doors were opened again and a warning voice called out from the gloom: 'No smoking; petrol case coming in,' and the casualty, reeking of petrol, hands and face burnt blue, was carried in. . . .

The doors opened; another case was rushed in. The MO glanced at the man lying on his stomach, one arm dangling over the side of the stretcher, his mouth open, as if he were snoring silently to himself.

'Resuscitation,' said the MO briskly; the stretcher was rushed out; another took its place; 'Evacuation,' said the MO from the other side of the room, and the newcomer was gently laid beside me; the doors opened and closed again; 'Resuscitation,' said the MO; the doors opened and closed. I began to wonder whether the whole of the British Army was not waiting outside, to be borne in, one by one, on those grey stretchers; and to be judged quickly by the clear-headed man, who never seemed to grow tired.

He was by my side again.

'You can smoke now,' he said and lit my cigarette; then he stood looking at me in a kindly way. 'You've made history today,' he said.

'Oh?' I said.

'Yes, it's a date that will never be forgotten; July the eigh-

teeneth; the day the armour broke through into the plain of Caen
and opened the road to Falaise.'

Even at this time, there were some bureaucrats to whom
the letter of Regulations was sacrosanct.

An irate little man came bounding into the room. . . .
'My ambulances are scheduled to run between the CCS
[Casualty Clearing Station] and the ADS [Advanced Dressing
Station]. I understand you sent some of them forward; is this
correct?'
'Yes,' said the MO in a tired voice. 'You see, we've had a lot
of casualties; there haven't been enough ambulances to go
round.'
'That's not the point,' said the little man irritably; 'not the
point at all. Regulations state that my drivers are not to go for-
ward of the ADS [where Captain Watney was lying].'
'As long as you realize that you've made a mistake, that's all
right,' said the irritable major. . . .
'Yes, yes,' said the MO wearily. 'I understand.'
The door closed behind him, almost before the MO had finished speaking; his assistant looked at him.
'Consider yourself reprimanded,' he said and grinned. . . .

The journey back to the main hospital was much smoother
Here he was brought inside a large marquee-type tent and
began to get delirious. He was convinced that a wounded
German near him had a grenade hidden under his blanket
which he was about to throw into the English casualties;
this, he had been told, had once nearly happened, being
only averted by the quickness of an orderly. But, 'this German would never throw a grenade; both his arms, badly
smashed, were tied together, between splints, in one en-
veloping bandage; his movements were the result of the
cramp and the pain in his arm'.
The last lap of the journey began. The long line of ambulances reached the sea. 'The doors were flung open and the
stretchers pulled out one by one; we were carried gently
down a ramp, over the extremity of which the sea lapped
noisily, and then up into the open bows of a small LCT;
there was no protection from the sun, which at that time of

the day was at its zenith; it beat down upon the hundred stretchers, lying side by side, with unmerciful strength.'

They soon reached the hospital ship with its nurses and orderlies lining the rails

I looked down at myself and realized, for the first time, how dirty and untidy I was looking; the back of my shirt had been cut away as well as the left sleeve, so that my shoulders and chest were bare; there was blood and dirt, in patches, here and there; my face was unshaven, my hair untidy. . . .

Ecstasy followed ecstasy; I was put in a comfortable bed; my ragged uniform was taken from me; I was washed in warm soapy water; I was given a pair of crisply ironed pyjamas; a cup of tea and, oh miracles of miracles, a poached egg that steamed gently on a clean, white plate.

He was on board the hospital ship and it had only been a little over 12 hours earlier that he had been wounded near the front line. The doctor's prediction had come true, he was back in England within 24 hours.

Others were evacuated by air. One badly burned tank trooper left an airstrip in Normandy at 6.15 pm; less than three hours later he was at the Special Burns Centre in Basingstoke! Over 100,000 wounded were brought out by air between D-day and 30 September without mishap.

The *Goodwood* offensive continued for two more days, but made little further territorial progress. The Germans had not been surprised at this offensive occurring when and where it did. They had, however, been temporarily stunned and overwhelmed by the sheer weight of the attack, but they recovered their equilibrium rapidly. Thereafter, they put their prearranged plans into effect and built up a powerful screen of tank and anti-tank guns; most of these were sited in and amongst the strongly built stone hamlets so profusely scattered in this region. Taking every advantage of the cover thus provided and exploiting their control of the ridge which runs both sides of the Caen–Falaise road, the Germans successfully resisted any break-through. Almost from the outset, the British had been hampered by low cloud which severely curtailed the support they could obtain from the fighter-bomber aircraft and the rocket-firing Typhoon machines which were so valuable in dealing with the German tanks. Owing to the congestion on the Orne bridges, the bulk of the artillery was stuck too far back to provide help. But the most serious deficiency was the shortage of infantry. *Goodwood* had been planned on the assumption that the armour would break through the main German defence. Once this had not happened, a dangerous imbalance between tanks and infantry quickly resulted. The armour could not get on until the infantry had cleared the many well-protected pockets of resistance and there were not sufficient numbers of good infantry for this purpose. It must be sadly admitted that *Goodwood*, in many cases, demonstrated a lamentable lack of cooperation between the infantry and armour. Nevertheless one regiment did its job with great determination and speed. The 8th Battalion of the Rifle Brigade took part in two major attacks in two days, they cleared two hamlets of the enemy, and captured about 400 SS troops (no mean feat in itself), as well as killing many Germans. In spite of all this, their own casualties were light.

On 20 July, a violent and prolonged thunderstorm rapidly transformed the churned earth into a glutinous morass of mud. Large-scale movement became out of the question. Though fierce fighting continued south of Caen, *Goodwood* itself had ended. On the map, the results looked unimpressive. After three days of battle, the British had just reached the edge of parts of the Bourguébus ridge to which they were clinging precariously. South and east of Caen, the great offensive had penetrated nowhere more than seven miles and this on a very narrow front. To achieve this the British had lost over 400 tanks, but many were later recovered and repaired.

Of the *Goodwood* battlefield an officer, who had landed on D-day, wrote in his diary that 'it was a scene of utter desolation. I have never seen such bomb craters. Trees were uprooted, roads were impassable. There were bodies in half; crumpled men. A tank lay upside down, another was still burning with a row of feet sticking out from underneath.

In one crater a man's head and shoulders appeared sticking out from the side. The place stank.' In one of the many German dug-outs, he found, incongruously, Paris fashion papers.

Although the Germans had completely foiled any British attempt at reaching Falaise, the *Goodwood* offensive had thoroughly alarmed them. This penetration of their carefully constructed defensive positions had shown the Germans that their hold on the Normandy front was very precarious, in particular, the close tactical use of heavy bombers had introduced a new and frightening element into the conflict. The scale of this attack also convinced the Germans that the Allies did not intend to make another landing on the west coast of Europe. From now onwards, formations were increasingly transferred from the 15th Army (largely stationed north of the Seine) to reinforce the Germans fighting in Normandy.

Hitler did not replace Rommel and the whole burden of running the Normandy battle fell on von Kluge who now combined the two posts of Commander-in-Chief West and Commander of Army Group B, Rommel's old job. As Montgomery had anticipated, von Kluge's immediate reaction to *Goodwood* was to move the German armoured reserves to plug the holes in the front opposite Caen, thereby weakening the American sector. Almost immediately these formations became involved in the battle there, so could not be withdrawn quickly.

Although he had made very little territorial progress, Montgomery had succeeded in locking up the German armour on the British flank. He had also managed quite effectively to 'write down' the German tank strength. Although their losses were far less than 400 suffered by the British, the Germans could ill afford to lose the numbers they did in *Goodwood*, since their total tank strength was much smaller than that of the Allies and replacements were virtually unobtainable.

10

The Uneasy Lull

'There is a turning point in all battles.'
– *General Sir Richard Gale*

THE WEEK 20–26 JULY proved one of the most momentous in the Second World War. In the first place, the long-delayed plot to assassinate Hitler came to fruition, but miscarried. Secondly the apparent failure of the *Goodwood* offensive aroused all Montgomery's opponents who made a concerted effort to have Eisenhower take over as Commander-in-Chief Allied Land Forces. Finally, by the evening of 26 July, the break-out from the Normandy bridgehead had definitely been accomplished. These seven days therefore covered a most dramatic transformation in the character of the struggle. From a stalemate in which both sides appeared virtually immobilized, the battle rapidly changed until it became one of the swiftest-moving campaigns in military history.

The 20 July Plot to assassinate Hitler did not affect the fighting capacity of the German soldiers in Normandy. On the other hand, amongst the most senior generals, all was hesitation, but von Kluge seemed to have been loyal to Hitler. He refused to do anything until he was sure Hitler had been killed. Rumours circulated all that day.

Only in Paris did a commander act. There von Stulpnagel arrested all the Gestapo and Nazi agents. However, he failed to persuade von Kluge to try to lead a revolt in the West and negotiate with the Allies, as Rommel might have done.

Once convinced that Hitler was alive, von Kluge sacked Stulpnagel who tried to commit suicide, but only managed to maim and blind himself. He was hanged slowly a month later.

The 20 July Plot unveiled the depths to which so many of the German General Staff had now sunk. The truth was that the majority of these proud Service chiefs had been reduced to little more than puppets over whom Hitler exercised an almost Mephistophelean power. One reason for the feebleness of these men lay in the manner in which Hitler could exert a hypnotic power over those who met him personally. The tough, efficient Production Minister Speer has testified about Hitler that all

who had worked closely with him for a long time were entirely dependent on and obedient to him. However forceful their behaviour in their own sphere, in his presence they were insignificant and timid. Cowardice alone does not account for this. As a result of their long cooperation, they not only developed an uncanny faith in him but also fell completely under his influence. They were in his spell, blindly subservient to him and with no will of their own.

Doenitz, whom Wilmot described as being 'regarded by his subordinates in the Navy as a hard and inflexible commander, makes a similar confession: "I purposely went very seldom to his [Hitler's] HQ, for I had the feeling that I would thus best preserve my power of initiative, and also because after several days there I always had the feeling that I must disengage myself from his power of suggestion."'

A rift within the ranks of the senior German generals weakened their position *vis-à-vis* Hitler. The older group of these men, like von Rundstedt, Keitel and Jodl, felt betrayed since, having somewhat haughtily backed Hitler's rise to power, they considered that the erstwhile corporal should regard himself as perpetually beholden to them, and ought always to take their advice in military matters. Instead, they were only too well aware that Hitler now distrusted them as much as they distrusted him. But the Führer had to rely on some highly trained professional soldiers to run the war and he had, to some extent, split the officer corps by retiring many of the older officers, and rapidly promoting to high positions a number of able and ambitious younger men drawn from outside the closely-knit circle of the German General Staff.

A place on Hitler's bandwaggon offered dazzling prospects of promotion, plenty of decorations and lavish financial rewards. Von Kluge had fallen for this form of bribery and accepted a personal gift of £20,000 from Hitler. Rommel had early on hitched his star to Hitler's. By these means, a bunch of more junior professional soldiers (not members of the General Staff) had come to the fore, owing almost everything to Hitler's influence. An uneasy fear of treachery within their ranks therefore embittered relations between the older senior German officers and their more youthful colleagues. In spite of this spirit of acrimony, most of the older German generals continued to serve on, reserving their devastating criticism of Hitler's direction of the war till he was safely dead. For his part, Hitler tended, after 20 July, to rely more and more on the political soldiers who formed the backbone of the SS formations: Model being one of the most prominent of these men.

Though long aware that a *coup d'état* was being organized against Hitler and the Nazi party, most senior German generals behaved very guardedly on 20 July. However sympathetically they felt towards the plot, they were determined to be sure which way things were going before giving the conspirators their backing. Some tried to excuse their equivocal behaviour by falling back on an oath of loyalty they had once pledged to Hitler. In a piece of reasoning reminiscent of that used by the victims of the Mau Mau oath, one aristocratic general (who claims in his memoirs to be a Roman Catholic) justified this inaction by arguing that he would not break this holy oath. He then admits that Hitler's subsequent conduct had invalidated the basis on which the oath had been taken! In an outburst of honesty about the 20 July plot he added that as 'SS men had been introduced into the troops fighting in the West, and in view of the attitude of the Marines and the Luftwaffe, revolt against Hitler, as he was alive, seemed to have no chance of success'.

The most compelling reason for the subservience of the German generals to Hitler lay therefore in their fear that he would strike back at them through their families. The Nazi machine was a satanic instrument of terror which tortured men, women and children with impartial brutality. As the war drew to its close, Hitler handed over more and more power to the Nazi party and especially to Himmler, who controlled, amongst other forces, the SS (*Schutzstaffeln* or Protection Squads). With his growing disgust of the conventional soldiery of the Wehrmacht, Hitler pinned his faith increasingly on these SS divisions, which got first priority in men and equipment. In return, they gave unswerving devotion to him.

These divisions came under Himmler's orders for nearly all things, except actual operational control in battle; they thus developed into an increasingly powerful private army inside the framework of the old German Army, or Wehrmacht. The aftermath of 20 July was greatly to increase the power of the SS and the Nazi party within the Wehrmacht, and even the Army salute was replaced by the Nazi one.

Many of the new senior commanders whom Hitler now promoted came from the SS divisions. Typical of these parvenu senior officers was Sepp Dietrich:

Short and squat, with a broad, dark face dominated by a large, wide nose, Dietrich resembled a rather battered bar-tender in appearance. He was a typical product of the Free Corps and the bullying gangs with which Hitler first made his advent on the German political stage. The First World War interrupted his plans to become a butcher, and after four years of fighting he had attained the rank of a sergeant-major. He spent the post-war years at a series of unsuccessful odd jobs and occupied his spare time as an enthusiastic adherent of the Nazi party.

In 1928 he joined the SS as a full-time member and in five years rose to the rank of *Brigadeführer* (Major-General) as the Commanding Officer of Hitler's personal bodyguard. He led the first SS division 'Adolf Hitler' in the French, Greek and Russian campaigns, and boasted that by 1943 only 30 of the original 23,000 men in his division were still alive and uncaptured. In Germany the Goebbels propaganda machine had made of 'Sepp' Dietrich an almost legendary figure, whose exploits as a fighting man of the people rivalled, if not surpassed, those of that other popular National Socialist personality, Erwin Rommel. Crude, conceited and garrulous, his meteoric career was undoubtedly achieved more by his hard and ruthless energy than by his military ability.

In Normandy, this utterly unscrupulous man first commanded I SS Panzer Corps, but in the last days of the battle he was given charge of most of the German armour. His 5th Panzer Army, as it was termed, replaced Panzer Group West and covered the German retreat to the Seine. Dietrich escaped to Germany. In the Ardennes offensive, Hitler put him in charge of the SS Panzer Army, when he lost several thousand more fanatical Nazis.

A somewhat similar character to Dietrich was the thirty-two-year-old Kurt Meyer, commander of the notorious 12th SS (Hitler Youth) Panzer Division. By mid-July, six of these SS divisions were in Normandy where they normally fought under one of the two SS panzer corps. Almost exclusively recruited from professional killers passionately devoted to Hitler and all he stood for, the SS formations already represented a most formidable concentration of political and military power.

Politically von Kluge seemed to have been remarkably naïve. He utterly misjudged the depths of savagery and suspicion which the 20 July plot had aroused in the Führer's twisted mind. On 23 July, von Kluge sent the injured Hitler a highly pessimistic assessment of the conditions in Normandy. This report was made even more unpalatable by being unabashedly based on a letter written by Rommel just before he had been wounded. (Rommel was known to have been, at least indirectly, implicated in the conspiracy.) Rommel's letter categorically stated that: 'The situation on the Normandy front is growing worse every day and is now approaching a grave crisis. ... The troops are everywhere

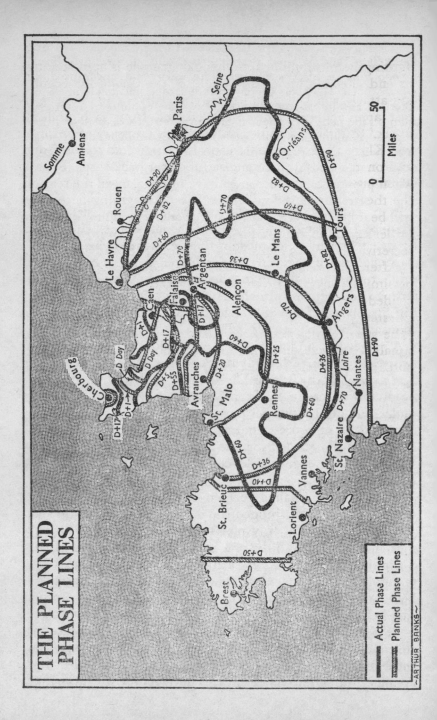

THE PLANNED
PHASE LINES

Actual Phase Lines
Planned Phase Lines

~ARTHUR BANKS~

0   50
Miles

Somme
Amiens
Seine
Paris
Le Havre
Rouen
D+90
D+82
D+60
Cherbourg
D Day
D Day
D+1→
D+1→
D+17
D+17
D+55
D+1→
D+17→
Caen
Falaise
Argentan
D+17
D+36
D+70
D+70
Le Mans
Orléans
D+90
D+82
D+60
Tours
D+82
Alençon
Avranches
D+20
D+60
St. Malo
Rennes
D+25
D+60
Angers
Loire
Nantes
D+36
D+70
D+90
St. Brieuc
D+60
D+36
D+40
Vannes
Lorient
St. Nazaire
Brest
D+50

fighting heroically, but the unequal struggle is approaching its end.' Reeling under the weight of the *Goodwood* bombing attack, von Kluge added prophetically: 'The moment is fast approaching when this overtaxed front is bound to break.' In his reply, Hitler only told his emissary to 'inform von Kluge that he should keep his eyes riveted to the front and on the enemy without ever looking backwards. If and when precautionary measures have to be taken in the rear of the theatre of operations in the West, everything necessary will be done by OKW and OKW alone.' From now onwards Hitler's fears of traitors in the Army made him extremely secretive about any plans for a withdrawal from Normandy.

After the *Goodwood* offensive had been halted, German pessimism was almost matched by the gloom which descended on the Allied side. Incredible as it now seems, Chester Wilmot did not exaggerate when he commented: 'The storm which burst over Caen on 20 July was a minor squall compared with the tempest which raged at SHAEF and at Leigh-Mallory's headquarters over what was regarded as Montgomery's "failure".' When *Goodwood* became bogged down it also struck a heavy blow at the morale of those participating in it. A regimental historian recalled that: 'At some level ... the *Goodwood* operation was advertised as the long-awaited break-out for which VIII Corps had been trained; the failure to break out (whether intended or not) cast the rebuffed troops into the depths of depression. From the point of view of the private soldier this battle was the biggest shambles of the campaign.'

Montgomery must bear some of the responsibility for this unhappy state of affairs. His directives and letters on the objects of the *Goodwood* offensive were ambiguous. Like the prophecies of the Delphic Oracle, his orders could be interpreted in several ways, depending on what the interested parties expected and hoped for.

In his orders about the *Goodwood* offensive, Montgomery mentioned the nearly magic and highly emotional name of Falaise. This gave the airmen the impression that Montgomery intended to reach that town, or its immediate outskirts. Montgomery stressed too that this attack was to be a very big one and he wanted all the air support possible. The airmen eagerly offered all the aircraft they could muster. At last, it seemed to them, Montgomery was about to make an all-out, if belated effort to fulfil the promised air plan by gaining control of the Caen–Falaise Plain. In anticipation, the senior airmen rejoiced at the prospect of having room to deploy their huddled-up aircraft, and also of being able to bring across the Channel hundreds of machines which, for lack of space in Normandy, were still being operated from English airfields.

To the consternation of the airmen, the *Goodwood* offensive ground to an apparently ignominious halt just east and south of Caen. Tedder, the Deputy Supreme Commander, remarked caustically '7,000 tons of bombs for 7,000 yards'. Over 400 tanks had also been lost. By the criterion of material expended for territory gained, *Goodwood* certainly seemed a most expensive operation. By 20 July, most of SHAEF and the other senior airmen, especially Leigh-Mallory and Coningham, made no secret but that they were profoundly disillusioned and disappointed at Montgomery's handling of the campaign. Three days later, Tedder, the Deputy Supreme Commander, wrote to the Supreme Commander. In this letter (only partially quoted in the official British History), he urged Eisenhower to take over as Land Force Commander, since he had lost faith in Montgomery's handling of the fighting on the British flank. Tedder also emphasized that he would support 'any action you may consider the situation demands'. This remark was tantamount to suggesting that Montgomery be replaced. Eisenhower refused to go to these lengths.

Nevertheless, at the SHAEF headquarters in England, the 'failure' of *Goodwood* seemed to Eisenhower and the Staff to be the last straw. They had interpreted Montgomery's plans as showing that he meant to break out, at any rate as far as Falaise, on the British flank. Isolated from the context, statements that, 'the whole eastern flank will burst into flames' and that, 'the time has come to have a real "show down" on the eastern flank,' all lent weight to such a view of Montgomery's plans. Thus when this offensive petered out on 20 July, Montgomery's critics at SHAEF turned on him, and these included several British officers who personally disliked him. Some felt he was too cautious and defensively minded to continue any longer as Commander-in-Chief of the Land Forces. Others considered that he was too blatantly ignoring the administrative problems, since more and more men and equipment were being crammed into an overcrowded beachhead which was one tenth of the area forecast on the build-up schedules for that date. Over one million men had been landed, more than all the forces on the Italian front. Also more than one million tons of supplies had been pumped in, enough, it was estimated, to fill a goods train at least 300 miles long.

Montgomery admitted he had misled the Press over *Goodwood*. On the evening of 18 July (the first day of the offensive), in an exultant mood, he called the first of the major (both ill-fated) press conferences which he held in the north-west Europe campaign. Next day the London *Times* carried headlines reporting that 'SECOND ARMY BREAKS THROUGH'. The paper continued 'ARMOURED FORCES REACH OPEN COUNTRY – GENERAL MONTGOMERY "WELL SATISFIED"'. The rspeonsible *New York Times* was even more cock-a-hoop. In rather more prominent type, it proclaimed, 'BRITISH RIP LINES EAST OF CAEN'. It also quoted a 2nd Army spokesman as saying, 'the advance had gone extremely well' and that 'a break-through was achieved'. Even as late as 20 July (the correspondent's dispatches of 19 July) *The New York Times* featured another headline, 'BRITISH TANKS DRIVE SEVEN MILES BEYOND CAEN'. That day their famous war correspondent Drew Middleton wrote, 'the penetration is already so deep and is expanding at such a rate that the enemy's chances of bringing the drive to an abrupt halt on the River Dives appear slight'. (Middleton was referring to that part of the Dives which lies east of Falaise.)

By 21 July, it was evident that the Press had wildly

overestimated the progress of *Goodwood*. On 21 July, the London *Times*, in an article conceded that the 'Second Army's break-through (break-in is the better term) had been halted'. All this had its effects on the morale of the troops who often received the newspapers the day they were published and these, with the BBC News, were their chief means of following the events in Normandy.

Even before *Goodwood*, it was becoming noticeable that Montgomery's handling of the Normandy battle was being reported more and more critically, especially in the American newspapers. The situation in the bridgehead was a frustrating one for the newsmen. For nearly seven weeks, a plethora of war correspondents had been cooped up in an ever more congested piece of territory. Some of them, like Moorehead, Wilmot, Pyle, Middleton, Baldwin to name a few, were highly experienced and very able men. Others knew little of military matters; one American quipped that, 'Practically every newspaper in the US sent a correspondent [to Normandy] except the *Dog World*'. Young, tough and active, many grew restless at the lack of exciting news. Despondency and a critical outlook affected some of them, as daily, by the jeepload, they made their fruitless journeys from one headquarters to another to be handed a comforting cliché-ridden communiqué. In their turn, some commanders found it hard to stomach the attitude of the war correspondents and one wrote sarcastically in his diary, 'On some days you'd think the war was being run for them.'

Both Montgomery and Bradley found this ill-informed Press criticism hard to endure. Yet, without briefing the Press on their true strategy, there was little to do except 'grin and bear it' and be comforted that the Germans would also be as likely to be misled as the Allied Press

During this stage of the battle the relationship between Montgomery and Bradley was most cordial and Bradley has gone out of his way to stress how harmoniously they worked together. In his own words, when, 'Montgomery bossed the US 1st Army as part of his 21st Army Group, he exercised his Allied authority with wisdom, forbearance and restraint.

... I could not have wanted a more tolerant and judicious commander. Not once did he confront us with an arbitrary directive and not once did he reject any plan that we had devised.'

Unfortunately the same happy relations did not exist between Montgomery and the more remote SHAEF. And the failure of the *Goodwood* offensive to gain much ground seriously undermined Eisenhower's confidence in Montgomery's conduct of the battle. Both commanders were agreed on the major plan, that the break-out should take place on the western or American flank. But soon after the landing they began to differ more and more on the method of executing this strategic manoeuvre. In *Crusade in Europe*, Eisenhower has explained how he, and his staff at SHAEF, as well as senior airmen, envisaged the course of the battle:

From the beginning it was the conception of Field Marshal Montgomery, Bradley, and myself that eventually the great movement out of the beachhead would be an enormous left wheel. . . .

An important point in our calculations was the line from which we originally intended to execute this wheel. . . .

Montgomery stated that the second great phase of the operation, estimated to begin shortly after D + 20, would require the British Army to pivot on its left at Falaise, to 'swing with its right towards Argentan–Alencon'. [Montgomery's own words]. This meant that Falaise would be in our possession before the great wheel began. The line that we actually held when the breakout began on D + 50 was approximately that planned for D + 5.

As has been shown, Montgomery soon found German resistance around Caen much more firmly based than either he or the *Overlord* planners had expected. He, therefore, considerably modified the orginally agreed 'master plan'. In his own words: 'It had been my original intention to secure the high ground between Caen and Falaise as early as possible, as being a suitable area for the construction of airfields; but this was not vital, and when I found it could not be done in accordance with the original plan without suffering unjustified casualties, I did not proceed with that venture.' Montgomery admits, disingenuously, that this unilateral and unannounced alteration of the master plan 'was not popular with the Air Command'.

In retrospect, there can be little doubt that Montgomery summed up the situation correctly and acted aright on the British flank. Nevertheless, it is unfortunate that to some of his equals and superiors his manner seemed off-hand and almost arrogant. The Normandy campaign was essentially a combined operation. As temporary Land Force Commander, Montgomery was one of a team of three, the other two being Ramsay the Naval and Leigh-Mallory the Air Commander. Montgomery sometimes acted as if the other members of the team did not exist, merely expecting them (and Tedder and Eisenhower his superiors) to display an unquestioning faith in his leadership and genius. He never met them to discuss and explain any alterations which he decided to make to the joint plans.

The Supreme Commander, his Deputy and SHAEF fared little better at Montgomery's hand. They received explanatory letters or copies of his directives which informed them of what he intended to do. Never once did Montgomery fly back to England to discuss matters with Eisenhower. SHAEF he avoided like the plague. He received Eisenhower in his headquarters whenever the Supreme Commander visited Normandy, which by early August, he had done ten times. An observer unaware of the command structure in Normandy might well have assumed that Montgomery was the Supreme Commander.

Montgomery did, however, carefully explain and discuss his plans with Brooke, the CIGS. He was the sole superior whom Montgomery respected and to whom he gave unwavering loyalty. Although officially not involved in the running of the battle, Brooke paid several visits to Normandy. He was Montgomery's confidant and was not only fully conversant, but also in entire agreement with the way Montgomery was fighting the battle in Normandy. In most cases, the two men thought alike, but Brooke was the dominant influence and guided Montgomery firmly in times of crisis. Both Brooke and Montgomery had a low opinion of Eisenhower's military, as opposed to his administrative and diplomatic ability. Furthermore, they seemed to have made little effort to conceal their view; but their poor estimation of Eisenhower was not shared by most Americans, nor by any means all the British senior officers.

Early in July, Brooke found himself having hotly to defend Montgomery against the Prime Minister's strictures. Churchill was complaining to the CIGS about the slow pace of the advance in Normandy. On 19 July, Brooke was just about to set off to see Montgomery when:

at 9.30 the PM sent for me. I found him in bed in a new blue and gold dressing-gown, but in an unholy rage! 'What was Monty doing dictating to him; he had every right to visit France when he wanted? Who was Monty to stop him?' ... At last I discovered that Eisenhower had told him that Monty has asked not to have any visitors during the next few days, and the PM had argued out that Monty had aimed this restriction mainly at him.

Eisenhower had imposed this ban because the work of the senior commanders was being dangerously hindered by a constant stream of important visitors. A day-trip across the Channel to see the sights of the Normandy bridgehead obviously ranked as a memorable and unique experience. Many important men had found that they had an urgent reason for making this short voyage. HM The King, the Prime Minister, the British and American Chiefs of Staff, de Gaulle were but a few of those who had, so as to speak, signed the Normandy visitors' book, and more recently a Russian observer team had installed itself and wanted to be taken everywhere. But the most serious event had been an American Cabinet minister's visit to Bradley's headquarters which lasted so long that the planning for an attack had been held up.

Brooke was apparently not affected by the ban on visitors, and flew over to Normandy. Directly he had arrived, he helped Montgomery compose a welcoming letter for the Prime Minister. Churchill was delighted and went across very shortly afterwards to spend three days in Normandy, living on a naval vessel.

Having previously stayed with Montgomery, Churchill knew the somewhat strange headquarters organization which Montgomery had evolved. It is worth describing this in some detail, since, though it was well suited to the needs of the almost independent commander of the 8th Army, it fitted less happily into the Normandy background.

Montgomery divided his headquarters into two unequal parts. Much the larger one housed all his principal Staff officers, this he called his Main HQ and it was here that all the routine matters were dealt with. Main HQ was presided over by his friendly approachable Chief of Staff, Freddie de Guingand. Moorehead has given a good picture of the *esprit de corps* which permeated this HQ. Explaining that some of these officers

were undoubtedly Montgomery's intellectual superiors, but, as with everyone else who worked close to him, they were devoted. They were the experts and they were allowed to work without interference. Consequently they found Montgomery the best of masters. . . .

It was one of Montgomery's ideas that as soon as you have picked your team you must stick to it. And so he carried this team with him wherever he went.

Montgomery completely detached himself from his Main HQ, living at his much smaller Tactical HQ which was always nearer the fighting than the main one. The rules were strict as Moorehead wrote: 'Except for senior officers no one without previous authorization was allowed within the precincts of this camp. All visitors except Royalty and those of Cabinet level were usually forbidden. . . .'

In this small and well-insulated headquarters Montgomery led a carefully regulated and strict routine. He rose and went to bed early, thus allowing himself plenty of time at both ends of the day in which to relax and think about the conduct of the battle. He spent most of the day at the front, returning in the evening when he telephoned de Guingand 'receiving information and laying down orders and plans for the next day. .... After dinner Montgomery would listen to the report of his liaison officers.'

De Guingand found this isolation of the Commander from all the rest of his Staff caused considerable extra work which Montgomery realized, but: 'used to say that he expected his staff to go mad, but he would take jolly good care that he didn't go that way himself! I gradually realized that once again Montgomery was absolutely right. He would certainly have gone mad if he had been surrounded by the activities of a "Main" headquarters. He would never have been able to exercise such intimate tactical command over his forces.'

Developed largely from his study of Wellington's and Napoleon's methods, Montgomery had introduced a unique element into his highly intimate Tactical HQ. Very carefully, he had hand-picked a dozen or so young men, mostly in their late twenties, whom he employed as his personal Liaison Officers, giving them the fullest authority to go everywhere and see everything. This they did fearlessly and several were killed in the process. In a way impossible for more senior officers to accomplish, these young and fairly junior officers enabled Montgomery to piece together, in an almost first-hand manner, what was happening on all parts of the battlefront. As de Guingand said of these young captains and majors:

They had drive and courage, and developed considerable judgement and a sense of responsibility. They would go anywhere and found out everything. To hear them giving their report to the Commander-in-Chief after dinner each evening was something not to be forgotten. One got a clear and vivid picture of the battle. One could sense the state of commanders, and the morale of their men. After each had said his piece, Montgomery would snap out a few crisp questions and receive equally sharp and crisp replies.

This band of what could almost be called intrepid young blood brothers (in Normandy they included some Americans), were the only occupants of his Tactical HQ. Montgomery's attitude to them was that of a Victorian father (or that somewhat similar figure a public-school housemaster) and he took a benevolent interest in all their doings amorous or otherwise. Churchill found this atmosphere congenial, for Montgomery writes that: 'one of his greatest delights was to sit in my map caravan after dinner at night and hear these young officers tell me the story of what was happening on the battlefront'. It was all very English, with romantic undertones of King Arthur and his knights at the Round Table. But de Guingand felt that the whole system had its dangers, since he noticed as the war went on Montgomery tended to become 'more dictatorial and uncompromising ... and we felt that this was not only due to the strain of war, but also because he did not live with officers nearer to his own age'.

A headquarters organized on such lines could hardly be expected to appeal to the more free and easy Americans. In particular, the friendly and approachable Eisenhower always seems to have returned from Normandy somewhat depressed after having visited his more battle-experienced subordinate; the somewhat self-conscious system of isolation in which Montgomery worked created a barrier between the two men, and Eisenhower was always much more at ease with Bradley who lived, worked and ate in the field with his staff.

The dispute between Eisenhower and Montgomery came to a head on 26 and 27 July. Paradoxically the issue between them had been solved, since as we now know the break-out had by then occurred. On 26 July, however, the situation on the American front still looked obscure, and it would have been premature to conclude that Cobra would result in a break-through of the German lines.

On 26 July, Eisenhower saw Churchill. Swayed by the mounting criticism of Montgomery voiced by his staff at SHAEF and stung by the hostility of much of the American Press, Eisenhower complained to the Prime Minister that Montgomery was slow and too defensively minded. The

Supreme Commander was also deeply disturbed by the prominent way in which many US newspapers were featuring a comparison of battle losses, and underlining the fact that the Americans had suffered 73,000 casualties, whereas the British and Canadian casualties were only 49,000 (At this date, about 770,000 American and 591,000 British and Canadian troops had been landed in Normandy.) The conclusion being drawn from these statistics was that the British forces were being spared at the expense of the Americans. Since Montgomery commanded the land forces, the Americans reckoned he must be responsible. Montgomery had never been a popular hero in the United States. Eisenhower, therefore, urged the Premier to put more pressure on Montgomery for the British to be offensively minded. Impressed by what he had observed during his recent stay in Normandy, Churchill was unresponsive to Eisenhower's pleas.

The discussion was resumed the next day when Churchill asked Eisenhower and his Chief of Staff, Bedell Smith to dinner with Brooke. This meeting cleared the air, though as a result of it, Brooke's opinion of Eisenhower sank still lower. That night he wrote in his diary 'Ike knows nothing about strategy.'

Next day Brooke wrote a long letter to Montgomery. In it he explained how he had emphasized a most important point to Eisenhower. 'I told him that in view of the fact that the German density in Normandy was 2½ times that on the Russian front whilst our superiority was only in the nature of some 25 per cent as compared to 300 per cent Russian superiority on the Eastern front, I did not consider that we were in a position to launch an all-out offensive along the whole front.' Eisenhower's invariable solution to the lack of progress in Normandy was to urge that a series of large offensives be launched. He never seemed to have properly grasped how effectively the British pressure was steadily eroding the German strength, nor did he appear, at the time, to have appreciated how continuously the British had been attacking the enemy.

Though this largely inter-Allied disagreement ended fairly amicably, its repercussions were even more widespread. For one thing Eisenhower became more determined not to be dominated by British strategic thinking. A few days later Churchill pleaded with him to cancel the proposed Franco-American landings in the south of France, known as *Dragoon*, but formerly called *Anvil*. When, early in July this invasion was agreed on, it had opened up attractive possibilities for breaking the stalemate in Normandy as well as providing extra ports for incoming American troops. The break-out considerably altered the situation. But Eisenhower refused to be stayed, despite the fact that this landing, by removing so many troops from Italy, would hamstring the advance there. The later effect of *Dragoon* was to strengthen immensely the case of those who wanted to pursue the Broad- as opposed to the Narrow-Front Strategy.

In spite of the most pressing pleas of his staff at SHAEF, Eisenhower refused to take over from Montgomery as Commander-in-Chief Land Forces. On 1 August he did, however, up-grade Bradley's command, which now became 12th US Army Group. This meant that Bradley had, on paper, an equal status with Montgomery who commanded 21st British Army Group. Nevertheless the general direction of the battle remained under Montgomery's control until 1 September, the pre-arranged date when Eisenhower assumed the dual role of Supreme Commander and Commander-in-Chief Land Forces. By then, the original *Overlord* plan had anticipated that the bridgehead stage of the battle would be over and a large enough town would be available to house the gigantic SHAEF headquarters.

This clash of views had an effect on the personal relationship between the two men. After the *Goodwood* offensive, Montgomery's influence on Eisenhower diminished. Later in August, when plans for the future strategy of the campaigns were being formulated, Eisenhower was much less prepared to listen to Montgomery's ideas than he had been before D-day. Hence Montgomery's advocacy of a single thrust into the heart of Germany did not carry the same weight as it would have done a few months earlier.

Especially on occasions of great tension, working with allies always produces problems. Great military leaders burdened with heavy responsibilities must hold strong opinions, and when they are of different nationalities these clashes of opinion are often more difficult to reconcile. In this case, it is now easy to see that Eisenhower, the senior airmen and most of the staff at SHAEF were too impatient with lack of territorial progress in Normandy. Furthermore, Eisenhower was too militarily inexperienced to be able to criticize, with any authority, his subordinate's handling of the battle. Yet if Montgomery had been of a less autocratic and self-righteous nature, he might have been sensitive enough to sympathize with the feelings of Eisenhower and the airmen. A personal, full and fresh explanation and discussion by Montgomery of his reasons for modifying the *Overlord* plan might have been sufficient to have smoothed over this admittedly frustrating patch in the fighting. To such a human gesture, the warm-hearted Commander-in-Chief would almost certainly have responded with that generosity which was so characteristic of him.

11

The Bridgehead Revisited

'All wars are infantry wars.'
— *Evelyn Waugh, Put out More Flags*

THIS CHAPTER IS intended to be a brief but necessary
interlude. It will try to draw together two aspects of the
Normandy battle which must be discussed if this campaign
is to be seen in perspective. The first of these subjects is concerned with casualties and the second with the unique life in
the bridgehead itself.

After more than seven weeks in Normandy the majority
of British Infantry battalions were becoming sadly depleted
both in quantity and quality. Some statistics will make the
quantitative point clear. An infantry division consisted of
about 18,000 troops, but almost all the battle casualties were
incurred by the 4,500 fighting men in the nine infantry
battalions. 3rd Infantry Division, which had landed on D-
day, had suffered 7,100 casualties by the end of the Normandy battle, of whom 904 had been killed. 15th Scottish
Division had arrived later and had lost 5,354 by the same
date. In the latter division, out of the 52 officers killed, 43
were from the nine infantry battalions (less than 14 per cent
of all the troops were infantry); of the remaining nine dead,
four were gunners (18 per cent of the total force), three
engineers (13 per cent of the total force). One officer from the
machine-gun battalion and one from the reconnaissance
regiment were killed in action. For the other ranks, the pattern was the same, except that eight soldiers in the RAMC
Field Ambulance Units had been killed. A battalion of 51st
Highland Division had 44 officer casualties (killed, wounded
and missing) during 7½ weeks' uninterrupted fighting in

Normandy; the magnitude of this total can best be appreciated when it is recalled that about 30 officers was the normal
fighting complement for a battalion. Even this figure of 44
fails to do justice to the facts, since several of these officers
might have been slightly wounded and thus not included in
the casualty lists.

Only those who have some first-class knowledge of it can
begin to appreciate the incessant dangers and discomforts,
as well as the cumulative stresses and strains, which the
front-line soldier is called upon to endure for weeks or
months on end, often without proper rest. The demands
made upon the fighting troops proved so heavy that few
men over forty could withstand the burden, and the average age for commanding officers in the 'teeth arms' units was
only thirty-five.

In the Second World War, as always before, the heaviest
battle casualties occurred among the infantry soldiers and
few of them managed to survive a year in action without
being wounded. Such a steady drain on their fighting manpower kept nearly all infantry battalions permanently under
strength as battle formations. They were further handicapped by the fact that many of their men, sent as replacements, tended to be imperfectly trained, and were new to
the conditions. All these factors, therefore, put a further
strain on those who remained to carry on. Of this problem,
which universally plagued all infantry battalions, Eric Link-
later wrote, 'however rapidly reinforcements may arrive,
reinforcements cannot restore a battalion to its previous
efficiency without a period for rest and training during
which its newcomers can be absorbed into and identified
with their fighting teams'. In Normandy, such periods of
rest and training were infrequent, and the record for continuous fighting was probably held by the Commando Brigade who spent 83 consecutive days in action. When judging
any lack of enthusiasm displayed in action, especially by
the veterans of the 8th Army, it must also be remembered
that, for most of the front-line soldiers, the bleak rule was
that you normally continued to fight on; either until you

were killed, or so severely wounded as to be unfit for further active service in the line.

Unavoidable though this grim state of affairs may have been, it did contrast very unfavourably with the conditions under which the RAF air-crews operated. Their losses were comparable with those of the front-line soldiers, but they flew a definite number of operational sorties, divided into two tours with a 'rest' in between. In the case of Bomber Command each tour consisted of 30 operational sorties, and for the fighter pilots each tour was 200 sorties or 200 flying hours whichever was the less. All aircrew who survived these two tours were then entitled to be placed permanently on non-operational flying duties. Although it is undeniable that the strain of warfare was less intense on the ground than in the air, it is nevertheless true to say that the cumulative effect of a year or more of modern infantry fighting proved too great for nearly all men to bear. Those who did survive frequently exercised greater caution in all they did, for not only had they been wounded too often themselves, but also they had seen too many of their comrades killed to be inclined to go on taking any risks. In the final stages of the Normandy battle, one exhausted infantry battalion in 3rd Division failed to go on, the reason was that; 'the old sweats had gone to ground when they heard a Spandau, and the young re-inforcement, in action for the first time, thought that what his elders and betters did he should do too. Such is the state to which too much hard fighting and mental exhaustion can reduce a fine formation.'

The army commanders were always acutely aware of this strain. Bradley paid this moving tribute:

the rifleman trudges into battle knowing that statistics are stacked against his survival. He fights without promise of either reward or relief. Behind every river, there's another hill – and behind that hill, another river. After weeks or months in the line only a wound can offer him the comfort of safety, shelter, and a bed. Those who are left to fight, fight on, evading death but knowing that with each day of evasion they have exhausted one more chance for survival. Sooner or later, unless victory comes, this chase must end on the litter or in the grave.

In Normandy, every effort was made to pull out the infantry, at least once, for a brief break from battle. Most divisions had rest camps where the troops could have a bath, change their underclothes and were given cigarettes and sweets. One officer recalls the pleasure in just bivouacking 'in the shade of the apple trees away from the din of the battlefield and all-pervading dust and traffic of the bridgehead'. Amusements were extremely limited. The mobile cinema seemed to have very limited repertoire and just showed continuous performances of *Four Jills in a Jeep*, a film which soon palled.

The time spent resting and re-equipping could be disturbed with forebodings. The historian of the Rifle Brigade commented:

When one's battalion has a period of rest in war delight in washing and sleeping, in drinking, perhaps, Calvados, and in buying eggs and butter, is tempered by the realization that this respite does not spring from the altruistic motives of the Higher Command, but that you are simply being fattened up, like pheasants in pre-war Septembers, for a particularly important occasion.

Like capital, courage is an expendable commodity and takes time to accumulate. With most soldiers, who were in continuous contact with the enemy, their stock of courage could soon be exhausted leaving them bankrupt and bereft of bravery. Medically this was known as battle exhaustion. During the later stages of the Normandy battle, such a condition accounted for a serious proportion of all casualties, amounting to nearly half in the case of one of the veteran divisions. In June, about 10 per cent of 2nd Army casualties were classified as being caused by battle exhaustion. By July and August, this total had risen to over 20 per cent. One of the gravest psychological problems was the way in which one or two neurotics could infect a whole formation. Sometimes this occurred when incompletely trained reinforcements were used as front-line troops and panicked. Nothing is more demoralizing than this kind of behaviour. Equally difficult to combat was the shock effect when really good officers were killed or gravely wounded. Such leaders had usually built up a sense of personal respect and trust which replacement officers could not quickly recreate. Often, too, officers were suddenly called upon to take over in a crisis and found that they were not able to cope with the demands made upon them. An example of this kind of thing happened when a good commanding officer was wounded at the height of a battle and the second-in-command moved up from the rear to take over. At brigade headquarters, 'he was given an erroneously optimistic picture of the situation' and when 'faced by a desperate military situation which would have taxed the skill of the most experienced commander, he became distraught' and of course had to be removed.

Psychiatric cases presented another problem. Some men hung on too long, their resistance snapped, they deserted and, on being caught, were severely punished. The more cautious reported sick, went to hospital, and no blame was attached to them. It seemed unjust. By July, exhaustion centres had been opened in Normandy, so that men did not have to return to England for treatment. Encouragingly, the Official Medical History records that, unlike the First World War, very few cases of self-inflicted wounds occurred.

Those who had been through the First World War sometimes commented critically on the lack of moral fibre of some of the troops fighting in the Second, considering them to be far too easily prone to psychiatric troubles. One of the reasons for this weakness, in what was never more than a minority of the younger generation, undoubtedly derived from the widespread preoccupation and interest in psychology. A contributory factor could have been the most comfortable and sheltered existence which most of the population enjoyed and which thereby made the horrors of war more difficult to endure. Together these two forces predisposed some to find quick release from pain and suffering in a nervous collapse.

Two approaches well summarize opposite attitudes towards casualties. One very brave officer wrote 'Most people seem able to accept casualties, which is just as well, but for my part I can never overlook the tragedy that each one means to someone far away, stricken at home. The sadness of it is always with me.' The other writer explained how for him and many others a kind of safety valve operated, 'all soldiers grow into a state of mind in which a friend killed yesterday became as remote in the memory as some half-forgotten schoolmate, to be talked of with some detachment'.

What has been written here about the rigours of infantry warfare, also applied to a greater or lesser degree to the tank crews and to some of those in the artillery and engineer units, but very few others were exposed to such continual danger. (In Normandy, about 44 per cent of the British served in the non-fighting, or services, arms whose troops very rarely came into contact with the enemy.) Certainly, no other troops had to fight for so long at a time against such dreadful hazards, as did the infantry. This point was well illustrated by the comparative casualties in *Goodwood*. The three armoured divisions engaged in this massive offensive suffered lighter losses than did the one and a half infantry divisions fighting on their left flank.

By the end of August, infantry casualties had reached such proportions that a division had to be broken up to provide reinforcements. The British Army's perennial shortage of infantry was, however, more than matched by the German deficiency in this arm. During one of the more crucial stages of the battle they were having to use a first-class engineer unit as an infantry. Truly all wars are fundamentally infantry wars.

Even at the risk of slightly contradicting what has just been written, one act of gallantry must be related because it epitomizes the almost universal spirit of self-sacrifice which prevailed in the bridgehead. A soldier in the lowly Pioneer Corps was helping build an airstrip when he noticed a badly damaged fighter preparing to land there. Directly in its path lay a piece of curled-up steel matting which he realized could wreck the plane. Unhesitatingly he threw himself on top of this, so that his weight flattened it out. The machine passed so close to him that its wheels skimmed against his shoulders, but the pilot landed it safely.

The second, and more cheerful, part of this chapter will review conditions in the bridgehead. By the end of July, life here had developed a unique character of its own. About one-third the size of the American sector, the British held a small and roughly rectangular-shaped piece of ground whose northern and western sides were both about 20 miles long; the southern side stretched for about 35 miles, whilst the eastern one was a mere 15 miles long. Into this tiny portion of France had been injected nearly 700,000 men (a little less than the population of Liverpool), 150,000 vehicles, and over three quarters of a million tons of stores; all these had to compete for space with, amongst other things, 11 airfields, more than three dozen villages, and the two towns of Caen and Bayeux. The congestion can be imagined when it is also remembered that many new roads had to be constructed and old ones widened. Furthermore, the figures for the size of the sector are to some extent exaggerated, since stores and airfields could not be placed too close to the fighting line, therefore, a belt of territory extending at least three miles behind the southern and eastern sides was not available for storage purposes.

Perhaps the most marked characteristic of the bridgehead was the ceaseless activity which went on everywhere. A sense of purpose pervaded the atmosphere. Nowhere could this be better observed than on the beaches themselves which always provided a fascinating spectacle. During the latter part of July, Churchill visited Normandy and spent much of his three days there watching, entranced, the routine on the beaches:

By day I studied the whole process of the landing of supplies and troops, both at the piers, in which I had so long been interested, and on the beaches. On one occasion six tank landing-craft came to the beach in line. When their prows grounded, their drawbridges fell forward and out came the tanks, three or four from each, and splashed ashore. In less than eight minutes by my stop-watch the tanks stood in column of route on the high-road ready to move into action. This was an impressive perform-ance, and typical of the rate of discharge which had now been achieved.

The British and US navies had brought the discharge of cargoes to a remarkable pitch of efficiency and a very flex-ible system of priorities had been worked out to meet the demands of the fighting forces. From their English ports, all vessels were routed to an area in mid-Channel, known as Piccadilly Circus. From there, they sailed along care-fully defined sea-lanes that had to be continuously swept clear of mines; these were chiefly dropped at night from German aircraft and provided the greatest single hazard to shipping. Once off the Normandy coast, each ship pro-ceeded to its allotted beach which would be expecting it. With its own piers, each beach worked as a self-contained inter-Service unit being responsible for the speedy discharge and turn-round of its incoming vessels. Early in July, the most easterly beach, Sword, had to be closed, since it was within range of the German guns round Cabourg and also could be shelled by the heavier coastal artillery from the mouth of the Seine. The abandonment of this beach meant that the length of the British beaches (the northern side of their territory) was reduced to 20 miles. During the whole campaign under 10,000 tons was lost out of the 1,400,000 tons of stores sent to the British sector beaches, a minute pro-portion.

The great artificial Mulberry harbour was always alive with vessels coming and going. Most of its piers and floating roadways radiated from Arromanches, and they stretched almost a mile out to sea. At any one time, it offered mooring space for 23 coasters and seven of the 7,000-ton Liberty ships which could only be unloaded in deep water. About 35 per cent of the British stores were landed through this harbour and these included some very awkward and heavy loads that would have been difficult to get ashore over the beaches. Nevertheless, some responsible critics regard the material, time and effort expended on constructing and positioning the Mulberries was out of all proportion to the value of the one harbour which survived the Great Storm.

Moving inland, the density of the traffic became immediately apparent. In a single day, 15,000 vehicles passed one check-point, the equivalent to one every five seconds. Amongst the stores required regularly, the hundreds of Allied aircraft in Normandy alone consumed a daily average of one million gallons of petrol and dropped 750 tons of bombs each day. All this had to be transported from the beaches to the airfields. Traffic jams were endemic and sometimes hindered operations by slowing up the movement of forces. The local roads soon began to collapse under the strain. It had been planned to use stone from quarries south of Caen for road repairs, but this source remained in German hands till August, and instead a soft limestone had to be used which did not stand up well to the pounding of heavy vehicles. Everyone who served in the bridgehead must have memories of hot days with the dust-caked Military Policemen patiently directing the flow of traffic and the equally begrimed squads of Pioneer Corps troops perpetually toiling away to repair the road surfaces. As new formations kept coming in, the quantities of signs multiplied, until crossroads looked like memorials to the output and ingenuity of countless signwriters. Even more bizarre were the occasional wayside calvaries draped with telephone wires.

Near the front, wounded animals roamed, often driven frantic by the noise and their pain. One officer recalls coming across 'a couple of black horses with a foal. They were running wildly about and both of the big ones had been wounded in the legs. It took a couple of hours to capture them, they were so wild. We fed them and cleaned up their wounds. I then sent them to the back areas where there is a special collecting station with a vet.'

With the pace of advance being so much slower than was predicted, unexpected socio-medical problems arose. No provision had been made for equipping formations with lavatories. The makeshift holes or abandoned trenches which were often used as latrines by the first arrivals soon became full up and a potential breeding-ground for flies. As numbers increased, the disposal of human excrement became a major medical headache. But it was found that reasonable lavatories could be made from the plentiful supply of old ration boxes. Another, though less pressing problem was the carting away and dumping of the tons of empty tins which daily accumulated. The doctors were, however, perturbed at the possibility of the streams and rivers being contaminated by all this effluent and also by the dirty water issuing from the mobile baths and laundries which were usually sited on their banks. Since much of the drinking water had to be drawn from the streams and rivers, this was an alarming prospect. By strict discipline and unremitting medical supervision, major epidemics were avoided, but a widespread, though mild, outbreak of gastro-enteritis occurred during the last few weeks of the campaign.

Being a rich dairy country, Normandy was full of livestock and these, and especially the cows, suffered heavily in the battle. Getting rid of their decomposing carcasses presented a permanent problem. One brigadier wrote home: 'I actually had to burn up a farm yesterday as the only solution to a stable full of dead horses and cows.' A day later he reported that he was having a tussle with the senior doctor over getting enough lime to restore a healthy smell to the atmosphere.

Not all the powerful smells were caused by decaying flesh. A story, probably apocryphal, went round the bridgehead about a factory near the front line, in the American sector, which stank to high heaven. The Americans assumed it was full of very bad meat. They decided to destroy it and use the occasion to demonstrate their skill with explosives. Some British officers were invited to watch. One of these visitors sniffed and sniffed again and then, to the horror of the other spectators, he rushed into the factory braving possible booby traps. As he had guessed, the factory was stacked high with deliciously ripe Camembert cheese; these he liberated and the factory was saved.

In the fertile area of Normandy, where the invasion took place, the German occupation had not materially affected life. The Wehrmacht formations stationed here behaved fairly correctly. The Normans had not experienced the thuggish treatment which the youths in the SS division meted out to the local population, raping the girls, getting drunk and breaking up the houses and pillaging. A kind of *modus vivendi* had been established between most of the Normans and their overlords but this was skin deep. 'The Normandy peasant had settled down to a policy of cheating the Germans, of swindling and opposing the Germans. . . . It was a sort of passive resistance which yielded good dividends. It helped them to preserve at least a vestige of their pride.'

The Normans hated the collaborators passionately, since they had often betrayed Resistance fighters to the Gestapo. For the women, the penalty was to have their heads publicly shaved. This treatment disgusted the Allied soldiers who frequently intervened to rescue the women. On the whole, the Allied forces had little contact with the Normans, who were soon greatly outnumbered by their liberators. The troops who arrived in the early stages of the battle resented the attitude of the 'locals'. The newspapers had led them to expect that all France was longing to be liberated, and most British soldiers regarded all Frenchmen as highly emotional folk who showed their feelings with an almost indecent lack of restraint. Thus the soldiers were keenly disappointed when their great crusade appeared so little appreciated. As an eye-witness wrote: 'Looking for cheers they found what looked like apathy. The soldier failed, in his enthusiasm, to realize that these civilians were numbed by bombardment, almost wholly Allied (though the French never reproached them for that).'

Moreover, some British soldiers felt they had been deceived about the conditions on the Continent. They thought that most able-bodied Frenchmen would be actively engaged in the Resistance movement, but Normandy seemed singularly devoid of such freedom fighters. Also, for so long they had heard about the starving peoples of the occupied countries that they could be excused for considering that this was universal throughout Europe. Instead, when the first soldiers went into Bayeux they could hardly believe their eyes; mounds of unrationed butter for sale, plenty of cream could be bought, to say nothing of large numbers of strong-smelling Camembert cheeses which many officers seemed, perversely, to relish. Nor did the farmers and their wives always endear themselves to those soldiers who tried to barter with them some of their monotonous tinned 'compo' rations for fresh vegetables or eggs, since the Normans usually proved themselves very hard bargainers. Yet there were touching pieces of evidence that the apparently unresponsive Normans did care and were grateful. The citizens of Caen, who had suffered more than most at the hands of the Allies, always kept fresh flowers on the grave of a Canadian buried in the outskirts of their town.

Strict orders had been issued to ensure that the rights of private property were respected. But it must be admitted that the British soldiers sometimes broke this regulation when they thought no one was about, and this did not always improve the relations between the British and the French. Captain Watney recalls one such incident.

one evening . . . I saw two of my men crawling on their stomachs up a gully between an uncut field of clover and a potato field; intrigued, I stopped and asked them whether they were stalking a sniper; they just put their fingers to their lips and pointed over the field towards the line of cottages that marked the outer fringe of La Délivrande; I looked round and saw a fat old peasant woman sitting on guard at the upper window of a small white house.

'This potato field', said one of my men, 'belongs to her; she won't sell. . . .'

I watched them entranced; and, although they were breaking an army order by stealing potatoes from the field, I could not help admiring their ingenuity; lying flat on their stomachs they dragged themselves from plant to plant, then, very gently, they uprooted each plant, stripped it of its new potatoes and replanted it in its old position; it was impossible, after they had passed, to tell by glancing casually at the plants, that anyone had been that way, but their sack became heavier and heavier. When we ate them that evening we calmed our consciences by telling each other that soon the whole bridgehead would become one vast car-park-cum-ordnance-dump, and that this particular field of potatoes would soon be trampled down and flattened by the feet and vehicles of the follow-up formations.

Unknown to the Allied soldiers, at the time, the Normans had a good reason for their early off-hand behaviour. The Germans had persuaded many of the French that the invasion was nothing more than a raid like the Dieppe one, but on a larger scale, and that the British and Americans would then depart leaving the Germans in charge again. Hence the cautious Norman peasant at first appeared somewhat incredulous about the duration of the whole thing. In one village it took a football match between British soldiers and the 'locals' finally to convince the French that the Allies were there to stay! It was not until after the break-out from this battle-scarred sector of Normandy that the British really experienced the exhilarating and never-to-be-forgotten thrill of seeing and hearing people showing their gratitude for being liberated.

Prisoners of war were remote from the fighting soldier, few of whom ever had the opportunity of seeing their disarmed opponents at close quarters. This was a pity. The prisoner-of-war cages offered a viewer as amazing a cross-section of humanity as had ever been assembled together. Alan Moorehead has written about his experiences interviewing prisoners near Cherbourg.

each nationality behaved exactly as you would have expected. The German officers and NCOs sat in taut and rigid little groups. . . . What they wished to convey was perfectly clear; dignity, pride, contempt, indifference. Strength in defeat. . . .

The German privates were sleeping in rows, striking no attitudes, simply resting. When a new truck-load of prisoners arrived, and they were ordered to make room for them, the Germans rose

in a body. They moved three paces to the right. Then they lay
down again in rows. . . .
     Then the Russians and the Poles. They stood like cattle. . . .
They were given biscuits and meat, and they showed no reaction
except to reach out and take the food. Had they been led out and
shot one by one they would probably have shown no surprise. . . .

     The most volatile were the Italian civilians employed by
the Todt Labour Organization. 'They came clamouring at
the wire. . . . Ah, Merciful God, he speaks Italian. Excuse.
Excuse. A great service! Will you explain to the American
soldiers that we do not fight? . . .'
     An hour or two earlier, these prisoners of war 'had been
fighting with a suicidal ferocity. Pill-boxes were being held
long after their eventual destruction was a certainty. The
Russians had been firing right up to the last few yards before
they threw up their hands. And now here in the prisoners' cage there was complete disintegration, an evident
hatred of the Germans.' Through an interpreter, Moorehead
questioned one of these prisoners, a Pole, as to why he had
fought so furiously for the Germans; the man replied

     'Like to see my back? It's got scars across it from the neck
down to the arse. They hit me with a sword. Either you obeyed
orders or you got no food. Certainly I went on firing from the
trench. There was a German NCO standing behind me with a
revolver. It wasn't enough just to shoot. You had to shoot straight.
If you didn't you got a bullet in the back. Like the Germans? I'd
like to tear their guts out.'

     At first by promises and bribes, later by threats, and finally
by a mixture of starvation and force, the Germans had, by
1944, assembled a most fantastically mixed army. The men
in it came from almost every nation in Europe as well as
from some Asiatic races. As Moorehead remarked the result
was 'the ludicrous anomaly of the Russian peasant firing at
the American doughboy in Normandy'.
     Finally, even after seven weeks' fighting in this tightly
constricted bridgehead its confines were still often ill-de-
fined.

If you have any doubt about how casual a battlefield is, I can give you the fact that we rode through the whole American front-line position and got beyond the advanced scouts to within, I think, two turns of the road of the Germans, not only without being stopped, but actually without seeing anyone. The week before, four German colonels had come down from Paris to look around and had similarly driven through both German and American positions. They pulled up in some bewilderment in our rear areas, thus making it from the fleshpots of Paris to the prisoner-of-war camps of Normandy in something under five hours without the least physical inconvenience.

The only reason we didn't make this trip in reverse is that we finally caught up with a Mark IV tank which was still burning and this seemed to call for a certain amount of consultation . . . two American boys in another jeep caught up with us . . . when we stopped them. It was they who told us that the front line *had* been where we were but that the division had pulled back two miles that morning to make room for the aerial bombardment.

A day later the *Cobra* offensive began.

12

The Break-Out

'Hard pounding this, gentlemen.'
– Wellington

THE TERRIBLE WEATHER, which had so hampered the British, forced the Americans to postpone their offensive, *Cobra*, which would not begin until 25 July. To erase the German defences, Bradley had produced a fairly simple plan. He proposed to lead in the attack with a crushing aerial bombardment on the forward German positions and for this to be effective good weather was essential. After the aerial attack, three infantry divisions were to clear the path for the armoured divisions of Patton's 3rd Army. These would be responsible for the actual break-out of Normandy which was to take place at Avranches on the base of the Cotentin peninsula. The next stage of the plan envisaged one part of the US forces driving southwards to the Loire, cutting off Brittany in the process. The other part of the American Army was to swing eastwards towards Le Mans and Alençon. It was anticipated that this manoeuvre would force the Germans to withdraw from Normandy and cross the Seine.

The initial success of this ambitious plan depended largely on two things. First the bulk of the German panzer forces had to be kept tied down on the other flank, by the 2nd Army, and secondly the bombing had to be followed up by a very rapid advance by the ground troops. The first of these requirements depended on Montgomery. He succeeded so well that on 24 July, the Germans, anticipating further attacks in the Caen area, had moved a panzer division from the American to the British sector. They also posted south of Caen another panzer division which had just arrived from the Pas de Calais. Therefore, opposing the Americans there were only 190 tanks, whereas about 645 German tanks were massed against the smaller British forces. Also, most of the deadly 88-mm anti-tank guns were stationed in the British sector.

To hoodwink the Germans still further and make them believe that another major offensive was about to be launched on the British flank, the Allies had in several places installed inflatable rubber models of guns and tanks. To add verisimilitude to these dummy weapons, at intervals loudspeakers blared out recordings of the noises of guns hooting and tracked vehicles moving. This kind of deception had been a favourite trick of Rommel's in the desert.

Bradley was particularly anxious to derive the greatest possible measure of assistance from the preliminary air bombardment. The effectiveness of the other aerial attacks, especially that on Caen, had been partially frittered away by the considerable pause which had elapsed between the departure of the bombers and the start of the ground advance. This breathing-space had enabled the Germans rapidly and skilfully to organize their defences. After much thought, Bradley decided to try to pulverize a piece of ground some 6,000 yards deep and 2,500 yards wide. To avoid the cratering that had always proved such an obstacle to the ground troops, he ordered that no bombs heavier than 100 lb should be dropped. This policy ruled out British Bomber Command whose machines were not equipped to drop high-explosive bombs of less than 500 lb weight. Nevertheless, 1,500 heavy American bombers were assembled and each carried forty 100-lb bombs. In all, Bradley estimated that some 60,000 small craters would be made by nearly 3,000 tons of bombs. In addition, he got the support of enough smaller aircraft to drop a further 1,200 tons of bombs.

To avoid casualties to his own troops and at the same time be able to place them very close to the bombing line (under a mile away), Bradley hit upon what appeared to him to be a fool-proof idea for *Cobra*'s aerial support. He asked that the bombing zone be set just south of a very clearly marked feature, namely a part of the twenty-mile straight stretch of road, that runs from St Lô to Priers. Thereby he envisaged that the aircraft could come in to bomb when flying parallel to, but south of this well-defined stretch of road, and thus they need never pass over the American troops. Bradley's plans for this aspect of the aerial bombardment painfully illustrate the kind of technical difficulties which beset inter-Service cooperation. Though agreeing to the bombardment, the airmen automatically rejected Bradley's fly-in route because they saw at once it would take too long for all these aircraft to approach this way and bomb the target. The air-planners, therefore, ordered the machines to cross the road at right-angles. To make matters even worse, by some mischance Bradley was not informed of this alteration.

On 24 July, the weather had improved sufficiently for the heavy bombers to attack and they set out. But in the meantime, the clouds closed in and they were ordered to return. This message did not, however, reach them all and some bombed short through the clouds, killing several score troops. It was only then that the horrified Bradley learnt that the bombers had come in on a course perpendicular to their target. Nearly seven years later, he wrote bitterly of this incident:

Had I known of air's intent to chance the perpendicular approach, I would never have consented to its plan. For I was unwilling to risk a corps to the split-second timing required in an overhead drop of 60,000 bombs from 8,000 feet.

Annoyed though I was by this duplicity [sic] on the part of the air planners, I had no chance but to consent to the attack or delay it indefinitely.

He added that he would have pulled his troops farther back, had he realized earlier the altered air plan. But a senior American airman commented: 'Any time heavies are used, there is a danger of casualties among our own forces.' In parentheses, it is worth mentioning that neither the British nor the American troops seemed to have been adequately

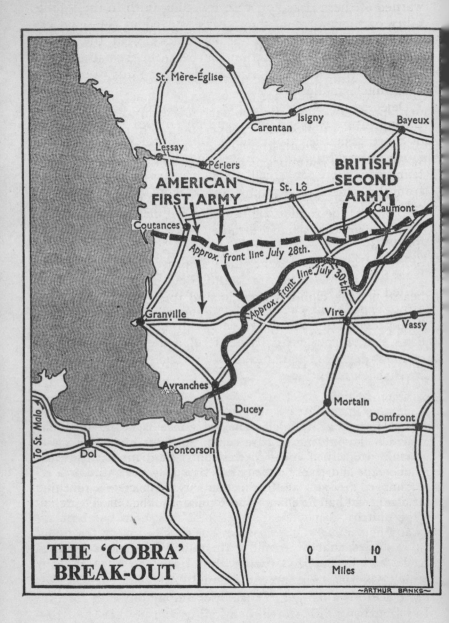

St. Mère-Église

Isigny

Bayeux

Carentan

Lessay

Périers

AMERICAN
FIRST ARMY

St. Lô

BRITISH
SECOND
ARMY

Caumont

Coutances

Approx. front line July 28th.

Approx. front line July 30th.

Granville

Vire

Vassy

To St. Malo

Avranches

Ducey

Mortain

Domfront

Dol

Pontorson

THE 'COBRA' BREAK-OUT

0   10
Miles

~ARTHUR BANKS~

warned of these risks, for, with touching faith in the infalli-
bility of their airmen, they always stayed in the open ex-
citedly watching these kinds of attacks. Had the Allied
troops been made to keep under cover, the casualties from
'shorts' in the close-support heavy bomber raids would have
been much smaller.

Dejected at the likelihood of this abortive bombardment
having given away his plan, and on edge at the possibility
of more casualties from the bombs, Bradley listened anxiously on 25 July to the full-scale aerial attack. His worst
fears were soon confirmed. Reports came in of more losses
from the American bombing and these included a divisional
commander. The confusion caused by these casualties (558
all told) amongst the forward troops inevitably slowed down
the initial momentum of the infantry attack. *Cobra*'s progress on its first day was disappointing. There were unspoken
fears that it might suffer the same fate as *Goodwood* and be
halted after a few small gains. The American anxieties were
groundless. Their enormous bombardment had fallen most
accurately on one of the two panzer divisions on the western
flank and, in fact, virtually obliterated the Panzer Lehr. Its
commander, Bayerlein, has drawn a vivid picture of the way
his division met its end:

> Units holding the front were almost completely wiped out,
> despite, in many cases, the best possible equipment of tanks,
> anti-tank guns and self-propelled guns. Back and forth the
> bomb carpets were laid, artillery positions were wiped out,
> tanks overturned and buried, infantry positions flattened and
> all roads and tracks destroyed. By midday the entire area re-
> sembled a moon landscape, with the bomb craters touching
> rim to rim, and there was no longer any hope of getting out
> any of our weapons. All signal communications had been cut
> and no command was possible. The shock effect on the troops
> was indescribable. Several of the men went mad and rushed
> dementedly round in the open until they were cut down by
> splinters. Simultaneous with the storm from the air, innumer-
> able guns of the US artillery poured drumfire into our field
> positions.

By 26 July, *Cobra* seemed to be making real gains, even

though most of the countryside was close *bocage*. The terran here resembed a huge chess board, each square being a small field (150 × 100 yards) which was surrounded by a broadly based-six-foot-high bank that was topped by a high hedge. The Americans had devised an ingenious kind of metal plough (made from salvaged German beach obstacles) that they welded on the front of their tanks. This enabled them to slice through these thick banks. Before this invention the Americans had used a laborious and ponderous sledge-hammer system of advancing, termed 'chess-board tactics'. It consisted in softening up each small area by artillery fire and fighter-bombers. The engineers followed this up by 'blowing' gaps in the embanked hedges to let the tanks drive into the next square.

Coutances was captured on 28 July and Avranches fell to the Americans on the 30th. Out of this town one vital road runs southwards and crosses a single bridge. This was the last place the Germans could hope to halt the Americans and they made frantic efforts to do so. But this part of the line was thinly held, the weather was excellent and the US Air Force was out in strength. The Germans had also now to contend with the forceful Patton whose 3rd Army consisted of over seven fresh, well-trained divisions. In a prodigious feat of drive and organization, Patton, in three days, pushed 100,000 men and 15,000 vehicles along that one road out of Avranches (a striking contrast to the traffic delays which hamstrung the *Goodwood* offensive).

On 1 August the American forces were reorganized. Bradley took over the newly constituted 12th US Army Group, composed of Hodges' 1st Army and Patton's 3rd Army. Since early in July, Patton had been kicking his heels in Normandy, but Bradley firmly refused to employ his forces in the fighting until the break-out was certain. By 4 August, Patton's 3rd Army had reached Rennes, the capital of Brittany. After this most of his divisions were ordered to turn eastwards in the general direction of Paris and the Seine. The long awaited break-out had taken place on the western flank. Montgomery's plan had worked and the battle for Normandy entered its final phase. As he expressed it, the Allied forces had 'unloosed the shackles that were holding us down and have knocked away the "key rivets"'.

Once Patton's break-out from Normandy had begun to make good progress, Hodges' 1st American Army started to move southwards to widen further this gap torn in the German defences. Judging that it was now opportune for the 2nd Army also to join in this drive, Montgomery secretly switched most of the British divisions across the front so as to get them on the left of the Americans. Therefore, by 30 July, three Armies, two American and one British, were all advancing southwards, parallel with each other, on the western flank of the Normandy front. To the 1st American and the 2nd British Armies fell the more costly and less thrilling task of trying to broaden the opening through which Patton's 3rd Army was pouring into the heart of France.

To achieve this three-pronged thrust, the British had to be hurriedly moved into the sector round Caumont. Before describing this offensive it is relevant to review briefly the more outstanding features of the terrain into which they were committed. The terrain through which the American 1st Army had to advance was somewhat similar.

Perched dramatically on a spur of high ground, Caumont has a breathtaking and panoramic view of all the countryside to the south. (For anyone who wishes to try to recapture something of the atmosphere of this campaign, a visit to this little town is a most rewarding experience.) Standing on the southernmost extremity of Caumont, it is even now quite easy to put oneself into the position of the British soldiers who, on that hot day at the end of July, surveyed a scene that has altered very little. Immediately in the foreground one's eyes are drawn downwards to where a straight dusty road plunges down a long steep hill at the bottom of which is a stream. Beyond this the road rises again to disappear over the brow of a small hill. On either side of the road are neat little fields encompassed by thick hedges.

Everything is now quiet and peaceful, but in 1944 the same stillness had an ominous and watchful air about it. Everyone then knew that the Germans were lurking somewhere below in well-prepared positions.

Still standing in the same place but looking up, the visitor is greeted by a sweeping view, something like the one from Box Hill in Surrey. Stretching away to a distant horizon is a network of irregular wooded slopes that rise gently, till they merge into a long series of ridges. This close and featureless region, known as the *Suisse Normande,* is broken only by the tall and unmistakable shape of Mont Pinçon, ten miles away to the south-east, which rises like some great bare head out of the surrounding foliage. Even to the most unmilitary observer, it is evident that this area must abound in good defensive positions. A glance at a map confirms this impression, since this is a very remote district strewn with small forests and steep little valleys that run in all directions. The few roads that exist are narrow and twisting and cross many bridges. Ironically, before the invasion, Montgomery had recognized the difficulty of advancing steadily through this country. He had warned that delays were likely to be encountered here. (Unfortunately, 2nd Army had forgotten Montgomery's earlier warning and issued timings which one who took part in these operations, castigated as 'optimistic to the point of fatuity'.)

The Americans had reached the Caumont sector by about 20 June. Since then, both sides had refrained from serious actions here. Thus the Germans had had ample time and opportunity to construct cunning defences, usually sited on the reverse slopes of the many wooded ridges. These they protected with minefields.

Known as *Bluecoat,* the immediate object of the British offensive was to capture Mont Pinçon and to get astride the good road that runs from Vire through Vassy to Condé sur Noireau. Six divisions were involved but the infantry ones, which had just come from the Odon battles, were tired. One of those who took part in this offensive summed up their attitude when he wrote:

For two months they had pinned down most of the enemy's divisions. When the offensive [Bluecoat] began they were already weary with the endless routine of marching and fighting, they were already punch-drunk with battle; so that for them there was no elation, no feeling of the great and wonderful days that had come at last, only the determination to stick it out a little longer, to conquer the numbing weariness, the fear that grew suddenly a hundredfold at the prospect of dying at the moment of victory.

The dogged courage and determination of the British foot soldier was a constant feature in this campaign. Never was it more fully displayed than during *Bluecoat*.

Especially for the infantry, this offensive proved a tedious and costly business. The narrowness of the few roads and the closeness of the country handicapped the tanks in an offensive role, the artillery could not reach many of the targets because of the steepness of the valleys, whilst the trees and dense undergrowth made it often impossible to locate a target sufficiently accurately to call up aircraft to bomb it. With the supporting forces so hampered, the pace was, inevitably, slow, but considering the difficulties it was often remarkable what progress was made. The type of country suited small but effective ambushes and the Germans consistently exploited this asset. A handful of them, with one or two well-sited machine-guns and 88-mm guns, would hold up a greatly superior British formation for several hours, and then would slip away whilst a more elaborate attack was being prepared against them. The same delaying tactics would be repeated a few hundred yards farther on. Another favourite German trick was to leave behind a small party which would suddenly appear with machine-guns, grenades and anti-tank weapons and shoot up the rear echelons and block the road. The historian of the 11th Armoured Division, which reacted very successfully to the difficulties of the *bocage*, has given an example of this kind of hide-and-seek tactics. 'The most usual party [of Germans] consisted of a few infantry accompanied by a tank or two; and on one occasion a force of four Tigers and thirty infantry cut the main divisional supply route and nearly intercepted a long column of ammunition trucks which were only saved by having taken a wrong turning and arrived safely by an alternative road.'

Tank crews found this kind of warfare very exhausting as this account shows.

To crash straight across country ignoring the easy route, taking in Churchillian [tank] strides small woods, buildings, hills, valleys, sunken roads and, worst of all, those steep high banks which divide up the Norman *bocage* like the ridges on a monstrous waffle; this was something for which we were not quite prepared by our training in the Dukeries.

There was no luxury and little comfort about the Churchills, save when driven slowly along a road: in the small fields of Normandy among the cider orchards, every move during the hot summer brought showers of small hard sour apples cascading into the turrets through the commanders' open hatches; after a few days there might be enough to jam the turret.

Five men in close proximity, three in the turret and two below in the driving compartment, all in a thick metal oven, soon produced a foul smell: humanity, apples, cordite and heat. Noise: the perpetual 'mush' through the earphones twenty-four hours each day, and through it the machinery noises, the engine as a background, with the whine of the turret trainer and the thud and rattle of the guns an accompaniment. The surge of power as the tank rose up to the crest of a bank; the pause at the top while the driver, covered with sweat and dust and unable to see, tried to balance his forty tons before the bone-jarring crash down into the field beyond, with every loose thing taking life and crashing round inside the turret. Men, boxes of machine-gun ammunition, shell-cases – and always those small hard apples.

The skill of the driver, and indeed of all those men in the crew, was remarkable: the operator struggling to keep the wireless on net and the guns loaded: the gunner with eyes always at the telescope however much the turret revolved and crashed around him; the hot stoppages in the machine-guns; the commander, with his head only above his hatches, choked with dust, not quite standing, not quite sitting during all those long Normandy days: always the wireless pounding at his ear drums.

After dark was the time for maintenance, when the 3-ton trucks from the echelon came up with petrol, ammunition and food; then the guns had to be cleaned and all repairs finished before first light and stand-to. Thanks to the tanks, repairs were not many, but crews could not go on for very long without a rest.

Mines provided a constant source of danger. The weather being extremely hot during this period, the rough roads were soon so thick in dust that the Germans could strew vast numbers of their Teller (plate) mines and easily camouflage them; some of these mines were so constructed as not to explode until three or four vehicles had passed over them. These mines packed 25 to 30 lb of TNT and, even under a tank, the effect was devastating. An American correspondent recalls coming upon the remains of a self-propelled gun in which the 'whole left side of the gun was wrecked. Two soldiers atop it were blown into the field bordering the road. One of them will live. Flames enveloped the gun and the bodies of the rest of the crew.' In the ditches and verges the soldier might step or crawl over the much smaller mines, known as pepper pots. These tiny mines were easily hidden and needed only 4 to 6 lb pressure to set them off. Even in one such small mine, the explosive charge was lethal and could kill a soldier who happened to lie on it; to tread on one could mean the loss of a foot and possibly a leg. Unsuspecting French civilians were also killed or maimed by these German mines which claimed a tragically large number of victims amongst children. Nevertheless, what most infuriated the attacking infantry was the German habit of fighting ferociously, inflicting heavy casualties and then coming out with hands up to surrender. Seeing all around comrades dead, dying and wounded and then to be expected to accept, as prisoners to be marched safely back, those who had slaughtered them, demanded more forbearance than could always be achieved in the heat of a battle. Also the Allies had to be extremely wary since the Germans (especially the SS) sometimes pretended to surrender in order to bring their adversaries out of their positions, when they were mowed down.

The historian of the Welsh Guards records one particularly macabre incident of this kind when a large German truck drove up:

with two men in the front cab and one on the roof. All but the driver had their hands up and when the truck stopped a corporal and two guardsmen covered them and stepped out to take them prisoners of war. At once the canvas cover in the rear was raised and two men with a machine-gun inside opened fire, wounding all three guardsmen. The Piat was promptly fired at the cab by two men who had remained at a roadside post and grenades were thrown into the body of the truck. All the Germans were killed instantly except the man on the cab roof. He knelt, terribly wounded, and swaying backwards and forwards began to sing a weird song, his voice growing fainter and fainter. The spectacle seemed to fascinate the men who, forgetting military caution, left their slit trenches and gathered round to gaze on this strange scene. One more compassionate, climbed up to help the wounded German down and at once a machine-gun opened from a farmhouse 150 yards away, killing him instantly. The others got to cover. But the shots set fire to the truck and the singing was finally subdued as the crackling flames made a funeral pyre for the singer and his comrades.

After eight days of this kind of intensive fighting the momentum of the *Bluecoat* offensive weakened. In some places little or no progress was made during the next week. By 6 August, the 2nd Army had pushed forward 12–20 miles on a front of about 12 miles. The most advanced divisions had by then reached the reverse slopes of the ridge which overlooks the Vire–Vassy–Condé sur Noireau road. In these excellent defensive positions two fresh SS panzer divisions were dug-in, with orders to hold up the British advance at all costs. The Germans were determined to control this road, since it was vital for them to do so if their forthcoming counter-attack was to have any hope of success. For the next week, the almost stationary western flank of the British 2nd Army pinned down here two of the best German panzer divisions which might otherwise have been involved in the Mortain counter-offensive. At the time, the exhausted British troops did not realize the important role they were playing and felt frustrated.

To the north-east, Mont Pinçon lay in the centre of the line of the *Bluecoat* offensive. On 6 August, it was captured by a remarkable feat of arms. In the grilling heat, the fighting at the foot of the mountain had been extremely vicious, one battalion being reduced to sixty men. In the thick of this battle, a few tanks of the 13/18 Hussars found a track. Under the cover of a smokescreen, they pushed up the steep sides of the mountain, one tank overturned, another had its tracks blown off, but eventually a mere seven tanks reached the summit. They were rapidly reinforced by more tanks and then the whole mountain was blanketed by fog. By the following morning, a good-sized force had been assembled and the Germans were driven off. That day the new XXX Corps Commander came up to survey the scene. Horrocks had been appointed to this post, and his dynamic presence soon made itself felt. To many, it seemed as if the almost miraculously successful capture of the forbidding Mont Pinçon had been rewarded by the reappearance of the universally trusted Horrocks, now recovered from his North African wounds.

13

On to Falaise

'The Germans were still fighting desperately just south of
Caen, where by this time they had established the
strongest defences encountered throughout the entire
campaign.'
– *General Dwight D. Eisenhower, Crusade in Europe*

WITH THE AMERICANS thrusting deep into France and
the whole western Allied front on the move, further
attempts were made to advance southwards from Caen. If
the Allies could stage a successful penetration here, they
might achieve a double envelopment of the German forces.

On 23 July, this eastern part of the line came under the
command of Crerar's newly constituted 1st Canadian Army.
About half the troops in it were Canadian and most of the
rest were either British or belonged to the 1st Polish Armoured Division. During the four weeks in which it slowly
and painfully worked its way from the southern suburbs of
Caen towards Falaise and Trun, this army became locked
in a series of some of the fiercest struggles of the whole campaign. The Canadian Army was not always as successful as it
should have been, but very many of the troops engaged were
new to battle, and some were not fully trained.

A vivid Press dispatch sets the picture in perspective:

I know nothing in this war which exceeds the bitterness and
strain of the battle the British and Canadians are fighting here
now, except the battles the Australians fought in New Guinea.
The Germans are fighting with almost the same fanaticism as
the Japanese, and they are digging-in in the same way. They go
to ground in elaborate earthworks when our bombs and shells
come over, then climb up to man their guns again. . . . Unhap-

pily, the only solution we have found so far is destruction – smashing every possible hiding place to the ground.

Neverthless even this treatment did not always succeed. The tiny hamlet of Tilly la Campagne with its solid stone houses was attacked, taken and retaken four times before its defenders eventually surrendered. A Canadian diarist commented on the results of one attempt to drive the German's out of it.

The Typhoons arrived and Tilly went up and down in a mass of smoking rubble. . . . Shortly afterwards our 'arty' played terrifically heavy fire into the rubble. . . . It is a seemingly impossible thing for anyone to live under such fire. Snipers continue to be very active and the seemingly impossible has happened because we are once again receiving MG fire from the streets of Tilly.

The advancing Canadians were fighting in a settled agricultural region with strongly built stone farm houses everywhere:

Occasionally there are hedges. . . . But all our infantry see, looking at the same fields straight on, is waist-high crops, and hedges and orchard walls which might hide anything. Country ideal for defence but heavily handicapped against attack: for the sniper can sit unseen in the corn, but when the infantry crawl up to get within hand-grenade range of him they are given away because the tops of the crops are disturbed. . . . This is good country for tanks. . . . But it is also good country for anti-tank guns. . . . [Since it] is dotted with clumps of trees, hedges, orchards, bushes, and 88-mm guns camouflaged to look like bushes.

The axis of the first two Canadian attacks *Totalize* and *Tractable*, lay along the Caen–Falaise road. Just over twenty miles separate these two towns and for three-quarters of this distance the Route Nationale No. 158 drives straight like a broad black arrow through the undulating cornfields. This, the Caen–Falaise Plain, has many stone hamlets, and some of the smaller ones, like Verrières, were not even marked on the 1/100,000 maps issued to the troops. Map-reading in this area was complicated by the innumerable side roads, drawn in red, which seam the Plain like little veins, and with the brown contour lines produced a bewildering effect on the map-reader. The little hamlets looked so similar, especially when half ruined, and as the pilot of an Auster noted: 'I found it very hard to distinguish one village from another. Hubert Folie looked very much like Ifs, the much-contested ruins of Tilly (La Campagne) looked little different from the others.' The problems of the map-reader were accentuated by names like Bretteville reappearing in several places, Bretteville sur Laize, for instance, was only about three miles away from Bretteville le Rabet. But even more confusing, some hamlets seemed to be joined to each other, as in the case of the tiny Cramesnil which appears on the map to be a continuation of the rather larger St Aignan de Cramesnil, a name which anyhow is definitely not designed to be pronounceable by an English signaller. These hamlets often had no distinguishing features, or when they had, in the heat of the battle, these could be misinterpreted with the most unfortunate results:

On all the maps we had used at home the sign for a church had been a small white circle with a cross on top. . . . In the village of Favières* was, on the map, a small *black* circle with a cross. Throughout the preliminary planning this had been referred to as 'the church', none of us realizing that the French had a habit of scattering calvaries or crucifixes about the countryside and that the sign for a calvary was a black circle and cross.

In normal circumstances, this mistake would have been obvious the moment the leading troops entered the village; but the circumstances were not normal. They were, in fact, thoroughly unpleasant. The companies were left with a deep sense of grievance over the shortage of churches in Favières, ignored the calvary, and (as the non-existent church was the landmark round which the whole operation had been based) were quite unable to say where they were. The artillery, mortars, and machine-guns were therefore unable for a time to fire a single round in their support for fear of hitting them.

The problems of accurate and speedy map-reading be-

* Favières is a hamlet, connected with Escures sur Favières, and lies some half dozen miles south of the railway junction of Mézidon.

devilled the advance of the troops here, and errors in inter-
preting maps, by the ground forces as well as the airmen,
caused several tragedies.

Called *Totalize* and begun on 7 August, the first major
Canadian attack had many original features and was the
brain-child of the forty-one-year-old corps commander, Simonds. He intended to try to push from just south of Caen
to Falaise. His major problem was, 'how to move a conspic-
uous tank across the bare plain without being knocked out by
the enemy tanks and anti-tank guns that were lying in wait'.
Adding urgency to solving this difficulty was that, unknown
to the Allies, another forty of the deadly 88-mm guns had
just arrived in this area.

To gain surprise, Simonds' plan for *Totalize* was to attack
by night with two armoured columns one each side of the
Caen–Falaise road. On the right of this road the Canadians
were to be organized in four parallel columns, whilst, on
the left, the British were to move in three columns. To give
them extra protection, some of the leading infantry were to
be transported in armoured carriers. Directionally the
groups were to be guided by a continuous line of tracer shells
fired from light anti-aircraft guns, by searchlight beams and
by compasses in the leading tanks. Farther out on the flanks,
the heavy bombers were to pulverize German centres of
opposition. Finally, the column was to be preceded, as far as
range permitted, by an artillery barrage of several hundred
guns. All enemy-held strong-points, like Tilly, were to be by-
passed. With the help of this juggernaut, it was intended to
break four miles deep into the German lines before halting.
In a second phase, when it was hoped to be clear of the main
enemy defences, rapid progress was to be made towards
Falaise.

Such a graphic account of this unique operation exists that
it deserves to be quoted at some length:

It was a perfect evening, warm and still. We stood about near
our tanks while the long summer twilight gradually turned to
dusk. Some smoked; few talked. At a quarter to eleven, as the
light was beginning to fail, the word was passed down the line:

'Get mounted.' Five minutes later the silence was shattered by the roar of tank engines starting up, and we began to move slowly to the start line, which was about a mile ahead. We had no difficulty over this part of the route as it had been marked by the military police with a double line of green and amber directional lights, and we were going very slowly – 1½ mph – so as not to forfeit surprise with too much dust and noise before we came properly into view of the enemy. We also wanted to make certain that we started off with the column well closed up.

The air bombardment was going on while we were moving up to the start line. There had been a great deal of fuss about the danger to our own troops, and we had received the strictest orders that every man was to wear ear-plugs. This night bombing was, in fact, far more accurate than some of the day bombing which we were to experience later, and, apart from a few flashes in the distance, we hardly realized that it was going on. The ear-plugs were quite unnecessary as we could hear nothing above the noise of the tanks.

So far there had been no enemy reaction, and at H-hour – half-past eleven – we crossed the road which was our start line and speeded up to 5 mph. This would, we estimated, bring us close up to the barrage when it opened fifteen minutes later about a mile ahead, just north of Tilly. All went well until the barrage started. The column was then immediately enveloped in a dense cloud of dust in which it was impossible at more than a few feet even to see the tail light of the tank in front. ... When the barrage started the needle immediately swung wildly in all directions, and the compass became useless.

In the dense dust-cloud the author's light tank disappeared into a bomb crater about ten feet deep. The two reserve navigators, following behind him, tried to avoid this crater and went into another.

The columns soon disintegrated into utter chaos. The confusion was indescribable. Everyone had been told to keep closed up and follow the tank in front, but it was soon apparent that it was the blind leading the blind. Great shapes of tanks loomed up out of the fog and asked who you were. Flails seemed to be everywhere and their enormous jibs barging about in the dark seemed to add to the confusion. It was not until you chanced on the road or railway that you had any idea of your position. Even so, this was no check on the distance travelled, and it was possible to go over the main road in the gloom without noticing it. In fact, some of the Canadians became mixed up with part of our column and one Canadian tank spent the rest of the night with us. [The parallel Canadian column was supposed to keep to the other, the west, side of the main Caen–Falaise road.]

There was very little sign of the enemy at this stage. We vaguely noticed a machine-gun spitting out of the darkness, but were too busy trying to find out where we were to pay much attention. The infantry, coming along behind in their open vehicles, had some trouble with this post, and a hand-grenade landed in a company headquarters carrier. This was thrown back with great presence of mind by one of the signallers, and the post was soon dealt with.

How long the confused mass of lost vehicles continued milling around in the fog between the road and railway it is difficult to say. After what seemed like a lifetime, Major Reid reported that he had found the hut on the railway at our selected crossing place. He put up a Verey light to show the rest of us the way, and before long a number of tanks had arrived, many of them being led by officers walking on foot. . . . Suddenly there were two flashes in quick succession, accompanied by showers of molten sparks as enemy bazookas, fired from behind the hut, hit the tanks. . . .

It was a fantastic scene. At first everything peaceful, then in a moment death, destruction, and fire. As the flames leapt from the turret of the tank the eerie light illumined the railway hut and shadowy figures could be seen running for shelter. Watched from a distance of less than a hundred yards one had a sense of unreality, as if it were some macabre scene at the theatre. . . .

It was now about two in the morning. The barrage had long ceased, the dust had settled, and a waning moon had risen in a clear, starlit sky. . . .

We spread out in a rough line and moved slowly forward firing our machine-guns into hedges and other places where bazooka parties were likely to be concealed. Control was the problem. Owing to the disorganization, normal methods were useless and it was no good just blundering forward individually. The infantry were completely in our hands and were still relying on us to put them down at the agreed debussing point. . . . The only thing to do now was to try to pick out landmarks and keep everyone together, particularly the infantry, by firing Verey lights.

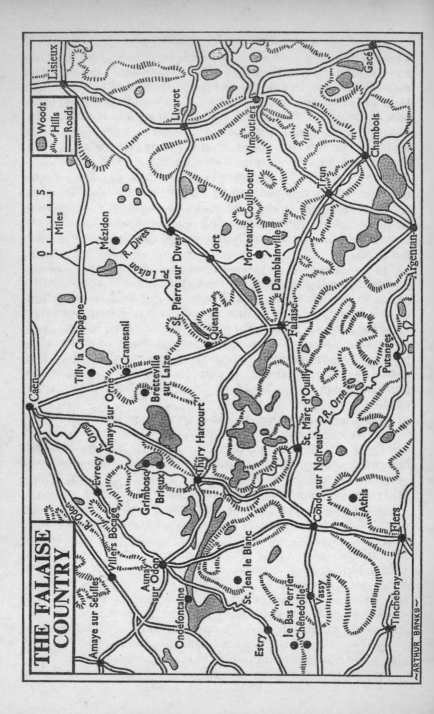

The small, square field with high elms surrounding it – that was a godsend, quite unmistakable. Now that we were in it should we ever get out? High bank and hedge ahead, rather like the *bocage*. Here we go – would she take it? – up, up – awkward to get stuck here – will there be a bazooka waiting the other side? – crash, we're through – across the road and into an open field. So we went on, the darkness streaked with red and white tracer from machine-guns. . . .

It was now about 3 am. Odd Germans were appearing out of the corn and giving themselves up to the infantry, who were soon out of their vehicles and going past us towards Cramesnil village in their usual confident and phlegmatic manner.

We were ordered to form ourselves into a rough 'close leaguer' for all-round defence while waiting for reports from the infantry about their progress in clearing the village. After about twenty minutes there was another of those now all too familiar showers of sparks and one of the tanks in the leaguer began to burn. This was perhaps the worst moment of all. We were a perfect target huddled together in the field, the black outlines of the tanks clearly visible in the moonlight. The shot had come from behind us so perhaps some enemy tanks, unseen in the dark, had trailed the column. We waited in suspense, and one wondered, selfishly, whether one's own tank would be the next to be hit. But there were no other incidents and we never solved the mystery of that last shot. . . .

The mist cleared about 8 o'clock and showed us another fine day with a cloudless sky. As we looked at one another we felt faintly surprised at seeing so many familiar faces. A tank driver probably expressed the feelings of us all as he produced a brew of tea with the words, 'Once or twice I didn't think we'd be having any more brews of tea, but here we are.' The brigadier came on the air to congratulate us and we began slowly to realize – like awakening from a nightmare – that all was well after all. Out of all the chaos and anxiety of the night had come success and the reassuring sunlight. Our weariness gave way to a feeling of exhilaration. It was a glorious morning and the fresh, unscarred countryside for a few brief hours belonged to us. Ours were the only track marks over the dew-laden grass, ours the only gaps in the hedges. Soon the trucks and lorries were to come and turn our track marks into dusty, busy highways so that we felt an irrational resentment that they should know nothing of how the tracks had been made and the hedges gapped during that anxious night.

Though they had anticipated an attack, *Totalize* created confusion amongst the German troops who had just arrived from the Pas de Calais to take over this sector. They were saved this night by the personal intervention of Meyer whose battered 12th SS Panzer Division was regrouping farther back (at this stage it had only forty-eight tanks of its own, though under its command were also nineteen Tiger tanks). When interrogated after the war, he said he realized that:

if I did not deploy my division correctly, the Allies would be through to Falaise, and the German armies in the West would be completely trapped. . . . Before me, making their way down the Caen–Falaise road in a disorderly rabble, were the panic-stricken troops of 89th Infantry Division. I realized that something had to be done to send these men back into the line and fight. I lit a cigar, stood in the middle of the road and in a loud voice asked them if they were going to leave me alone to cope with the enemy. Hearing a divisional commander address them in this way they stopped, hesitated and then returned to their positions.

The Germans now reacted rapidly to this deep penetration of their lines. Their experienced tank and 88-mm gun crews were formed into a most effective screen which became the backbone that gave the necessary depth to defensive positions skilfully chosen and well camouflaged.

The impetus was lost by the time the Allied advance was resumed in the afternoon of 8 August. Also, everything seemed to conspire to go wrong for the Canadians during the next few days. In the second phase of *Totalize*, two armoured divisions, one Canadian and the other Polish, took over and both were untried formations. Just outside Caen and about six miles before reaching its forming-up positions, the Canadian armoured division had a totally unexpected baptism of fire. Coming from a strong-point, by-passed during the previous night's advance, this German firing had a most demoralizing effect on the Canadians whose leading troops halted at once. Soon the inevitable traffic jam developed on the sole available road, Route No. 158. (With the vehicles close together, an armoured division on the move covers some five or six miles of highway.)

Worse was to follow. About twenty of the American heavy bombers, who were supporting this second phase of *Totalize,* dropped their loads on to the densely packed columns which had been held up near Caen. This bombing created terrible confusion and further delays. Thus when the attack eventually began, it went in without many of its tanks and guns. Fully alerted, the Germans broke up these and later Canadian attacks. Within 48 hours they had destroyed about 150 Allied tanks whose smouldering hulks dotted the rolling wheatfields of the Caen–Falaise Plain. The inexperienced Polish division had underestimated the strength of the German opposition and attacked with more verve than skill, and in the process one of their squadrons had lost 26 of its 36 tanks in a few hours. A little later, an entire Canadian armoured regiment losing its way, became cut off and was obliterated by the Germans. One of the main stumbling blocks to the advance was the large Quesnay Wood which had been turned by the Germans into what was almost a redoubt; an attack on it was fairly easily beaten off when the unfortunate Canadians went in with no armoured support, the Poles who were to have provided it having been very badly hit by the American bombing two days earlier. In all, about nine miles of ground had been gained before the *Totalize* attack was called off on 10 August.

Once again premature hopes of a rapid advance to Falaise had been shattered. Nevertheless, as has happened time and again in war, an apparent local success caused a major miscalculation in strategy. In this case, by 9 August, von Kluge felt that the success in warding off the offensive on Falaise meant that he must obey Hitler's order to try to mount a counter-attack towards Avranches. If the *Totalize* offensive had proved more menacing, von Kluge would almost certainly have anticipated the likelihood of an encirclement and might have thus felt justified in ordering the 150,000 German troops, still west of the Orne, to begin a slow and orderly retreat eastwards across the Seine. Such a manoeuvre would have avoided trapping so many of the German forces in the Falaise Pocket.

14

The Falaise Pocket

'They perform the most prodigious feats so long as their madness keeps them going.'

– Hans Kirst, Officer Factory

BETWEEN 7 AND 21 AUGUST 1944, the battle for Normandy reached its climax. For much of this time, the conflict became extremely complicated and even an historian, with all his advantages, has difficulty in constructing a lucid narrative. Naturally, therefore, those attempting to direct the battle frequently found themselves handicapped in making decisions against this background of uncertainty. Indeed it would be hard to think of another campaign in which a victory so complete was bedevilled, up to the last minute, by such delays and setbacks. Before describing the fighting, the major events in relations to the German and Allied plans will be sketched in.

On 7 August the Mortain counter-offensive was launched. Looking at the map in his east Prussian hideout, Hitler had seen that only twenty-five miles still separated the forward German troops from the coast at Avranches and he ordered an armoured group to be assembled to break through the American forces and reach the sea there. Only a relatively light screen of American forces had been left to guard this sector of the narrow corridor through which Patton's forces were pouring out of Normandy. If successful, this thrust would have isolated Patton by depriving him of his essential supplies and his armoured columns would soon have been halted. Hitler's grandiose plan next envisaged this panzer group turning north to create chaos in the American rear areas. Quite out of touch with the realities of the situation, Hitler argued that such a master stroke would demoralize the Allies and dramatically revive the German fortunes in Normandy. Feebly acquiescing, von Kluge drained his front of most of its armour to form Panzer Group Eberbach which consisted of about 185 tanks, though many of these never got as far as the starting line for this counter-offensive.

As usual, in his plans Hitler had made no allowances for the Allied air superiority. The Mortain counter-offensive made little headway, and soon foundered against ceaseless air attacks, the rocket-firing Typhoons being used to particularly deadly effect. The promised German air support never materialized because it was broken up by the Allied fighters long before reaching the battlefront. In fact after two days, the American ground forces had mastered this counter-attack and began to drive the Germans back. Not until 14 August, did Hitler finally abandon the idea of this counter-offensive and accept the inevitability of a retreat.

During all this time, undeterred by German threats, Patton surged on unchecked towards Chartres and Orleans. Elsewhere the relentless pressure of the other Allied armies was everywhere slowly forcing the Germans back.

August 15 proved a very black day for Hitler, since the Allies landed in the south of France. But, more ominously, he lost all contact with von Kluge who was cut off from the outside world for two days when visiting the forward troops. Quick to sense treachery after the 20 July plot, Hitler immediately concluded that his despairing general was independently negotiating surrender terms with the Allies. On 16 August, von Kluge got back and reopened communications with Hitler, advising him that the only hope was to retreat across the Seine. In fact this was already happening. Infuriated, Hitler sacked von Kluge.

Hitler appointed Field-Marshal Model to command the German forces in Normandy. Model arrived on the 18th and found a chaotic situation. Under von Kluge's direction, the German forces had been retreating steadily since the 16th. At first this had been a fairly orderly process, but by

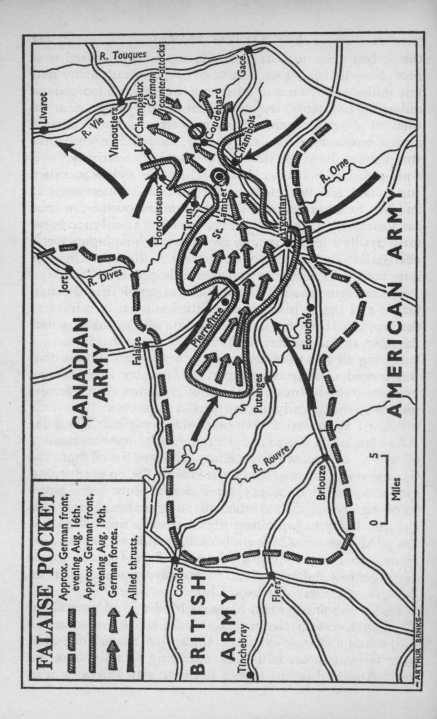

FALAISE POCKET

Approx. German front, evening Aug. 16th.

Approx. German front, evening Aug. 19th.

German forces.

Allied thrusts.

R. Touques

Gacé

Livarot

R. Vie

Les Champeaux

German counter-attacks

Coudehard

Chambois

Vimoutiers

R. Orne

Hordouseaux

Trun

St. Lambert

Argentan

CANADIAN ARMY

Jort

R. Dives

AMERICAN ARMY

Pierrefitte

Ecouché

Falaise

Putanges

Miles

R. Rouvre

Brîouze

0   5

Condé

R. Rouvre

BRITISH ARMY

Flers

Tinchebray

—ARTHUR BANKS—

the 17th, the air attacks had reduced the withdrawal to a rout. Nonetheless, though most of the German Army had lost its cohesion, several small and well-disciplined groups did exist and were struggling desperately to get clear of what the German senior officers now saw to be the jaws of a trap, known as the Falaise Pocket. Model discovered that von Kluge had earlier withdrawn the relatively well equipped II SS Panzer Corps. This was awaiting orders just outside the Pocket. On 20 August, Model used some of its units to break into the Pocket, from the outside, to help extricate some of those who were cut off. The only roads remaining open to the trapped groups were those between the villages of Trun and Chambois which, situated between Argentan and Falaise, are about six miles apart.

By 22 August the Allies had sealed off the Falaise Pocket. Outside it, the Germans were still conducting a retreat to the Seine, near Rouen, where they held a bridgehead across the river, and there they kept at bay an American force that had moved down the Seine to try to encircle, from the rear, those who had escaped from the Falaise Pocket. This bridgehead was withdrawn on the night of 23 August, and the organized battle ended. In barest outline, such were the events which led to the defeat of the German Army in Normandy.

Turning to the Allied reactions; until the Mortain counter-offensive, Montgomery had always considered that the Germans would try to escape from Patton's sweeping advances by making a steady withdrawal towards the lower Seine, and would then try to hold this river-line. Hitler's inept interference in ordering a counter-offensive opened up the possibility of a new and much greater victory. It now seemed feasible for the Allies to trap all the German forces in Normandy. Accordingly, it was decided to swing a part of Patton's 3rd Army northward to Argentan where it would link up with the Canadian Army which would advance there via Falaise. Simultaneously with this thrust, the 1st American and 2nd British armies were to drive the enemy back from the salient around Mortain. With a strong Allied line extending from Falaise to Argentan, the retreating Germans would, it was planned, find their escape routes barred. Thus securely bottled-up, either they would be forced to surrender, or would risk annihilation in trying to break through the encircling troops.

Such, very briefly, was the Allied plan for converging on and then trapping the German Army in Normandy. It very nearly came off, but just as the Germans had found, under much more favourable circumstances at Dunkirk, a completely successful encirclement of this magnitude rarely happens when the attacking force is confronted by good troops well led. As will become evident, the weakness of the plan was that the jaws of this trap, set between Argentan and Falaise, could not be sprung quickly enough. The timetable proved too optimistic, the Canadian rate of progress towards Argentan falling badly behind schedule. Also, after the formation of 12th US Army Group, Montgomery no longer exercised the same degree of control over the Allied forces. In the words of the Canadian Official History, 'there was an element of committee in the Allied system of command during this month of August'. Bradley now took important decisions without prior reference to Montgomery and an unfortunate absence of clear-cut authority made itself felt just when speedy and precise timing was the essence of success.

The final stage of the campaign can be said to date from 13 August, when Patton's force, driving north to close the Falaise Pocket, was halted by German opposition just south of Argentan, about fifteen miles from Falaise. The Canadians were poised eight miles north of Falaise, and thus less than twenty-five miles separated the armies. As Patton's troops were preparing to continue northwards to Falaise, Bradley forbade them to go on. Though this decision was taken with Eisenhower's agreement (he was with Bradley when the order was issued), Montgomery apparently was not consulted. Patton naturally flared up at this restriction. He wrongly blamed Montgomery for this delay and characteristically asserted that if allowed to 'go on to Falaise we'll drive the British back to the sea for another Dunkirk'.

The halting of Patton's army at Argentan was one of the most momentous and controversial decisions of the war and the reasons for making it have been the subject of much discussion. It has now become hard to disentangle fact from post-war justification, especially as Bradley has produced several explanations for his action. (Montgomery has been reticent about his part in this rather conflicting affair.) As far as can be judged, three main reasons influenced Bradley. First, both he and Montgomery believed that the forthcoming Canadian offensive, *Tractable* (due to start on 14 August), would succeed. Only eight miles from Falaise, the Canadians seemed to stand a better chance of getting there before the Americans.

Secondly, there was the problem of the air offensive. The Allied pilots were taking an enormous toll of the retreating Germans in the Argentan–Falaise region. If Patton had continued his advance through this featureless district, it would have been too dangerous to have permitted the Allied airmen to operate, since the pilots of high-speed aircraft cannot easily distinguish friend from foe when attacking. Therefore, the air attacks would have to have been stopped when they were having a most devastating effect.

The third, and probably most compelling, reason for halting Patton's forces was that Bradley thought the Germans were already retreating in strength and would overwhelm the Americans who were very much out on a limb. In his own words, he preferred 'a solid shoulder at Argentan to a broken neck at Falaise'. He was however misinformed about the speed of the German withdrawal which did not begin on any scale until the 16th. But looking at a map, one can appreciate his anxiety about the American divisions at Argentan which were at the end of a tenuous fifty to sixty mile supply line running through Alençon; and Hitler had, in fact, hoped to attack the Americans in the Alençon area. Possibly too, the Mortain counter-attack being fresh in his mind, Bradley did not want to take any undue risks at this juncture. Nevertheless, it now seems certain that on 14 August, but probably not later, Patton's forces could have advanced relatively easily, most, if not all, of the way to Falaise, and thus have greatly narrowed the gap through which the Germans would have to retreat. Patton waited impatiently for two days, and when no authority was forthcoming for renewing his advance, with Bradley's consent, he removed over a quarter of the force at Argentan. When, on 18 August, the weakened American forces resumed their advance they found the opposition much stiffer and only managed to link up with the Canadians in any strength on the 20th. This happened near Chambois.

Before describing how the Falaise Gap was closed, it is necessary to summarize the events elsewhere. The formations of the 1st and 2nd British Armies had the unspectacular task of squeezing-out the Mortain salient and subsequently compressing the Germans into the narrowest part of the Falaise Gap. Comparatively little progress was made against the Mortain salient from 6 to 13 August, but from 14 August the Germans began what was at first a slow withdrawal. Everywhere the situation now became very confusing, since the Germans often fought the kind of rearguard actions in which they were so skilful. Sometimes the British were misled by appearances, as at Tinchebray where, from all reports, the Germans had decided to defend the town to the last. One regimental historian wrote of this event:

Everyone sat in or within reach of his slit trench enjoying the sunshine, while a fire-plan of vast proportions, employing a huge number of medium guns, was worked out. When everything was ready and the total destruction of Tinchebray had become a regrettable certainty, the most forward troops were shocked to see one of the Norfolk's water trucks motoring back up the road from the doomed town. . . . The driver had gone belting down the road much too fast to notice that there were no heads popping out of the slit trenches anywhere, and had motored straight into Tinchebray where he had found no-one except the excited populace whom he therefore liberated.

By getting lost, the driver providentially saved the town and prevented a second battle of Tinchebray (the previous one had been during the Hundred Years War).

By the 16th the retreat was in full swing, the Germans streaming back into a small salient west of the Argentan–Falaise road. Hereabouts the country is a mass of tracks with thick plantations and sausage-shaped hills with very steep sides. As the pace quickened, many units were soon lost. In desperation, one British artillery officer was forced to test the accuracy of his whereabouts on the map by ordering his own guns to fire at the point where he supposed himself to be. When he picked out the smoke from the shot it had landed 1,000 yards away to the east of where he was standing!

By 19 August the most incredible enemy targets were presenting themselves:

the floor of the valley was seen to be alive with stuff. Men marching, cycling, and running, columns of horse-drawn transport, motor transport, and as the sun got up, so more and more targets came to light. Soon the whole Regiment was banging away with all it had, and the cry for more ammunition went up on all sides. It was a gunner's paradise and everybody took advantage of it. . . .

Away on our left was the famous killing ground, and all day the roar of Typhoons went on and fresh columns of smoke obscured the horizon. From our position we could just see one short section of the Argentan–Trun road, some 200 yards in all, on which sector at one time was crowded the whole miniature picture of an army in rout. First a squad of men running, being overtaken by men on bicycles followed by a limber at a gallop, and the whole being overtaken by a Panther tank crowded with men and doing well up to 30 mph, all with the main idea of getting away as fast as they could.

In this final phase of the campaign, the most crucial and savage conflicts were waged round Falaise. The brunt of this fighting fell on the Canadian Army whose vicissitudes will be followed in some detail. But first, a few words may not come amiss about some of the more peculiar characteristics of the conflict on the Caen–Falaise Plain, a district on which the eyes of the world were suddenly focused. To those fighting there, this area seemed to have been dedicated to battle by the Germans, who had evacuated all the inhabitants and most of their livestock. From the end of July until after the middle of August, the sun was so hot here that, by early afternoon, any man touching exposed metal burnt his bare skin. Vast numbers of vehicles pounded the dry ground and the dust was so dense that desert veterans recalled their North African days with nostalgia. Driving at anything except a snail's pace raised a huge cloud of this dust and, in the forward areas, shelling and mortaring inevitably resulted. Well-provided with long-range Moaning Minnies, the Germans knew the range to most targets; the huge notices saying DUST CAUSES DEATH emphasized the dangers of speed to all who neared the forward troops. One effect of this chalky dust was to turn everyone's hair grey, youth seemed to have departed, leaving only an army of prematurely aged and grimy men.

Dry weather had ripened the tall uncut corn, which could not only hide snipers, but also caught fire easily; many a wounded soldier was literally roasted to death when he lay helplessly on the ground, the corn all round set ablaze by a mortar bomb or a smoke shell. A drought added to the discomfort, little water could be found locally and it had to be brought up in the water trucks, whose arrival came to be the most important event in the day, even more eagerly awaited than the mail from home.

Finally, the insect life flourished. In the daytime persistent hordes of flies swarmed round the soldiers and their food; great fat flies bloated from their feasting off tens of thousand of human and animal corpses which lay rotting on the battlefield itself, or its environs; others fed off the large quantities of human excrement which lay on the hard, dry ground. Stomach upsets became common. By night, the mosquitoes took over to plague the troops. They were larger and more ferocious creatures than any that even the most hardened veterans had encountered elsewhere and seemed to find little inconvenience in making their nightly journey from the Ore or Dives Valleys to the Caen Plain. 'If a mosquito decided it would dine off your knees, then dine it did, battledress or no battledress; and as it sucked, its friends would be wriggling happily inside your gaiters to nibble your ankles while others clamped down in hordes upon your wrists and face.' They appeared to relish the anti-mosquito paste.

Even in the most unpleasant conditions, little incidents break the tension. The Poles (who were fighting with the Canadians) provided one by describing how the Germans, who feared instant death if captured by them, would try to bluff their captors. A prisoner would claim in Polish: 'I am a Pole. My mother was born in Poznan.' The Poles questioned him in Polish. 'What is your name?' He answered, 'I am a Pole. My mother was born in Poznan.' They said: 'It's a very hot day today, isn't it?' He replied: 'I am a Pole. My mother was born in Poznan.' Also the Poles were always supposed to keep a lorry full of new clothing with their forward troops, so that the Polish prisoners could be immediately stripped of their Wehrmacht uniform and join their comrades; having no reinforcements in Britain, the replacement of casualties was a major problem for the Polish Division.

On 14 August, the Canadian Army mounted a new armoured offensive, called *Tractable*. This was intended to overwhelm the German positions blocking the way to Falaise; after this the Canadians were to push on to Argentan and so link up with Patton's forces. The axis of the new offensive lay to the east of the Caen–Falaise road, and the initial break-through was to be made in daylight, the direction being concealed from the enemy by a smoke screen. Heavy bombers from the RAF were to precede the attack by bombing the main German strong-points, such as the Quesnay Wood.

Heartened by the Russian offensive, encouraged by Patton's successes and reassured by newspaper articles comparing August 1944 with August 1918, a sense of optimism prevailed amongst the waiting troops; it seemed as if the war was almost over. As the sky became filled with the black shapes of Lancaster and Halifax bombers, many soldiers climbed on to the roofs of lorries to get a grandstand view of this massive assault. No one doubted the accuracy of

Bomber Command which had made six previous raids without causing a single Allied casualty. There was a popular joke that, when the British bombed the Germans ducked; when the Germans bombed, as they did every night, the British ducked; but whenever the Americans bombed both sides ducked. From a distance the first wave of bombers seemed to drop their loads on the targets. Tragedy now dispelled premature elation. From the second wave of planes, bombs could be seen falling well behind the forward lines. Yellow smoke-flares were fired, a sign that the position was a friendly one, but, by some inconceivable oversight, Bomber Command had not been informed of the significance of this signal. Bombs continued to fall on the massed troops. Four hundred Allied casualties resulted from this fatal misjudgement. Some Austers went up, hoping to show the bombers their error. The Poles, who suffered most, reported that one such pilot, 'flew in front of the on-coming waves of aircraft, carried out expressive manoeuvres and flapped his wings, thus earning the gratitude of us all'. Whether or not owing to the initiative of the Auster pilots, the third wave of bombers dropped their loads on enemy-held territory.

Indeed, *Tractable* seemed dogged by calamity. The day before it started, a Canadian officer got lost, drove into the German lines and was killed. He had on him (though this was contravening the strictest standing instructions) the plans for *Tractable*. Hence the Germans possessed full information about the impending offensive and were able to site their troops and guns accordingly. The Allied commanders were not aware, until afterwards, that the Germans had this invaluable knowledge.

In spite of the demoralization and disorganization caused by this bombing of our own troops, *Tractable* had to go on. Strangely, it began well, since the Germans were blinded by the smoke screen. But later the dust clouds raised by the bombing and a mass of armoured vehicles obliterated all landmarks. The Canadians steered as best they could by the sun. Considerable confusion soon occurred, but about four miles of territory were gained. On the ridge overlooking

Falaise, the main German defences were reached and the attack petered out. The Canadians were now once again battering against troops of 12th SS Panzer Division which was literally fighting to the death; the last sixty of them held out for three days in Falaise and when they ceased to resist only four wounded prisoners were taken. The SS troops everywhere kept the less enthusiastic forward troops in position by shooting, from behind, any of them who tried either to surrender or retreat. Increasingly, the SS elements used the ordinary Wehrmacht formations as a protective screen behind which they tried to make their escape. This policy explains why apparently poor-quality troops should have fought with such desperate bravery against hopeless odds.

On 17 August, the Canadians captured the ruined Falaise. The previous day Montgomery had directed the Americans to move on beyond Argentan to Chambois and draw closer to the Canadians, so narrowing the neck of the Falaise Pocket. This was easier said than done. Patton had lost all interest in these isolated and depleted divisions which were now transferred to the 1st US Army, a process which caused friction and delayed getting them on the move again. Hence it was not until 18 August that the Americans were ready to begin trying to join up with the Canadians who had by now managed to get within ten miles of Chambois, the proposed meeting-place. The Americans showed no willingness to coordinate their efforts with the Canadians'. A tenuous and partial link-up was achieved on 19 August, though the neck of the 'pocket' was not tightly sealed until the 21st.

From 17 to 21 August inclusive, the Official Histories explain that the battle of the Falaise–Chambois area had entered into 'a very fluid state'. In less military terms, this meant that pretty well all effective higher control of the fighting had been lost. To make this point is not to criticize the Allied high command. If a battle is to be fought on some kind of prearranged lines, the enemy too must react in a reasonably predictable manner, otherwise it is impossible to collect and collate the intelligence material on which plans are based. During these five days, however, the German higher formations lost their cohesion and disintegrated into small battle groups led by men hell-bent on breaking out from the 'pocket'. In these groups, many were accustomed to retreats on the Russian Front where no quarter was given. Writing of the commander of the 12th SS Panzer Division and some of his followers, a German historian glowingly depicts this Götterdämmerung-like scene:

they met an armoured column of 1st SS Panzer Division, which was just then getting ready for attack. Meyer's group joined them. But the enemy anti-tank barrier proved too strong. They fell back. They rallied again. They launched another attack. This time they were successful. They swam across the Dives. On the hillside sloping down to the river the enemy was established and was firing down at them. The river-bed had become a death-trap for the horse-drawn artillery. Dead horses, limbers, guns, with human bodies scattered along them – that was the scene on the muddy banks of the Dives.

The group moved on. Canadian infantry was overrun. Meyer with his 200 men tore through the enemy positions like a ghostly hunt. The men did not yell. Almost without a sound they burst from the hedges. The Canadians, in panic, fell back in the face of this assault. It was led by the commander himself, his head in a bloody bandage and his pistol in his fist. Charging alongside him, with a machine-pistol, was Mikhail, a Cossack from Dnepropetrovsk who had accompanied Meyer throughout the campaign. . . .

They leapt over a ditch full of German dead.

Out! That was their one thought. Out of this inferno.

The inexperienced Canadian armoured division which bore the main impact of this violent disorganized fighting tended to become confused as sudden attacks burst on them from almost every direction. From 17 to 21 August this involved conflict raged in the thick country around Trun, St Lambert and Chambois, and here friend and foe were often inextricably intermixed in the steep-banked narrow lanes, small fields and innumerable orchards. This kind of fighting demanded the highest initiative from relatively junior officers and in some cases this occurred. A Canadian major gained the VC after three days of hand-to-hand fighting at St Lambert, where he repelled wave after wave of German counter-attacks; in the end, his company had been reduced to a mere handful. Fighting at such close quarters, it was impossible to exploit the very close aerial support in which the Typhoon pilots specialized. But in spite of snipers and the general confusion, the artillery observers usually managed to direct their guns on to the hemmed-in enemy with unprecedented effect. Both Canadian and British regiments joined in this activity, since, by 16 August, the 2nd Army's guns were within range of the Germans from the western end of the pocket. The effectiveness of the British and Canadian artillery was once more demonstrated here and confirmed many in their belief that the Royal Artillery was the most efficient service in the Anglo-Canadian armies.

One must conclude by remarking that in this maelstrom the Canadians' advance was frustratingly sluggish, and, in retrospect, it was unfortunate that the better-trained British 2nd Army could not have been employed to close the Falaise Gap.

One more account remains to be told about the ground fighting. It concerns the Polish Division which, somewhat unjustifiably, had not impressed observers during the *Totalize* offensive. But its epic stand at the Falaise Pocket has earned its immortality.

It is necessary to go back to 17 August, when this division made a most remarkable night march from the eastern flank. Driving across twenty miles of unknown territory, the Polish tanks broke through the enemy defences and moved round, in an arc, behind the Germans who were trying to break out from the Falaise Pocket. At dawn on 18 August, the Poles were installed athwart the major German escape route, the main road running from Chambois to Vimoutiers. Cut off from all supplies for three days, the Poles sat astride a dominating ridge of ground, which, from its shape, they called the Mace. Assailed from all sides, they were sandwiched here between the Germans trying to break out and troops of II SS Panzer Corps who had already broken out, but were trying to return to save their trapped comrades. The Polish divisional history gives a vivid and authentic picture of the death throes of the German Army:

an uninterrupted flow of German vehicles was moving – an endless column casually composed of tanks, guns, various types of motor cars and horse-drawn vehicles. All of them were loaded up with men and material.

There, behind a small horse-drawn cart carrying a mountain of bundles, rolled a Panther, behind it horses, tired out with the steep climb and mercilessly beaten by the crew, were pulling a gun, there was an ambulance, and on both sides a snake-like trail of pedestrians accompanied the column.

The column was moving with the speed of a tortoise. The rate of progress was dictated by the starved and tired horses trying to ascend the steep slope.

The Polish tank crews were waiting for these Germans:

The Shermans deployed as though on manoeuvres, took in the greatest possible length of road and fired simultaneously from all their guns and machine-guns. ... The German column halted immediately. The men riding on top of the tanks, trucks and carts disappeared in a twinkling. Flames and wreaths of smoke burst forth. ...

Anti-tank shells whistled past, German tanks within the German column tried to offer resistance, but in vain. Imprisoned in the traffic jam, in a cutting, they could do no harm to the Shermans. Their shots went high, whilst our 17-pounders firing from a height at the German Panthers hit their targets again and again. ...

(The road was soon) littered with smashed vehicles, the bodies of men and horses, the immobilized guns and tanks in which the ammunition continued to explode.

White flags shot up, handkerchiefs tied to sticks or branches. The prisoners, giving up all thought of further resistance, all attempt at escaping from the 'bulge', abandoning their foredoomed efforts, moved towards us; the wounded crawled along begging for help.

The ruthlessness of some of the Germans passed all belief, as this next incident demonstrates:

White handkerchiefs were waved and a whole crowd of Germans appeared, walking towards the tanks with their hands up There were quite a lot of them, probably over a hundred.

Karp [a Pole] ceased firing, and leant out of the turret. He had never before taken so many prisoners all at once. But there seemed to be something the matter with the crowd of Germans, some of them fell down wounded or killed. Who was firing at them? German tanks! Germans must not surrender, rather should they die, if necessary by German shells.

Shells and mortar bombs fell on the Poles and their prisoners indiscriminately, causing 'appalling destruction among the crowds of German prisoners; after each barrage huge red stains appeared in that grey mass of humanity'.

There was at least one suicidal assault when:

a German company which, for some unknown reason, chose to climb the steepest slope of the 'Mace', and which, scattering grenades, went forward shouting madly, only to break down in the terrible fire of the tracers of the anti-aircraft tanks. Within a few minutes the company ceased to exist, and the shouts, which were meant to buoy up their spirits in the assault, changed into the horrible cries of men dying in the midst of burning grass.

Amongst the Polish prisoners was a German corps commander – one of the few messages that got through was said to have been a request for orders as to what to do with him if, as then appeared probable, they were overrrun. 'Shall we shoot him; yes, no?' came the anxious query; the reply of the Canadian corps commander has not been put on record.

On 21 August, the exhausted Poles linked up with the Americans at Chambois. Later some Canadians reached them and reported that the 'picture was the grimmest the regiment has so far come up against. ... The Poles cried with joy when we arrived.'

Nevertheless, the most spectacular work of destruction was accomplished by the pilots of the Allied Tactical Air Forces. From the beginning of August, the Germans had been obliged to move increasingly by day. As the Falaise

Pocket became more constricted and the number of roads reduced, it became impossible to conceal these movements; nor by mid-August was it any longer feasible to restrict to night marches the traffic flowing back along the roads to the Seine.

Ranging widely, the fighter-bombers found an almost unbelievable profusion of targets, and the pilots flew up to six sorties every day, diving repeatedly to attack. One pilot reported that an unidentified column must be Germans, since he could see their helmets and their square heads! He had brought his fighter down to 50 feet to make certain of the identity of those in the vehicles. A pilot has recounted the technique employed to destroy the German columns.

When the Spitfires arrived over the small triangle of Normandy, bounded by Falaise, Trun, and Chambois, the Typhoons were already hard at work. One of their favourite tactics against long streams of enemy vehicles was to seal off the front and rear of the column by accurately dropping a few bombs. This technique imprisoned the desperate enemy on a narrow stretch of dusty lane, and since the transports were sometimes jammed together four abreast, it made the subsequent rocket and cannon attacks a comparatively easy business against the stationary targets. Some of the armoured cars and tanks attempted to escape their fate by making detours across the fields and wooded country but these were soon spotted by the Typhoon pilots and were accorded the same treatment as their comrades on the highways and lanes.

Immediately the Typhoons withdrew from the killing-ground the Spitfires raced into the attack. The tactics of the day were low-level strafing attacks with cannon shells and machine-guns ... the ground crews worked flat out in the hot sunshine to re-arm and refuel the aircraft.

After some Typhoons had been fired at by lorries with Red Crosses painted on them, the pilots gave up trying to avoid hitting these so-called ambulances which formed a great proportion of the German wheeled transport. Nor could they do anything when 'sometimes the despairing enemy waved white sheets at the Spitfires as they hurtled down to attack'.

The road leading eastwards out of Vimoutiers provided an especially favourable hunting-ground:

In one part the road winds steeply down to a small stream whose bridge had been effectively bombed thus causing a traffic jam. An armoured carrier lay nose-down in the stream, and for the mile of road up the hill vehicles lay burnt and inextricably mangled in their dozens. Almost the only civilians I saw were an old couple who had returned to find their cottage virtually undamaged, but were driven out by the stench of three dead horses that lay, maggot-infested along the verge beside their narrow front garden.

15

The End of it All

'If every civilian in the world could smell this stink, then
maybe we wouldn't have any more wars.'
— *Technical Sergeant Haguall of the
Graves Registration Unit*

O N 22 AUGUST the battle was over. It rained. The air in
the Falaise Pocket became unbearably heavy with the
smell of death:

After we left Falaise behind, all the roads were so choked with
burnt-out German equipment that it was quite impossible to continue the journey. The bloated corpses of unfortunate domestic
animals also lay in our path, so we took to the fields and tried to
make some progress across country. Each spinney and copse
contained its dreadful quota of dead Germans lying beside their
wrecked vehicles, and once we came across the body of what had
been a beautiful woman lying sprawled across the back seat of a
staff car.

Eisenhower thought that only Dante could have done
justice to the scene, saying that 'It was literally possible to
walk for hundreds of yards at a time stepping on nothing
but dead and decaying flesh.' The stench of the carnage was
so great that it penetrated the cockpits of aircraft a thousand feet above.

Moorehead likened it to:

one of those crowded battle paintings of Waterloo or Borodino
— except of course the wreckage is different. Every staff car — and
I suppose I have seen a hundred — is packed with French loot and
German equipment. There is a profusion of everything: field-
glasses and type-writers, pistols and small arms by the hundred,
cases of wine, truck-loads of food and medical stores, a vast mass

of leather harness. Every car is full of clothing, and every officer seems to have possessed a pair of corsets to take home.

No one could count the dead, but it was estimated that at least 10,000 bodies were there and about 50,000 prisoners were taken. Surmises of the numbers who managed to escape vary from 20,000 to 50,000, the latter being the highest German figure, but many of these must have later been killed between the 'Pocket' and the Seine.

From 22 to 27 August, the German formations in Normandy remained a fighting force only on the northernmost Allied flank, where they continued to conduct a skilful retreat and were aided by the bad weather which grounded aircraft. On 26 August, Patton summed up the situation when he sent a telegram to the Supreme Commander saying, 'Dear Ike, Today I spat in the Seine'.

The battle for Normandy had thus ended in the complete rout of the German forces whose casualties amounted to over 300,000. Though always on the offensive, Allied ground forces had lost 209,672 (including 36,976 killed), a wonderfully small total considering this included the D-day figures. (In the First World War, the unsuccessful Dardenelles Campaign cost the Allies about 250,000 troops.)

Backed by the navies and air forces, the Allied armies had won a conclusive victory far more economically and much more quickly than any had dared hope. On the British troops had fallen some of the hardest and least obviously rewarding parts of the fighting and they had shown a tenacity and endurance which impressed both their Allies and the enemy. Finally, Montgomery's handling of this battle further enhanced his reputation as a very great commander.

In conclusion, every battle carries with it an accompaniment that is rarely mentioned. This is the unromantic and gruesome task of the burial squads who have to clear up the remains of the soldiers for whom victory and defeat now meant the same thing. The men detailed to do this ghastly job usually remain silent, but one of them has spoken out on an aspect of war that many prefer to ignore:

Sure, there were lots of bodies we never identified. You know what a direct hit by a shell does to a guy. Or a mine, or a solid hit with a grenade, even. Sometimes all we have is a leg or a hunk of arm. . . .

There's only one stink and that's it. You never get used to it, either. As long as you live, you never get used to it.

British and German Equipment

British Artillery

FIELD GUNS
25-pounders, maximum range 13,400 yards, normal rate of fire 3 rounds per minute, calibre 3.45 in. (approx. 86 mm).
MEDIUM GUNS
5.5 in. (approx. 140 mm), firing either 100-lb shell with maximum range 16,200 yards, or 80-lb shell 18,100 yards, normal rate of fire 1 round per minute.

German Artillery

FIELD GUNS
105 mm, maximum range 12,000 yards, firing a shell of 34 lb.
MEDIUM GUNS
150 mm, maximum range 14,500 yards, firing a shell of 96 lb. In artillery pieces the Germans were greatly outnumbered by the Allies, but they made up for this deficiency, to some extent, by their most effective Nebelwerfers.

German Nebelwerfers

Mobile multi-barrelled (5–10 barrels) mortars. There were five regiments equipped with these mortars, each regiment having 60–70 of these weapons which had a very high rate of fire. They were of three sizes:

	PROJECTILES	RANGE IN YARDS
150 mm	75 lb	7,300
210 mm	248 lb	8,600
300 mm	277 lb	5,000

British and American Fighters and Fighter-Bombers

These were mainly Spitfires, Typhoons, Mustangs and Thunderbolts, all single-seater, single-engined machines with maximum speeds of 400–480 mph. A Spitfire could carry up to 3 bombs with a total weight of 1,000 lb, the Typhoon could be armed with either eight 60-lb rockets or 2,000 lb of bombs. The American Thunderbolts could carry two 1,000-lb bombs and in a few cases were armed with rockets. In addition all these machines were equipped with 4–6 guns of either 0.303-in or 20-mm, or 0.5-in calibre.

Code Names

ANVIL

Original name for the Allied landing in the South of France in August 1944, later rechristened DRAGOON.

BLUECOAT

British 2nd Army's offensive towards Mont Pinçon and Vire, begun on 30 July.

COBRA

American break-out by St Lô begun on 25 July.

EPSOM

British 2nd Army's offensive to cross the Odon and Orne rivers south-west of Caen, 26 June–1 July.

GOODWOOD

British 2nd Army's offensive south-east of Caen, 18–21 July.

GOOSEBERRY

Artificial breakwaters for the offshore anchorages and Mulberry harbour(s), largely composed of blockships known as CORNCOB.

MULBERRY

Artificial harbour(s) off the Normandy coast.

OVERLORD

Plan and operation for the invasion of France.

TOTALIZE

1st Canadian Army's offensive towards Falaise, Phase I: 8–11 August.

TRACTABLE

1st Canadian Army's offensive towards Falaise, Phase II: 14–16 August.

Armoured Division

DIVISIONAL HQ

Assault Arms

ARMOURED BRIGADE	INFANTRY	ARTILLERY	ENGINEERS SIGNALS	RECONNAISSANCE REGT
3 armoured regts	3 battalions	2 field regts each with 24 guns	2 field squadrons	armoured cars
1 motor battalion	independent machine-gun company		field park squadron	
		anti-tank regt		

Services

RASC	RAMC	RAOC	REME
4 transport companies	field ambulance	ordnance field park	3 workshops
	field dressing station		12 light aid detachments

Total

724 officers, 14,240 other ranks, 3,414 vehicles, 246 medium tanks, 44 light tanks

---

THE DIVISIONS ENGAGED WERE

BRITISH	CANADIAN	POLISH
Guards, 7th, 11th	4th	1st

British Liberation Army and Major Forces under British Command

Army Group, Twenty-first

ARMIES
British, Second; Canadian, First (from 31 July)
CORPS
British I, VII, XII, XXX; Canadian II
ARMOURED DIVISIONS
BRITISH Guards, 7th, 11th
CANADIAN 4th
POLISH 1st
INFANTRY DIVISIONS
BRITISH 3rd, 15th, 43rd, 49th, 50th, 51st, 53rd, 59th
CANADIAN 2nd, 3rd
AIRBORNE DIVISION
BRITISH 6th

Divisions, Main Fighting Units

ARMOURED 1 armoured brigade of 3 armoured regts, 1 motor battalion, 1 armoured reconnaissance regt.
1 infantry brigade of 3 battalions (about 800 men each).
TOTAL 724 officers, 14,240 other ranks, 3,414 vehicles (246 medium, 44 light tanks, 100 armoured and scout cars).
INFANTRY 3 brigades (9 battalions), 1 reconnaissance regt (134 armoured and scout cars).
TOTAL 870 officers, 17,477 other ranks, 3,347 vehicles (no tanks).
AIRBORNE 2 parachute brigades (6 battalions).
1 airlanding brigade (3 battalions, 1 armd recce regt).
TOTAL 702 officers, 11,446 other ranks, 1,708 vehicles (including 904 'Jeeps' and 16 light tanks).

Divisional Supporting Formations

ARTILLERY ?field regts (each 24 guns), armd 2, inf 3, a/b 24, 75mm pack howitzers.
1 anti-tank regt, armd 78, inf 110, a/b 68, guns 6 and 17 pounders.
1 anti-aircraft regt, armd 141, inf 125, a/b 23 (20mm).
HEAVY MACHINE GUNS armd 1 indep co, inf 1 battalion, a/b none.
ENGINEERS 1 field park, armd 1 squadron, inf 1 co, a/b none.
field companies, armd 2 squadrons, inf 3, a/b 1.
bridging unit, armd & inf only.
SIGNALS divisional signals unit.
RASC TRANSPORT COMPANIES armd 2, inf 4, a/b 3.

RAMC field ambulances armd 2, inf 3, a/b 3.
field dressing station, armd 1, inf 2, a/b none.
ORDNANCE (RAOC) 1 field park, *Provost* 1 co.
REME workshops, armd 2, inf 3, a/b, 1.

Other Major Fighting Formations

79th Armd Div, containing specialised armour, eg amphibious and mine-clearing (flail) tanks.
7 British, 1 Canadian Independent armoured and tank brigades each with about 3,400 men, 1,200 vehicles (190 medium and 33 light tanks).
2 special service brigades each of 4 commandos (464 men each).
1 Belgian, 1 Netherlands inf brigades.
2 SAS and 2 French para regts.
Artillery army groups RA, 5 British, 1 Canadian. 5 heavy regts each of 16 guns (8 7.2″ howitzers and 155mm guns) and 24 medium regts each of 16 5.5″ guns. Also 8 fld regs. Total strength about 40,000 men. Anti-aircraft brigades 8. 18 heavy A-A regts each of 24 3.7″ guns, 21 4 A-A regts each 54 40mm guns. 1 searchlight regt.

These War Establishment figures could be soon reduced by casualties: Aug. 1944, British troops only 660,000 of whom 56% fighting troops (incl Signals). Figures, etc from L. F. Ellis, *Victory in the West*, vol L, Appendix IV, HMSO 1962.

BIBLIOGRAPHY

ANON., *Incidents with the 7th Bn. Somerset Light Infantry* (published privately).

ANON., *A Short History of the 7th Armoured Division* (published privately).

ANON., *Taurus Pursuant: History of the 11th Armoured Division* (published privately: 1945).

BARCLAY, C. N., *History of 53 (Welsh) Division in the Second World War* (William Clowes & Sons Ltd: 1956).

BARNARD, W. T., *Queen's Own Rifles of Canada* (Ontario Publishing Company).

BARON, A., *From the City, From the Plough* (Cape: 1948)

BBC, *BBC War Report: June 6th 1944 – May 1945* (Oxford University Press: 1946).

BLUMENTRITT, G., *Von Rundstedt* (Odhams: 1952).

*BORTHWICK, A., *Sans Peur: History of the 5th Seaforth Highlanders 1942–1945* (Mackay: 1946).

*BRADLEY, O., *A Soldier's Story* (Eyre & Spottiswoode: 1952).

BRERETON, L. H., *The Brereton Diaries* (Morrow: 1946).

BRYANT, Sir A., *Triumph in the West* (Collins: 1959).

BUTCHER, H. C., *My Three Years with Eisenhower* (Heinemann: 1946).

*CARELL, P., *Invasion – They're Coming!* (Harrap: 1962).

CHURCHILL, Sir W. S., *The Second World War*, Vol. VI, *Triumph and Tragedy* (Houghton Mifflin: 1953).

CLARK, R. W., *Great Moments in Battle* (Phoenix House: 1960).

CLAY, E. W., *The Path of the 50th: The Story of the 50th (Northumbrian) Division in the Second World War* (Gale & Polden: 1950).

*CLOSTERMANN, P., *The Big Show* (Penguin: 1950).

CREW, F. A. E., *Army Medical Services Campaign*, Vol. IV (HMSO: 1962).

DE GUINGAND, Sir F., *Operation Victory* (Hodder & Stoughton: 1960).

EISENHOWER, D. D., *Report to the Combined Chiefs of Staff on the Operations in Europe of the Allied Expeditionary Force* (HMSO: 1946).

EISENHOWER, D. D., *Crusade in Europe* (Heinemann: 1948).

EHRMAN, J., *History of the Second World War: Grand Strategy*, Vol. V (HMSO: 1956).

*ELLIS, L. F., *Victory in the West*, Vol. I, *The Battle of Normandy* (HMSO: 1962).

ELLIS, L. F., *The Welsh Guards at War* (Gale & Polden: 1946).

ELLSBERG, E., *The Far Shore* (Gibbs & Phillips: 1960).

ERSKINE, D., *The Scots Guards 1919–1945* (William Clowes & Sons Ltd: 1956).

ESPOSITO, V. J., (Editor), *West Point Atlas of American Wars*, Vol. II (Praeger: New York).

*ESSAME, H., *The 43rd Wessex Division at War 1944–1945* (William Clowes & Sons Ltd: 1952).

ESSAME, H. and BELFIELD, E., *The North-West Europe Campaign* (Gale & Polden: 1962).

FERGUSSON, B., *The Watery Maze* (Collins: 1961).

*FLOWER, D., *History of the Argyll and Sutherland Highlanders (5th Bn.)* (Nelson: 1950).

FLOWER, D. and REEVES, J., *The War 1939–1945* (Cassell: 1960).

FULLER, J. F. C., *Decisive Battles of the Western World*, Vol. III (Eyre & Spottiswoode: 1956).

GALE, Sir R. N., *With the 6th Airborne Division in Normandy* (published privately).

GILL, R. and GROVES, J., *Club Route in Europe* (Hannover: 1946).

GREENFIELD, (Editor), *Command Decisions* (Methuen: 1960).

GUDERIAN, H., *Panzer Leader* (Michael Joseph: 1952).

HARRIS, Sir A., *Bomber Offensive* (Collins: 1947).

*HASTINGS, R., *The Rifle Brigade 1939–1945* (Gale & Polden: 1950).

HILL, R. J. T., *Phantom was There* (Arnold).

*HORROCKS, Sir B., *A Full Life* (Fontana: 1962).

INGERSOLL, R., *Top Secret* (Partridge Publications: 1946).

JACKSON, G. S., *Operations of VIII Corps* (published privately).

JAMAR, J. (trans. Slomozanka, M. C.), *With the Tanks of the 1st Polish Armoured Division* (Hengelo: 1946).

JOHNSON, J., *Wing Leader* (Penguin: 1959).

JOLLY, A., *Blue Flash* (published privately).

KINGSTON-MCCLOUGHEY, E. J., *The Direction of War* (Cape: 1955).

*LIDDELL HART, B. H., *The Tanks*, Vol. II (Cassell: 1959).

*LIDDELL HART, B. H., *The Other Side of the Hill* (Cassell: 1951).

*LIDDELL HART, B. H., (Editor), *The Rommel Papers* (Collins: 1953).

*MARSHALL, S. L. A., *Night Drop* (Macmillan: 1962).

MARTIN, H. G., *The History of the 15th Scottish Division 1939–1945* (Blackwood: 1948).

MILLS-ROBERTS, D., *Clash by Night, A Commando Chronicle* (Kimber: 1956).

MONTGOMERY, Field-Marshal Viscount, *Normandy to the Baltic* (Grey Arrow: 1961).

Memoirs of Field-Marshal Montgomery (Fontana: 1960).

*MOOREHEAD, A., *Eclipse* (Hamish Hamilton: 1947).

*MOOREHEAD, A., *Montgomery* (Hamish Hamilton: 1947).

MORISON, S. E., *The History of the US Navy in the Second World War*, Vol. XI (Little, Brown & Company: 1960).

MUIR, A., *First of Foot* (Blackwood: 1961).

NORTH, J. W., *North West Europe 1944–1945* (HMSO: 1953).

OGORWKIEWICZ, R. M., *Armour* (Stevens: 1960).

*OPPITZ, K., *The Soldier* (Muller: 1954).

OWEN, R., *Tedder* (Collins: 1952).

PAKENHAM-WALSH, R. P., *History of the Corps of Royal Engineers*, Vol. IX (Institution of Royal Engineers: 1958).

PARHAM, H. J. and BELFIELD, E., *Unarmed into Battle* (Warren: 1956).

PATTON, G. S., *War as I knew it* (W. H. Allen: 1950).

*POGUE, F. C., *The Supreme Command: US Army in World War II* (Office of the Chief of Military History Department of the Army, Washington, DC: 1954).

ROSSE, Earl of, and HILL, E. R., *The Story of the Guards Armoured Division* (Bles: 1956).

*ROSKILL, S.W., *The War at Sea*, Vol. III (HMSO: 1962).

SALMOND, J. B., *History of the 51st Highland Division* (Blackwood: 1953).

SAUNDERS, H. St G., *Green Beret: Marine Commandos* (Michael Joseph: 1949).

SAUNDERS, H. St G., *Story of the Parachute Regiment* (Michael Joseph: 1950).

SAUNDERS, H. St G., *The Royal Air Force 1939–1945*, Vol. III (HMSO: 1961).

SCARFE, N., *Assault Division, A History of the 3rd Division* (Collins: 1947).

SCHWEPPENBURG, Geyr von, *The Critical Years* (A. Wingate: 1952).

SHERWOOD, R. E., *The White House Papers of Harry L. Hopkins*, Vol. II (Eyre & Spottiswoode: 1949).

*SHULMAN, M., *Defeat in the West* (Secker & Warburg: 1947).

SPEIDEL, H., *We Defended Normandy* (Michael Jenkins: 1951).

*STACEY, C. P., *Victory Campaign: Official History of the Canadian Army*, Vol. III (The Queen's Printer: 1960)

STOKES, R. R., *Some Amazing 'Tank' Facts* (pamphlet).

THOMPSON, R. W., *The Price of Victory* (Constable: 1960).

VERNEY, G. L., *The Guards Armoured Division* (Hutchinson: 1955).

VERNEY, G. L., *Story of the Desert Rats* (Hutchinson: 1954)

WALLACE, B. G., *Patton and his Third Army* (Military Services Publishing, Harrisburg P.A.).

*WATNEY, J., *The Enemy Within* (Hodder & Stoughton: 1946).

WEBSTER, C. and FRANKLAND, N., *Strategic Air Offensive against Germany 1939–1945*, Vol. III (HMSO: 1961).

WILMOT, Chester, *The Struggle for Europe* (Fontana: 1959).

WOOD, A., *The Falaise Road* (W. H. Allen: 1945).

WOODWARD, D., *Ramsay at War* (Kimber: 1957).

YOUNG, D., *Rommel* (Collins: 1950).

SUPPLEMENTS TO 'THE LONDON GAZETTE'

MONTGOMERY, Field-Marshal Viscount, *Operations in N.W. Europe from 6 June 1944 to 5 May 1945* (4 September 1946).

LEIGH-MALLORY, Air Chief Marshal Sir Trafford, *Air Operations by the Allied Expeditionary Force in NW Europe from 15 November 1943 to 30 September 1944* (2 January 1947).

RAMSAY, Admiral Sir Bertram H., *The Assault Phase of the Normandy Landings* (30 October 1947).

PERIODICALS

CARVER, R. M. P., 'Tank Policy 1939–1945', *Royal Armoured Corps Journal*, 1959.

'Musketeer', 'Campaign in NW Europe. Some aspects of Administration', *Journal of the RUSI*, February 1958.

WYATT, W., 'Letter from France', *Horizon*, October 1944.

UNPUBLISHED DIARIES

Belfield, E. M. G.

Jennings, M.

Wood, A. C.

*VALUABLE WORKS NOT CONSULTED BY THE AUTHORS

FLORENTIN, E., *Stalingrad in Normandy*.

MCKEE, A., *Caen, Anvil of Victory*, Pan.

SIMOND, P., *Maple Leaf Up*.

Pamphlet: 'Boisjos Côte 262' (An account of the exploits of the Polish Armoured Division on Hill 262). Dufresne Vimoutiers, 1965.

*Denotes books of unusual interest recommended for further reading.

INDEX